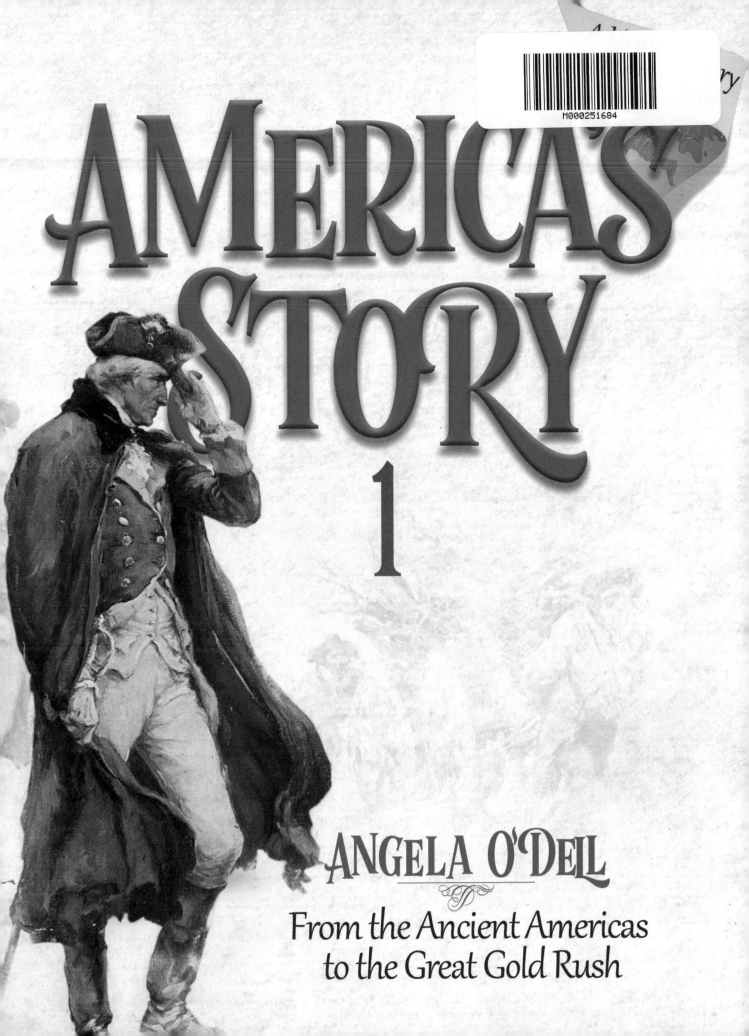

AMERICA'S STORY
1

ANGELA O'DELL

*From the Ancient Americas
to the Great Gold Rush*

First printing: February 2017
Fifth printing: July 2020

Master Books®, P.O. Box 726, Green Forest, AR 72638

Master Books® is a division of the New Leaf Publishing Group, Inc.

ISBN: 978-0-89051-979-0
ISBN: 978-1-61458-583-1 (digital)
Library of Congress Number: 201795874

Unless otherwise noted, Scripture quotations are from the New King James Version of the Bible.

Printed in the United States of America

Please visit our website for other great titles:

www.masterbooks.com

For information regarding author interviews, please contact the publicity department at (870) 438-5288.

Dedicated to my favorite students,
who were also my teachers.
I love you!
Soli Deo Gloria

Master Books®
A Division of New Leaf Publishing Group
www.masterbooks.com

Image Credits

All images are public domain (PD-US, PD-Art, and LOC), except for:

Science Photo Library - 22BL, 23B

Shutterstock - 5, 6, 10, 11, 12TL, 12C, 12B, 13TL, 13TR, 14R, 15, 18T, 21, 26T, 26B, 34R, 35, 51T, 51B, 53, 54R, 55, 59, 61, 62BL, 64L, 64R, 71, 74L, 74R, 75R, 76B, 84L, 84R, 94l, 94R, 101B, 102T, 102BR, 103TR, 104R, 105, 109B, 114L, 115, 117B, 119T, 119B, 120, 123BR, 124R, 125, 135, 144L, 147T, 154L, 154R, 155, 157B, 160, 164R, 165, 166, 167T, 169T, 170T, 174R, 175, 176B, 182TR, 184R, 185, 195, 196T, 196B, 199, 201B, 204R, 208, 211B, 214R, 215, 224R, 225, 230B, 246R, 247, 249C, 249B, 250T, 251BR, 252T, 254TR, 254BR, 255, 258, 264B, 266, 267T, 269, 274R, 275, 276, 279T, 279B, 282B

SuperStock- front cover

Wikimedia Commons: Images from Wikimedia Commons are used under the CC0 1.0, CC BY-SA 2.0 DE, CC-BY-SA-3.0 license or the GNU Free Documentation License, Version 1.3. CC0 1.0 - 21B, 95, 202T; CC BY-SA 1.0 - 45; CC BY 2.0 - 65, 132TR, 144R, 263BL; CC BY-SA 2.0 - 37B, 44R, 122B, 194R; CC BY-SA 2.0 DE - 23M; CC BY 3.0 - 142B; CC BY-SA 3.0 - 12TR, 22T, 23T, 32TL, 32 TR, 32C, 32BL, 32BR, 33TL, 33TR, 33BL, 33BR, 40TL, 40B, 72TL, 72BR, 101T, 132TL, 132M, 132B, 133TL, 133BL, 133BR, 141, 162T, 164L, 183BR, 191B, 192T, 193BR, 203T, 205, 222TL (GuidoB), 236R, 271BL, 271BR; CC BY-SA 4.0 - 73T, 133TR, 173BL, 265 (© Raimond Spekking).

L = left, TL = top left, BL = bottom left, C = center, CR = center right, CL = Center left, R = right, TR = top right, BR = bottom right

TABLE OF CONTENTS

Welcome to America's Story! This book is a unique combination of storybook and history curriculum. It is written in the same style that I have used with my own children, and many of the stories are the same ones I have told them as we have woven our tapestry of historical knowledge throughout that time.

History truly does need to be taught as History… HIS story. However, you must know that not every person in American history was a Christian. That does not mean that God did not use these people for His plan and glory. Those people fit into God's picture just the way He needed.

In our family, we firmly believe in providing a living education. This means making relationships with what we learn. It means that we learn about both heroes and villains. We learn about famous men and women and not-so-famous men and women. We make friends in history instead of just memorizing dates and names. We reach out and touch nature and learn to be observant of the small things in life. We see God's love for us in the flaming-red sunset, as well as in the busy little ants laboriously gathering their food. We work diligently to hide God's Word in our hearts.

Our goal is a living relationship with our Heavenly Father and wise hearts that love His world!

Blessings,
Angela O'Dell

CHAPTER 1

WHO LIVED HERE FIRST?

Starting Point: Following the events at the Tower of Babel, people groups moved throughout the world taking their languages and customs with them. Some of these people groups came to the Americas, where they formed a very diverse group of Native American cultures throughout the United States, Canada, as well as Central and South America well before Europeans arrived to colonize the lands.

Spot Light

Cahokia Mounds, Illinois

Mysteries of the Mound Builders: Today we find large Indian mounds, some in the shape of animals, throughout the midwest and eastern states. These are some sites of the mysterious Mound Builders that included a number of the Native American societies, including the Mississippian, Fort Ancient, and Adena cultures. These amazing builders chose dirt to make their monuments, and represent some of the largest cities, such as Cahokia, and advanced cultures in early history.

READY TO EXPLORE?

1. How do you think people first arrived in the Americas originally?

2. What do you think life was like in the Americas before visitors from Europe arrived?

Are you ready to enjoy an interesting story? This is the story of our great country and how it came into being. When I was a little girl, I used to wonder who had lived in my house before me. How many other children had climbed the trees I played in? What were they like, and what kind of clothes did they wear? I had a lot of questions. Do you ever wonder about these kinds of things?

Have you ever wondered who the first Americans were? Would you believe that there were millions of people living in *North* and *South America* by the time our Savior, Jesus Christ, was born? Well, there were! Historians (people who study history) believe that the first people came over from *Asia* through the *Bering Land Bridge,* which is now the *Bering Strait,* into *Alaska.*

Throughout hundreds of years, these people formed many nations. These nations are the ancestors of today's Native American Indians and the tribes that still exist in the jungles of South America. Artifacts have been found in both *North and South America* that are thought to be thousands of years old. These artifacts tell us a little about how these people lived. There really isn't any other way to know much about these people, for there are not many written records of their ways of life. They did not have pens, pencils, or paper like we do, and they all spoke in their own languages. Many of them did not have a written language, making it very hard to leave information for the following generations.

North America

South America

CONTINENT: a large body of land. The earth is divided into seven continents.

I think it is fun to contemplate the way the ancient American people could have lived. Can you imagine being a little boy or girl in those times? You would have had toys, but nothing like the toys you have now. These people had no plastic, rubber, or metal. Everything was made from animal skin, bones, wood, or even rocks. If you were a young boy, living in one of these tribes, you would probably own a toy bow and arrow. If you were a young girl, you might go to sleep at night cuddling your doll made from corn husks.

Corn husk doll

These people's houses were different from ours, too. Various tribes had different types of houses; some were made from animal skins, while others were constructed from mud or wood. These homes were heated by a fire right in the middle of the floor. It is easy to think that there were only adults who lived in these houses, but all civilizations have children, too. Close your eyes and imagine being you, but living back in one of these ancient tribes. How different your life would be!

We know that there were fishermen, hunters, weavers, and priests in these ancient tribes. We also know that they did not worship the One True God like we do. Many of the tribes worshiped the crops that they grew and ate, while others worshiped nature, which was around them. They thought of themselves as "brothers" with the animals and plants.

These early American people moved around much of the time. If the tribe mainly hunted for a living, they followed the great herds of buffalo. The men would hunt and kill the animals with long, sharp spears. The women and children followed behind them carrying the tribe's belongings. Do you know what Indian babies were called? They were called papooses, and they were carried on their mothers' backs. What a fun way to ride! All the people in the tribe had responsibilities; even the children had jobs. Do you have chores? They are probably different from the early Indian children's jobs.

If a tribe was mainly fishermen, they did not move around as much. However, their diet consisted mostly of fish. Do you like fish? Would you like to eat it every day for almost every meal? The farming tribes had to move to stay in warm enough places to grow their crops. These tribes, along with the hunting tribes, had smaller houses that were easier to move around. These houses were made from buffalo or deer skin stretched over long poles. You may have heard of these houses; they are called teepees. When I was a child, I used to make "teepees" by throwing blankets over chairs or tables. I used to sit inside my teepee and imagine I was an Indian. It's fun to do this, but can you imagine not having a house that was made to stay in one place? How strange it would be to travel with your whole town from one location to another, but that is exactly what most of these ancient North American tribes did!

Papooses

NARRATION BREAK

Tell how the early Americans came to be here.

Not all ancient Indian nations were nomads (wanderers).Some of the South and Central American nations were highly advanced civilizations with cities and governments. The Incas (ING-kus) in Peru, the Mayans (MY-ins) in Central America, and the Aztecs (AZ-teks) of modern Mexico are some of these nations. They are very old civilizations! Maybe someday you will have the chance to explore the discovered ruins of temples and cities left from hundreds of years ago. You can learn more about these ancient Americans in resources from your local library.

You probably have heard the names of many of the Native North American Indian tribes, but I will tell you about some of them.The Ojibwa (o-JIB-way), the Iroquois (EAR-u-koy), and the Wampanoag (wam-pa-NO-ag) tribes made up the Algonquian (all-GON-quin) nation.These people lived around the *Great Lakes* and the *Eastern Coast of North America.* They mainly hunted and fished for their food. Their houses, called wigwams, were dome shaped and made out of wood, animal skin, and bark. They were similar to the teepee, but they were round instead of having a pointed top.

Down to the south of the Algonquian nation, lived the Seminole (SEM-in-ole) tribe. This group of people once lived in what is now *Georgia.* They were peaceful people who lived by farming the land. As more settlers from other parts of the world came to North America, the Seminoles ran away, leaving their farms to live in the *Florida* swamps. They had to change their ways of living to adapt to their new home. They became hunters and fishermen, and they built a different kind of house called a chickee. These houses had open sides and were built on stilts. Can you think of the reason the Seminoles built houses like this? What kinds of animals live in the Florida swamps, or as we call them, the Everglades?

Hunters stampeding buffalo herd

Have you ever seen a buffalo or a bison? There are not very many of them now, but back hundreds of years ago, vast herds of them roamed the *Great Plains.* If your home is in one of the states right in the middle of our country, you have probably heard some of the names of the Indian tribes who lived there. In fact, they still live there on what is called reservations. Later, we will learn more about the Indian reservations, but back in the time we are reading about now, the Plains Indians roamed about hunting buffalo for food.

The Blackfeet, Comanche (com-AN-chee), Cheyenne (shy-ANN), and Sioux (SUE) were great hunters. They used the buffalo for many things besides just for meat. They made clothes and houses from the skin, and they also used the bones. Have you ever seen a buffalo bone necklace? Many Native Americans wore them as decoration.

Other tribes, such as the Apache (u-PACH-ee), Hopi (HOPE-ee), Pueblo (PWEB-lo), and Navajo

(NAH-vi-hoe) Indians lived in the south western corner of North America. These tribes made houses out of adobe (u-DOBE-ee), a straw and clay mixture dried hard by the sun. They were mostly farmers who grew corn and cotton as their crop. Just like in all the other tribes, everyone worked very hard. Women and children did most of the garden work, while men worked on building projects. Some of them made large cities out of hardened earth. Many of the houses in these cities were built right on the side of a mountain and were many stories high, similar to an apartment building.

There were many interesting people who lived on our continent for a very long time. As we wind our way down the path of American history, remember you too are a part of our great country's story. Would you like to learn more about the Ancient Americans?

NARRATION BREAK

Tell what you learned about the different tribes.

Group of Siksika (Blackfeet) men and one woman singing in front of teepee

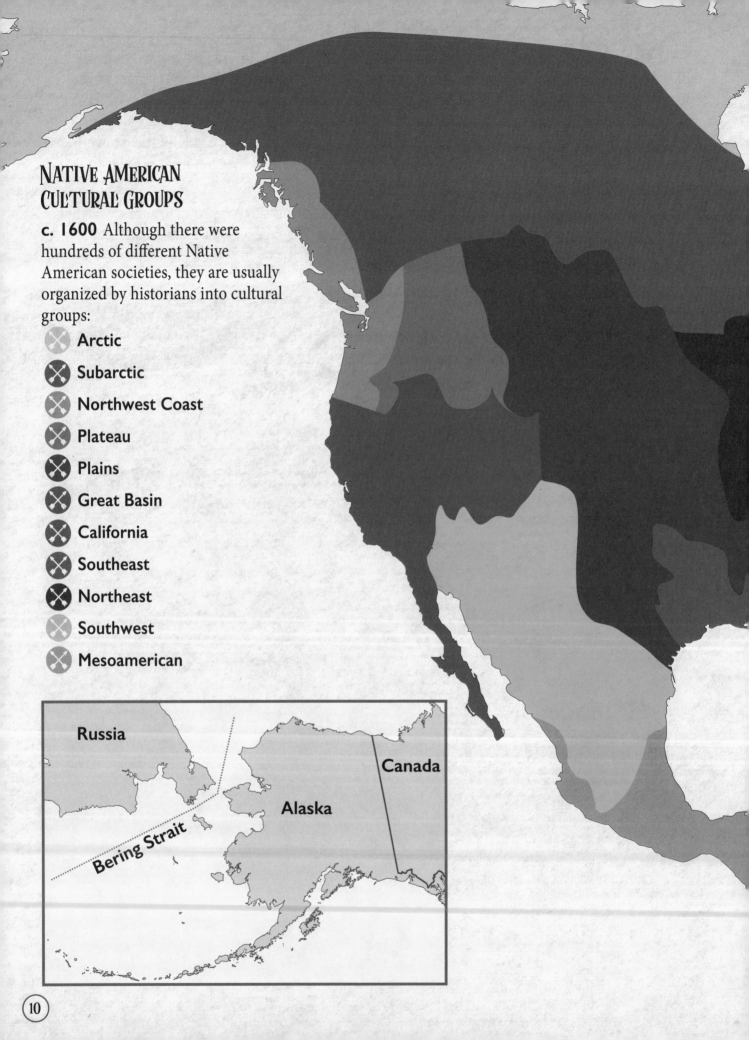

NATIVE AMERICAN CULTURAL GROUPS

c. 1600 Although there were hundreds of different Native American societies, they are usually organized by historians into cultural groups:

- Arctic
- Subarctic
- Northwest Coast
- Plateau
- Plains
- Great Basin
- California
- Southeast
- Northeast
- Southwest
- Mesoamerican

Russia

Canada

Alaska

Bering Strait

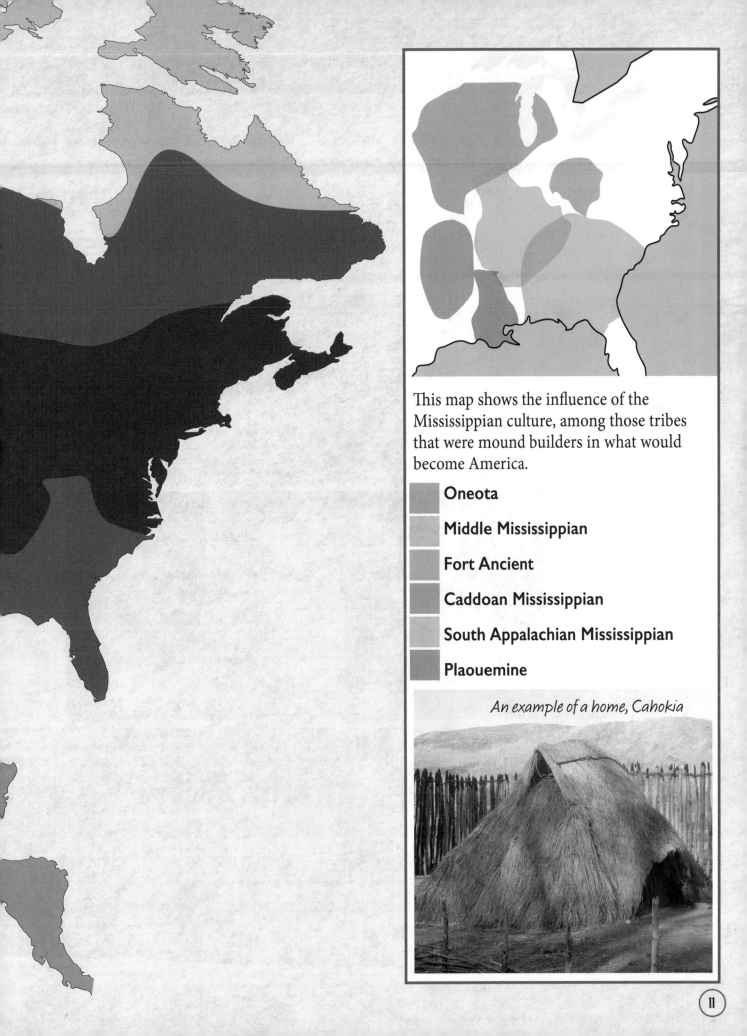

This map shows the influence of the Mississippian culture, among those tribes that were mound builders in what would become America.

Oneota

Middle Mississippian

Fort Ancient

Caddoan Mississippian

South Appalachian Mississippian

Plaouemine

An example of a home, Cahokia

▲ A waddle and daub house, made of wooden strips and combination of soil, clay, straw, or sand, used by groups like the Mississippian culture.

▲ Cliff Dwellings at Mesa Verde in southwestern Colorado

Example of ▶ a birch bark wigwam such as the Algonquian Indians used.

An example of a ▶ longhouse, similar to those used by the Iroquois

▲ A hogan, an earthen house in the style of the Navajo

▲ An earthen house or lodge; styles varied among the Navajo, Sioux, as well as some tribes on the west coast of America.

▲ Teepees were designed to be moved and easily put up again.

Reconstruction of ▶ a Timucuan chickee on display at Ft. Caroline National Monument in Jacksonville, Florida

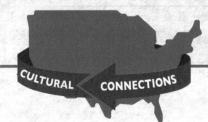

CULTURAL CONNECTIONS

Native American recipes are part of the foods we eat today. Corn was a very important crop for many of the tribes and societies. Corn varieties were adapted for different growing seasons and areas of the country. There are many other areas of the Native American culture that you can learn about through reading and visiting nearby sites.

Native Americans raising corn

Different colors and varieties of corn

THOUGHTS TO REMEMBER

1. We learned that people first arrived in the Americas by crossing over the Bering Land Bridge, which is now the Bering Strait. Although we cannot be 100% sure this is the route of their migration, archaeological finds largely support this theory.

2. Life for some Native Americans was mostly nomadic. We also learned how various tribes lived by hunting and farming, formed communities, and what types of abodes different groups lived in.

CHAPTER 2

LEIF ERICSON, THE CHRISTIAN VIKING

Spot Light

Starting Point: We learned in our last chapter how people have been living in North and South America for a very long time. We need to remember that back in the time of our story there were no televisions, radios, or computers. There was no easy way to get information across the Atlantic or Pacific Ocean.

The Very Large Solar System: Ancient and Medieval scientist and philosophers taught that the earth was the center of the entire universe. Now we know that our solar system is a tiny but divinely significant dot in a universe too vast for comprehension.

READY TO EXPLORE?

1. What did ancient people believe about earth and its place in the universe?

2. Do you understand why they believed this?

Leif Ericson journeys to the Americas	European nations (including Portugal) search for new ocean routes	Navajo, Apache, and other native tribes move from the north to the southwest of North America
1000 A.D.	~1400	~1400

Many of the people on the other side of the world, in *Europe, Asia,* and the other, more "civilized" continents, did not even know that North and South America existed!

Most of these Europeans believed all kinds of things that might sound funny to us. We know that the world is round, right? Actually, it is a sphere, which means it is shaped like a ball. How do we know this? If you had never seen a globe or a picture of our planet Earth from outer space; if you had always been told that the earth is flat, and the sun goes around it, you would believe it, right? It is easy to believe something when you do not know any differently. These people did not know any better, so they made up all sorts of stories about the world. Some believed that the earth was a huge plate-shaped disc that was carried on the back of an even bigger turtle!

SPHERE: an object having a round, solid, 3-dimensional shape like a ball.

Other stories included being able to fall off of the earth if you went too far. Many people believed in giant sea monsters and dragons that could swallow whole ships. At that time, the very idea that you could set sail from Europe heading west and eventually come back around to your own continent, was a crazy thought! No one had ever done it before.

Can you imagine how surprised these people would be, if they could see our modern jet planes flying across the great Atlantic and Pacific Oceans? They did not even know that there are two huge oceans on our earth. Let's take a few minutes right now to look at a globe. Find the Atlantic Ocean; it is the ocean that lies between the continents of Europe and Africa, and North and South America. Now spin your globe or look at your map at the other side of the Americas. That huge area of water you see is the Pacific Ocean.

Viking ship replica

Living around this time, in the countries of Norway and Sweden, was a tribe of sailing men. You may have heard their name before; they were called the Vikings. They were fierce people who believed in many gods. In this way, they were not unlike the Native American people about whom we have learned.

There are many varying stories about these people. Over the years, many of these stories have turned into legends. Legends are stories that are somewhat true with no one really knowing which parts are fairy tale and which parts are factual. We do know that a Viking man named Leif Ericson "discovered" North America around A.D. 1000. This story has been passed down for many generations.

NARRATION BREAK

Tell what you have learned so far about what people thought the world looked like.

Leif Ericson Discovers America

Among the Vikings, there lived a man named Erik the Red. He was even more fierce and worse tempered than the other Vikings. In fact, he was so ill-tempered, he was expelled from the country of Norway for picking fights! Erik moved his family to *Iceland*, where he built a farm. They lived peacefully for a while, but again, Erik's temper got the best of him. Again, he was punished and forced to leave for picking more fights.

This time, Erik decided to move to a place where he could live by himself with just his family. He chose to live in *Greenland*. When I was a young girl, I used to be very confused about Greenland and Iceland. I thought it was strange that Greenland is mostly ice, and Iceland is very green. Erik the Red chose Greenland because it was so icy, and he thought nobody else would want to live there. He wanted to be by himself with just his family. They called their new home in Greenland, Brattali.

Erik the Red had three sons. We are going to get to know his youngest son, Leif, a little better, for he is an important person to our country's history. Thankfully, Leif did not inherit his father's bad temper! He was a curious young boy, but he had a much more gentle spirit. As he grew, he became a wiser and more self-controlled man than his father was.

When Leif, who became known as Leif Ericson (also spelled "Erickson," "Ericcson," or "Erikson") grew up, he decided to sail back to Norway. He had heard of a wise and powerful king named Olav, who ruled in Norway at that time, and he wanted to meet him. While Leif was in Norway, he was converted to Christianity by King Olav, who indeed was a good man.

Erik the Red

On his return voyage, Leif became lost in a fog storm and was blown off course for several days. When the fog cleared, he could see that he was nowhere near his icy home of Greenland. Instead, he was in sight of a place he had never seen before! This land had beautiful trees and thick vegetation.

Leif and his men went ashore to explore. What they found was the most remarkable land they had ever seen. There were wild berries and grapes growing everywhere, and the wild animals were plentiful. There was such abundance that they named this new land, Vinland or Wineland. They stayed and explored this land for several months.

When Leif and his men returned to Greenland, they told everyone about this strange and wonderful new land. Leif also told them about the new God, whom he had learned about in Norway. Erik the Red was not happy that his son did not worship the old Viking gods anymore, but Leif's mother soon became a Christian. This made Leif very happy.

Soon, other members of Leif's family decided to go to this new land that Leif had told them about. Within a few months, there were over one hundred people who had moved to Vinland. These Vikings had a big surprise though! They soon found that they were not the only inhabitants of this land. Remember the Native Americans we learned about in the last chapter? That is right — Vinland was actually the northeastern coast of North America!

At first, the Native Americans were friendly, but soon they realized that these pale-skinned, blue-eyed visitors thought that they owned this land. Fighting broke out between them, and the Vikings were outnumbered. They decided to return to their homes in Greenland where they had lived peacefully.

There, Leif became the new leader of his family after his father's death. It is said that the Norsemen (another name for Vikings) returned to North America to harvest trees and other natural resources, but none of them actually lived there again. As years passed, and generations came and went, the new land was all but forgotten.

The Last Sea Fight

The only memory of this land was kept alive through the legends and tales, which were told around the fires at night and passed down from generation to generation. North America was to remain a land shrouded in mystery for five hundred more years. However, God had a plan for the great continent, the future home of the United States of America.

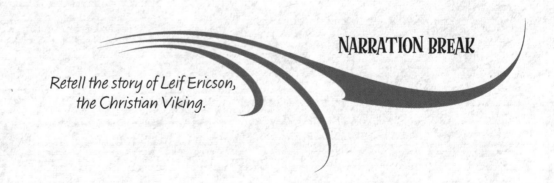

NARRATION BREAK

Retell the story of Leif Ericson, the Christian Viking.

THE VINLAND MAP

Fact or Fake? The Vinland Map caused a sensation when it was discovered in 1957, interestingly before the discovery of a Norse site in Newfoundland, Canada. Found in a very old book, the Vinland Map continues to stir controversy over its authenticity. Not only would the map have been the first known to show America, if true, it would have been evidence of the exploration of America by the Vikings.

There are few archaeological clues to how much of the Americas that the Vikings may have explored. Vinland is mentioned for the first time in a historical text written around 1075, and reveals that the name was connected to the abundance of grapes that grow there. It was described as an abundant land beyond which were no islands, just constant fog and ice.

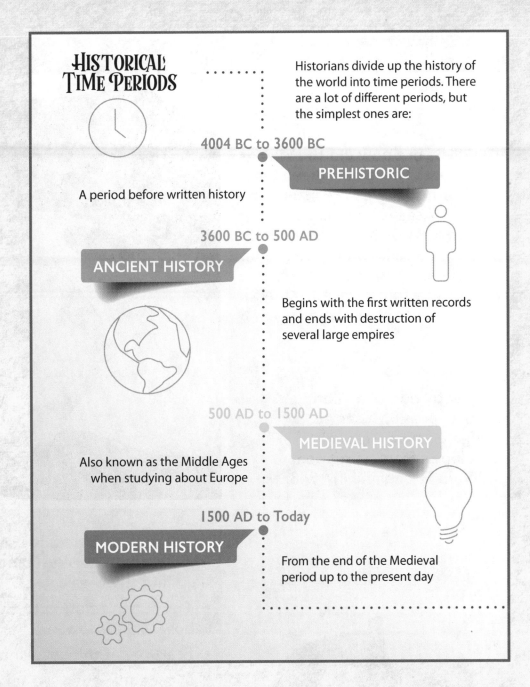

HISTORICAL TIME PERIODS

Historians divide up the history of the world into time periods. There are a lot of different periods, but the simplest ones are:

4004 BC to 3600 BC

PREHISTORIC

A period before written history

3600 BC to 500 AD

ANCIENT HISTORY

Begins with the first written records and ends with destruction of several large empires

500 AD to 1500 AD

MEDIEVAL HISTORY

Also known as the Middle Ages when studying about Europe

1500 AD to Today

MODERN HISTORY

From the end of the Medieval period up to the present day

Historians and cartographers (people who draw and study maps) continue to debate various positions of whether or not the map is a fake or real, as they study the parchment, ink, lettering, marks, and other details.

Church of Hvalsey, the best-preserved Nordic ruins in Greenland.

Sailing across the ocean required strong navigational skills – but how did the Vikings do that? There have been hints of something called a sunstone in their sagas, the tales of great adventure and history, which helped sailors find the sun on cloudy days. Some feel these sunstones were a mineral, possibly Icelandic spar. ▶

An illustration of a Viking sundial, possibly used to navigate; the design is developed from a fragment found in Greenland in 1948. ▼

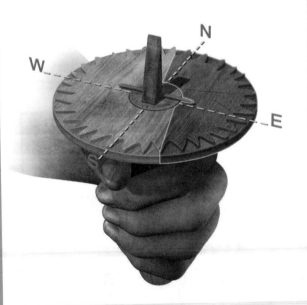

In addition to a possible sunstone, the Vikings could have used other clues to help find their way:

- The sun in relation to the horizon – how high or low

- Features of the coastlines

- Directions found in their sagas or narratives

- Weather patterns of rain or wind or even storms in certain areas

Crops were grown, homes were built, businesses thrived, as well as beautiful crafted items like clothing, swords, combs, musical instruments, and jewelry — artifacts of which have all been found.

Science Photo Library

HOW DID VIKINGS LIVE ON LAND?

Trelleborg, one of the seven known Viking ring castles ▶

Reconstructed long house in the Viking Museum in Borg, Norway ▼

The Norse had a form of government and a social order — royal families, clan chieftains who were landowners and of noble blood, freemen who owned smaller farms, or skilled craftsmen like shipbuilders or fishermen. At the bottom of the social order were the slaves. Many extended family groups lived together in large groups.

Example of a Viking ring fortress ▼

Science Photo Library

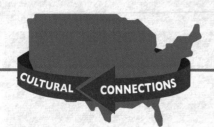

Although the Age of the Vikings ended almost 500 years before European explorers (whom you will learn about in our next chapter) set foot on the continents of North and South America, they still have an immense impact on our culture here in the United States of America. The Vikings not only came to North America and created settlements, but they also traveled broadly all over Europe. Some of their interactions with the peoples in these countries were friendly and productive to both parties, but many of them were raids. The Vikings were known for their pillaging and stealing! When they raided these countries, they sometimes overthrew the leaders and government, setting up their rulers instead. After centuries of this behavior, the Vikings had successfully planted themselves in England and France, spreading the influence of their Scandinavian culture and creating whole new family lines with all new mixed English/Viking and French/Viking surnames (last names). Years later, when the settlers from those European countries settled in America, they brought all of those customs and words with them! We can thank the Vikings for these words, which we still commonly use.

Club — *a heavy wooden, blunt weapon.*

Ransack — *to rip a house/room apart in search of something.*

Law — *a rule meant for all people to follow.*

Bug — *an insect.*

Reindeer — *a large antlered mammal.*

Dirt — *the common ingredient of the ground.*

Rotten — *decay.*

Did you know that you speak Norse (Viking)?

A Sami family in Norway, 1896. The Sami are a native people group that had interactions with the Vikings. Some involved trade, marriages, or even conflict.

THOUGHTS TO REMEMBER

1 and 2. We learned in Chapter 2 that the ancients held the belief that the earth was the center of the universe. It is easy to see why they believed this — after all, we can't feel the earth moving as it spins and turns its way around the sun! It does indeed feel like the earth is the center with all other planets and stars circling around and around us.

CHAPTER 3

CHRISTOPHER COLUMBUS AND OTHER EUROPEAN EXPLORERS

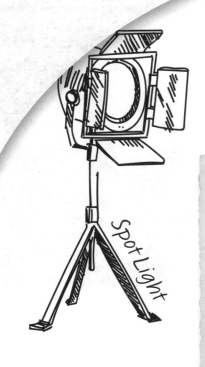

Spot Light

Starting Point: Stories of a "new land" had been told across Europe since the time of the Vikings, and Christopher Columbus was interested in finding it. One of a group of adventurous European explorers of the time, Columbus would set sail in an effort to reach Asia. Others would soon follow.

San Sebastian de la Gomera, Canary Islands

Mistaken Location: Christopher Columbus believed he had landed on an island off of the coast of the Indies. This is why he called the natives he encountered "Indians."

READY TO EXPLORE?

1. What war were King Ferdinand and Queen Isabella of Spain fighting when Christopher Columbus first asked them to fund his explorations?

2. From what country did Columbus come?

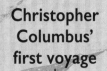

Christopher Columbus' first voyage	European slave ships begin transporting abducted Africans to Central America	Walseemüller map, the Universalis Cosmographia
1492	early 1500s	1507

Nearly 500 years after the adventures of Leif Ericson, a young man from *Genoa, Italy*, heard the story of this Viking who found a new land. The young man's name was Christopher Columbus. Christopher was interested in sailing across the *Atlantic Ocean*, something no one of his day had ever done before. Let me tell you more about our young Mister Columbus before we go on.

Christopher was born the son of a weaver in Genoa, Italy. From a very young age, Christopher knew he did not want to be a weaver like his father. Instead, he wanted to become a sailor. He spent many long hours of his childhood daydreaming of being out on the sea. By the age of 13, Christopher was working on a ship's crew, where he learned much about sailing and ships. He had many adventures, including being chased by pirates!

Inspiration of Christopher Columbus

When he became a grown man, Christopher moved from the boot-shaped country of Italy to nearby *Portugal*. There he married a lovely lady from Madeira, and they had a son. Christopher was known as a gentleman of the sea, but he still longed for adventure and discovery. He still dreamed of crossing the Atlantic Ocean.

Unlike many people of his day, Columbus believed that the world is round. He knew that the great explorer Marco Polo had said that there was a great "sea" on the eastern side of Asia. Nobody knew that the continents of North and South America existed, so Christopher thought surely this "sea" must be the Atlantic. He believed that he would be able to sail west from Portugal and reach *China* and *India*. He was a little confused about the size of our earth!

It was around this time that he heard the legend of Leif Ericson and how he had found an unfamiliar, rich land. Columbus reasoned that this must have been China or perhaps India, and therefore Ericson's travels proved that he too could do the same.

Let's take a few minutes to look at a globe. Can you see what Christopher Columbus was mistaken about? If you completely removed the continents of North and South America and combined the Atlantic and the Pacific Oceans, it would look a

GLOBE: a spherical representation of the earth, usually on a pedestal or stand.

lot different, wouldn't it? It would take you a very long time indeed to reach China, Japan, or India sailing west from Europe!

The first thing Columbus needed to do was find a rich king to finance his long voyage. He went to the king of Portugal with his request, but the king believed he was crazy to even think about it! Christopher then went to King Ferdinand and Queen Isabella of *Spain*. They were interested, but they were at war and did not have the money to give Columbus.

During this time, Christopher's beautiful wife died, and he was left to raise their little son, Diego, by himself. He waited seven years for the war to be over; by that time, he was nearly broke himself. Finally he received word that Spain had won the war, and King Ferdinand and Queen Isabella were ready to help him.

The king and queen promised to give him great rewards if he was able to cross the Atlantic and bring back riches from this faraway land. The queen, who was a Christian, was eager to spread the gospel to the "heathens" in the new land. The king, who was a little concerned about the emptiness of his kingdom's treasure boxes, was eager to get his hands on the riches of the land that he supposed was China or India.

At last, Christopher Columbus had his ships! The **Niña, Pinta,** and **Santa Maria** were small ships, but they were sturdy and strong. He had another difficult task now; he had to find enough men to be crews on his ships. This was not easy, because so many sailors thought that if you sailed out too far, you could fall off the edge of the world. They thought Columbus was crazy to think you could sail all the way around the earth.

The three ships finally set sail on August 3, 1492. The sailors that Columbus had found to sail the ships were nervous and afraid to leave their families. They were not at all sure that they would ever see their homes again. Many thought they were following a crazy man to the edge of the earth.

They sailed out to sea and soon were farther than any European sailor had ever been before! The crew became increasingly nervous. They grumbled and complained that there was nothing out there but water and more water. Their food became moldy, and they complained about that, too. The fresh water ran low, and the men truly began to panic! Have you ever heard the saying, "Water, water everywhere but not a drop to drink?" You cannot drink ocean water because it is too salty! You would just get thirstier and thirstier.

Columbus, departing on his first voyage, takes leave of the king and queen.

NARRATION BREAK

Retell what you have learned about Christopher Columbus so far.

Just as everyone was convinced that they were going to die, they started seeing signs of land. Then, on October 12, 1492, Columbus spotted land. He thought perhaps he had reached an island off of the coast of China or India. When they reached shore, the people they saw did not resemble Chinese people, so they concluded that they must be near India; this is why Columbus called them Indians. He named the place they had landed *San Salvador*, which means "Holy Savior." Of course, we know that they had not landed on China or India, but they did not know that the continents of North and South America even existed. The island on which they had landed was very near present-day *Cuba*.

Columbus spots land.

The natives of the island treated Columbus and his men like gods. They had never seen a large ship before, and they thought the sails of the three ships were clouds that had brought foreign gods to their shores. The men took gifts and even people from the island when they went home to Spain. The explorers were treated like heroes, and the king and queen gave Columbus an enormous reward.

Columbus made three more voyages, and even though he had found riches on the island on his first voyage, he never did discover any great and glorious fortune as he had hoped. Christopher Columbus died in 1506, never knowing that he had landed on a new continent.

Columbus's explorations opened the door to other explorers, and over the next hundred years, Portugal, *Spain, France,* and *England* claimed huge areas of North America. An explorer named Amerigo Vespucci proclaimed that South America was a new continent, and in 1507 it was added to the map. The name America comes from this explorer's name.*

Columbus lands.

* Amerigo Vespucci's claim of finding a new world was discredited when it was discovered he had made the entire tale up with intentions of gaining attention, but it was too late — America had been named.

Ponce De Leon, the aging governor of *Puerto Rico*, was looking for the mythical Fountain of Youth. There was a legend that said if he could bathe in this fountain, he would be young again. Instead of finding the fountain, he found a beautiful new land that he named Tierra *Florida* because of the bright-colored wildflowers he found growing everywhere. Florida is the Spanish word for "flowery."

In 1540, another Spanish explorer named Coronado explored what is now the southwestern corner of the United States. He was looking for the legendary Golden Cities of Cibola. He wanted to find the famed cities and claim all the gold for Spain. Of course he never found them, but he did claim the area that is now *Texas, Oklahoma,* and *Kansas.*

Spain claimed an even larger area when De Soto landed on the Florida coast and traveled northwest until he reached the *Mississippi River*. Meanwhile *France* claimed most of what is now *Canada. England* did not want to be left out and sent an explorer, John Cabot, to claim the eastern coast of what is now our country, the United States.

Ponce De Leon

As more and more Europeans settled in central and northern South America, the need for cheap labor grew. In 1503, the first slave ships started arriving on our shores. Sadly, this was the beginning of the African slave trade. We will see how the slave trade spread like a plague, darkening the future of what would be our country.

Piece by piece, North America was being claimed by European countries. Spain built a city-settlement in Florida. Saint Augustine is the oldest European-built city on North America. It was English settlers, however, who determined the destiny of our country. We will learn about the first lasting English settlement in our next chapter.

I hope you are enjoying the journey through the history of our great country. The ride is about to get a little bumpy, so fasten your seat belts! In our next chapters we are going to meet a real princess, hear about the mystery of a disappearing colony, and learn how one man saved the life of an entire settlement.

Amerigo Vespucci

NARRATION BREAK

Retell the rest of the story of Christopher Columbus and the other explorers.

AMERICA ON THE MAP

History is a fascinating study of how people live, travel, and record the details of their lives. Maps are among the more interesting artifacts of history. They reveal what certain people or countries knew about the world at any given time. It shows their ability to either share information found on maps from other cultures or proves they were capable of traveling to these places themselves.

The Vinland Map shown in the last chapter is an example of a mappa mundi — that is a Latin phrase that simply means it is a map of the world, thought to have been created during the Middle Ages or medieval period of history. So is the Waldseemüller map known as Universalis Cosmographia. Finished in 1507, the map incorporated the knowledge of explorers like Columbus and Amerigo Vespucci into his work.

Closeup of the Martin Waldseemüller map showing South America and the word "AMERICA"

It is thought Waldseemüller guessed the ocean was there or theorized the lands of this New World couldn't be the same as China, India, or Asia because of the known information at the time, and so he simply separated it with a body of water

The United States Library of Congress purchased the Waldseemüller map for $10 million.

The Waldseemüller map is the first one to show that the Americas were separate from the continent of Asia, and it actually uses the name "America" on the part of the continent we know as South America. It also shows the Pacific Ocean, though it was not named that at the time.

A copy of Martin Waldseemüller's map, on display in the Treasures Gallery, Library of Congress (Jefferson Building), Washington, D.C.

▲ The *Santa Maria* was a carrack (or nao). The *Pinta* and *Niña* were smaller naval ships.

▲ Columbus and his officers stayed in the toldilla in the stern (back) of the ship. Here, Columbus has a navigational tool called a quadrant on his desk.

The crew ▶ wore their own clothes and went barefoot.

◀ The *Santa Maria* was run aground in Hispaniola.

The rigging allowed the crew to operate the mast and sails. ▶

▲ The crew's food supplies included sea biscuits and salted meat

▲ Other crew members did the manual labor onboard the ship, including cleaning the deck and operating the sails.

▲ The crew's schedule was organized by six four-hour watches. Rodrigo de Triana was on watch when he sighted land.

▲ The *Niña* was captained by Vicente Yáñez Pinzón on this voyage and, like the *Pinta*, completed the trip. It would follow Columbus back to the Americas on his next two voyages. In fact, she was his favorite of the ships on the first voyage, and he eventually became a part-owner.

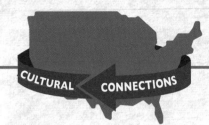

It is interesting to note the different and unique motivations behind the five major European countries' explorations of the New World. Generally speaking, the Dutch came from the Netherlands to trade with the Natives and other settlers in the New World, the Portuguese came to explore and trade, the English came because, more than anything, they wanted more land, the French wanted to outwit the English in any and all of their endeavors, and the Spanish came to get rich. Mexico is our neighbor to the south. This land was once ruled by great ancient civilizations such as the Mayans and Incas. When the Spanish came, they overthrew these civilizations and set up their own way of life, including the introduction of the stolen Africans, who were sold into slavery, and the arrival of Catholicism. Over the centuries, this mix of people became the countries of Central America. If you were to visit Mexico today, you would see many Catholic churches, old Spanish missions, and Aztec ruins. The heritage of many Mexicans can be traced back to the Aztec, Spanish, and Africans of the exploration period.

Ruins of Papantla, Mexico, 1883

Chichen Itza archaeological site of Maya ruins in Mexico

THOUGHTS TO REMEMBER

1. We learned that the king and queen of Spain were unable to help Columbus with the finances needed to complete his explorations because they were in the middle of fighting a long and expensive war. This war was an ongoing battle with the Islamic forces attempting to take over European thrones. Queen Isabella was well-known to be a Christian (Catholic) monarch.

2. Columbus was originally from Italy.

CHAPTER 4

SETTLEMENTS, MOSQUITOES AND AN INDIAN PRINCESS

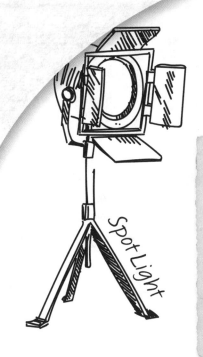

Spot Light

Starting Point: Discovering the new lands brought hope for opportunities to many, but not everyone would live to see their dream realized. And while it was a new life for many Europeans, Native Americans began to see their way of life come to an end.

Jamestown National Historic Site

The Settlement of Jamestown: The Settlement of Jamestown was the first lasting English colony in America. Its original population was entirely male. These men came to America for financial gain.

READY TO EXPLORE?

1. How did the colony of Roanoke go down in history as the Lost Colony?

2. What do you know of the Indian princess, Pocahontas?

Do you like a good mystery? History is full of them, and today we are going to learn about one of the most enduring mysteries in our country's history — the mystery of a disappearing colony! A colony is another word for a settlement where a group of people live together in a community and work together to achieve a common goal.

While *Spain* and *France* were exploring and claiming land for their respective countries, England was struggling to start a settlement in the New World. In 1587, a group of English settlers started a colony on Roanoke Island off the coast of North Carolina. They called their island settlement "Cittie of Raleigh," (yes, that is the way they spelled it) after Sir Walter Raleigh, an explorer whose men first spotted this island.

After getting his people settled in for the winter, John White, the governor of the settlement, went back to England for more supplies. He was delayed because of a war being fought over the passageways in the Atlantic Ocean, but finally, he was able to return to his colony in the New World.

A Croatoan village of the Secotan in North Carolina by John White

ISLAND: a small piece of land completely surrounded by water

When he returned, the people of the "Cittie of Raleigh" were completely gone. The houses were tumbled-down, and everything was overgrown with weeds and bushes. There were no signs of struggle — it was as though the inhabitants simply disappeared. The only clue was the word "Croatoan" carved into a tree. Governor White knew that the Croatoan Indians lived on a nearby island that is known to today as *Hatteras Island*.

John White discovers the word "CROATOAN" carved at Roanoke's fort palisade.

Poor Governor John White. His daughter, Eleanor Dare, along with her husband and infant daughter, were among the lost settlers. He searched frantically, but to no avail. The weather was nasty, and his ships were badly damaged in a storm. He realized that he needed to return to England for help. Sadly, John White never got that help or returned to look for the settlers.

To this day, the colony is called the Lost Colony of Roanoke. Many people believe that the settlers were kidnapped and forced to leave the island, while others believe that perhaps the people were starving and willingly left with the Indians. What do you think happened?

In 1607, another group of English settlers came to the New World. These were not families looking for a new life; they were men and boys mostly from the upper class in England. They were searching for the legendary riches of the New World. They were convinced that there was gold and other treasure here; they were looking for adventure. The one thing they were not looking for and not ready for, was hardship. Instead of riches, hardship is exactly what they found in the New World.

Sir Walter Raleigh

These adventure hunters lacked survival skills needed to settle this wild, new land. They built their settlement, Jamestown, too near a swampy area. Do you know what happens when you camp close to a swampy, wet area? Soon, you are being visited by a very unwelcome and unpleasant guest, the mosquito! These unfriendly little insects did more than annoy the Jamestown settlers though; they spread malaria, a disease that killed 72 of the men in one year!

Marsh wetlands on the island proved to be a breeding ground for mosquitoes.

NARRATION BREAK

What do you remember? Retell the story of the Lost Colony of Roanoke.

Pocahontas saves John Smith.

Among the Jamestown settlers, there was one man who was used to hardship and adventure. Captain John Smith was not going to let some pesky mosquitoes get him down! He was a tough man who made the rule, "He who will not work, shall not eat." I am sure that the English gentlemen did not like to hear this. They were used to having servants work for them, and they were not used to hunting for their meat or planting their own vegetables. Arguing and fighting broke out among the men, but they soon realized that John Smith was right; they had no servants or slaves to do their work for them here in this New World. If they wanted to live, they would have to work!

Soon, John Smith was considered a leader in the group, and even though a lot of the other men did not like him, they did listen to him. He also interacted with the local Indians, becoming good friends with the daughter of Chief Wahunsunacawh of the Powhatan Indians. There are many opinions about Captain Smith. Some people think he was a remarkable, upright man, while others think he was a bit of a scoundrel. Maybe he was a little of both! At the time of the Jamestown settlement, he was 27 years old and had already had an extremely adventurous life. He also seemed to have a knack for getting in and out of trouble. He was arrested many times but always escaped being hung or executed.

John Smith was always getting into scrapes with his fellow Englishmen and with the Indians. He was quick witted though, and usually found a way around the disagreement. His fellow settlers grudgingly admitted that he was the only one who could get them through the long, cold winter.

I mentioned before that Captain John Smith became friends with the daughter of an Indian chief with a really long name — Wahunsunacawh! You probably have heard the story of Pocahontas, the Indian maiden who saved Captain John Smith's life. Did you know that she was not much older than you probably are? Historians believe that she was between 11 and 13 years of age when she met Captain Smith. Pocahontas may have been a child, but she did something very brave; she stopped her father from killing Captain Smith when there was

a big disagreement between the Indians and the English settlers. She wanted her people, the Powhatan Indians, to live peacefully with these Englishmen in Jamestown.

Like so many other interesting people in history, not much is actually known about this Indian princess — even though there seems to be plenty of legend! We do know that she persuaded her father to help the men at Jamestown by allowing her to take them food through the winter, therefore saving the men from starvation. They had not hunted and planted enough to get them through the winter.

The relationship between the Indians and the settlers did not stay friendly for long. Captain Smith returned to England after he was badly injured in a gunpowder accident. When she was 17 years old, Pocahontas was kidnapped by the Englishmen, but she was treated kindly by most of the settlers. Many of them remembered how she had helped them.

John Smith

Later, Pocahontas married one of the Englishmen, John Rolf. Her marriage did bring some peace again between her people and the settlers. She became a Christian and took the name Rebecca. Shortly after she married Rolf, Pocahontas went on a voyage to England to meet her husband's family. While in England, she became ill and died, leaving behind a two-year-old son. Her son eventually returned to the land of his mother's people.

Wedding of Pocahontas and John Rolf

NARRATION BREAK

What do you remember? Retell the story of Jamestown and Pocahontas.

Finding Roanoke Colony

Roanoke Island is among the Outer Bank islands of North Carolina. The island used to be considered part of the lands of Virginia. The Lost Colony was the second attempt at colonizing the island.

Map drawn by John White in 1585. Roanoke is shown circled in the center of the map.

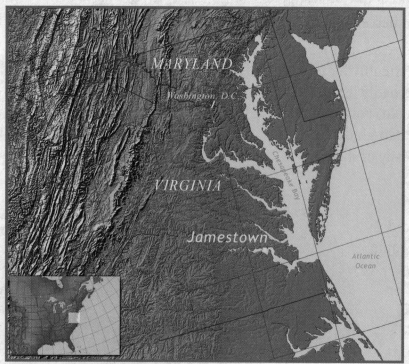

The site of the Jamestown Settlement, which managed to survive as the first permanent English community in America.

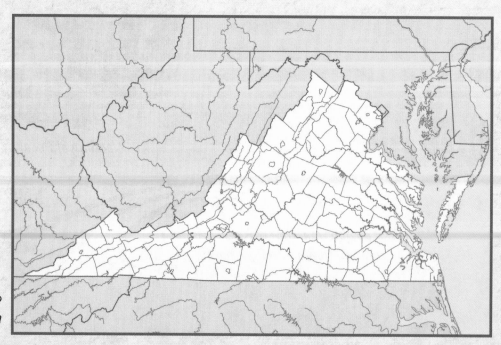

Location map of Virginia

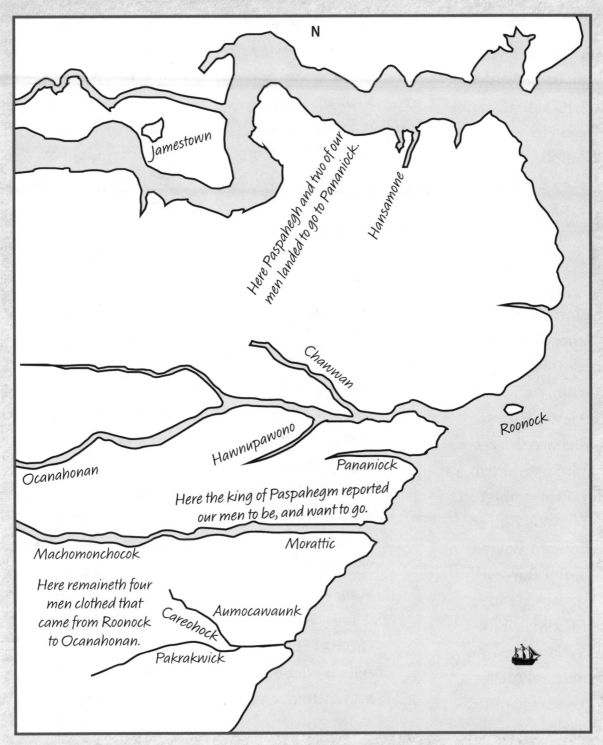

N

Jamestown

Here Paspahegh and two of our men landed to go to Pananiock.

Hansamone

Chawwan

Roonock

Hawnupawono

Pananiock

Ocanahonan

Here the king of Paspahegm reported our men to be, and want to go.

Morattic

Machomonchocok

Here remaineth four men clothed that came from Roonock to Ocanahonan.

Aumocawaunk

Careohock

Pakrakwick

Map similar to the one drawn by a Jamestown settler in 1607, it makes references to possible survivors of Roanoke being seen among the Indian settlements and evidence of techniques learned from the colonists.

THE PEOPLE OF THE LOST COLONY*

ADULT MALES

John White, governor
Roger Bailie, assistant
Roger Prat, assistant
George Howe, advisor
Nicholas Johnson
Ananias Dare
John S. Meyer
Thomas Warner
Anthony Cage
John Jones
John Tydway
Ambrose Viccars
Edmond English
Thomas Topan
Henry Berrye
Richard Berrye
John Spendlove
John Hemmington
Thomas Butler
Edward Powell
John Burden
James Hynde
Thomas Ellis
William Browne
Michael Myllet
Thomas Smith
Richard Kemme
Thomas Harris
Richard Taverner
John Earnest
Henry Johnson

John Starte
Thomas Crowley
Richard Dange
William Lucas
Arnold Archard
John Wright
William Dutton
Morris Allen
William Waters
Richard Arthur
John Chapman
William Clement
Robert Little
Hugh Tayler
Richard Wildye
Lewes Wotton
Michael Bishop
Henry Browne
Henry Rufoote
Richard Tomkins
Henry Dorrell
Charles Florrie
Henry Mylton
Henry Payne
Thomas Harris
William Nicholes
Thomas Phevens
John Borden
Thomas Scot
Henry Sturges
William Willes
John Brooke

John Bright
Clement Tayler
William Sole
John Cotsmur
Humfrey Newton
Thomas Colman
Thomas Gramme
Marke Bennet
John Gibbes
John Stilman
Robert Wilkinson
Peter Little
John Wyles
Brian Wyles
George Martyn
Hugh Pattenson
Martyn Sutton
John Farre
John Bridger
Griffen Jones
Richard Shaberdge
James Lasie
John Cheven
Thomas Hewet
William Berde
Edouard Jourdan
Walter Raleigh

ADULT FEMALES

Eleanor (Elyoner) Dare,
John White's daughter
Margery Harvie

Agnes Woo

Wenefrid Powell

Joyce Archard

Jane Jones

Elizabeth Glane

Jane Pierce

Audry Tappan

Alis Chapman

Emme Merrimoth

--- Colman

Margaret Lawrence

Joan Warren

Jane Mannering

Edeva Sturges

Rose Payne

Elizabeth Viccars

CHILDREN AND TEENAGERS

John Sampson

Robert Ellis

Ambrose Viccars

Thomas Archard

Thomas Humfrey

Thomas Smart

George Howe

John Prat

William Wythers

Virginia Dare, John White's granddaughter

Virginia Dare Flavoring Extracts label, 1923 ▶

THE ENDURING STORY OF VIRGINIA DARE

Every member of the Lost Colony of Roanoke had dreams of a new future here in the New World. The birth of one little girl highlighted the promise of this future and her mysterious loss amplified the tragedy.

Baptism of Virginia Dare ▼

Virginia was born on August 18, 1587 and while how and when she died is not known, she has not been forgotten in American history. She has appeared in stories, monuments, names of different places, advertising, a commemorative coin, and even a postage stamp in 1937.

CUT ON HEAVY BLACK OUTLINE AND FOLD BACK WINGS ON DOTTED LINE

You get the natural flavor when baking with VIRGINIA DARE Double Strength Extracts

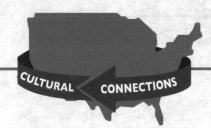

CULTURAL CONNECTIONS

America has always been the land of opportunity and innovation! The history of Jamestown, the first permanent English colony, attests to that. Although the men who came to settle this colony were not particularly prepared for the hardship, the mosquitoes, or the Native Americans, Jamestown did survive. In our story of history, you will learn that the history and the culture of our country are defined by the men and women who have given everything to live in freedom. This stubborn will to make it and do what needs to be done, to not only survive, but to thrive, is what makes America "the land of the free and the home of the brave." It is important that you, the next generation of Americans, understand that this is your heritage as a citizen of this country. You will learn that nothing, especially freedom, is free — someone always pays for it. This chapter's cultural focus is an invitation for you, the student, to pay attention to, and to learn from, the sacrifice of those you will learn about in this history story, because you are an important part of that story.

Jamestown: Building a Fortified Village

Remains of the 1639
Jamestown Church tower

THOUGHTS TO REMEMBER

1. We learn in Chapter 4 that the colony of Roanoke mysteriously disappeared. The mystery has never been truly solved.

2. We learned that Pocahontas was brave and showed mercy to the new arrivals to her land. By providing food, she helped them survive. Though her life held difficult challenges, she served as a bridge between her tribe and the new settlers.

44

CHAPTER 5

PILGRIMAGE TO FREEDOM

Spot Light

Starting Point: Freedom has been at the heart of this new land, America, since the beginning. The story of the Pilgrims is a great example of why a new land was so important in order for them to be able to live their faith in peace and security.

Replica ship Mayflower II

The Pilgrims Great Sea-Voyage: The Pilgrims voyaged to America on the *Mayflower*. You can visit a replica of the *Mayflower, Mayflower 2*, at Pilgrim Memorial State Park pier in Plymouth, Massachusetts.

READY TO EXPLORE?

1. Why did the Pilgrims go through such hardship to come to America?

2. What is the National Monument to the forefathers?

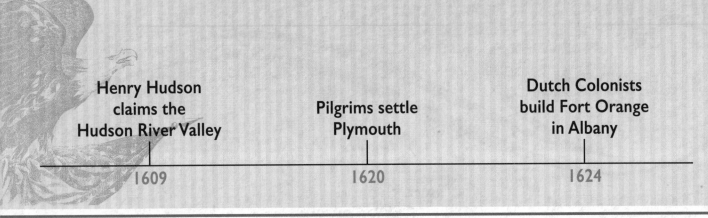

Today, our story takes us back across the Atlantic Ocean to *England*, the small island country from which the settlers in our last chapter came. However, this time we are going to follow the story of a different type of New World settlers.

First, let me acquaint you with a small village in England, which is the backdrop for the beginning of our story. *Scrooby* is a rural village in the Yorkshire province of England. With lush, green, rolling hills and quaint farms dotting the countryside, it looks rather like a picturesque land in a storybook. In fact, this part of England is the setting of a very famous story that I am quite sure you have heard. The village of Scrooby is very close to Sherwood Forest, where the famous Robin Hood and his merry men lived.

In the late 1500s and early 1600s a group of people lived in this area who called themselves Separatists. That is an odd name, isn't it? The name comes from the word "separate." They chose this name because they wished to separate themselves from the Church of England. At this time in history, King James of England was the boss! He believed he had the right to tell everyone how to worship God. Of course, he was wrong. No one has the right to tell anyone how they should worship God; that is a personal decision.

The Separatists, led by William Brewster, John Robinson, and later, William Bradford, met secretly at Mr. Brewster's home in Scrooby. There they worshiped the way they saw fit. What they were doing was illegal, and the brave church leaders were arrested and imprisoned many times for disobeying King James.

The small group soon began planning a move to the nearby country of *Holland*, where the government did not interfere with the churches. They would be free to practice their faith as they chose. They were heartbroken to leave their homes and country. After they gathered their crops, sold their houses, and said tearful goodbyes to their friends and loved ones, they boarded the ship they had hired to take them to Holland. The captain of the ship was not their friend, though; he had turned traitor and sold them into the hands of the English soldiers.

The Pilgrims, for that is what they called themselves now, were again put into prison. King James was very angry! He did not know what to do with these people who refused to obey him. Now he wondered what to do with them, for they had sold all their homes and had no place to live! The women and children stayed with family and friends while the men were kept in prison for several months. Meanwhile, King James was befuddled! What was he going to do with these people now? They were becoming more trouble than they were worth.

After they had been released from prison, William Brewster, William Bradford, and John Robinson yet again planned a journey to Holland. Maybe by this time King James was tired of dealing with this wayward group, for he did not do much to stop them.

Embarkation of the Pilgrims

PILGRIM: a person who journeys to a sacred place for religious reasons.

Their second attempt at escape was successful, and they arrived in Holland at last. The Pilgrims were delighted to have the freedom to worship God as they pleased and adjusted well to their new home. The children made friends and learned the language easily.

They had lived in Holland for 11 years, when the church leaders became concerned that their group was becoming too comfortable with the "worldliness" of Holland. Even though their neighbors and the Dutch (that is what the people of Holland are called) government was very friendly and allowed them to gather and worship as they pleased, they feared losing their identity as a group.

William Brewster and William Bradford began talking about going to the New World. They liked the idea of having land to farm and plenty of space in which to spread out. They also knew that there would be no one else around to influence their children in a worldly way.

Some of the Pilgrims did not want to go to the New World. They were comfortable in Holland. They owned homes, and their children had married Dutch people. Settled and comfortable, they did not want to leave their friends, and they were fearful of the legendary "savages" of the New World.

There was a man in the Pilgrim congregation named Myles Standish. Mr. Standish was an English captain who enjoyed adventure! He was a fighting man and offered his services to the Pilgrims who wanted to go to America. It is said that Myles Standish had a sword, named "Gideon," which had been given to him by an old sword maker whose life he had saved.

Mr. Brewster returned to England and applied for a land patent that would allow the Pilgrims to settle in the New World. It was 1619 by the time they finally received the land patent for land near Jamestown in Virginia.

Can you imagine the hustle and bustle of the preparations? The women and children busily knitted hats and mittens to be worn on the voyage and in the New World. Food items were carefully prepared and stored for the voyage and the arrival in the New World. Everyone who wanted to go sold everything they could and gathered the money to buy a ship.

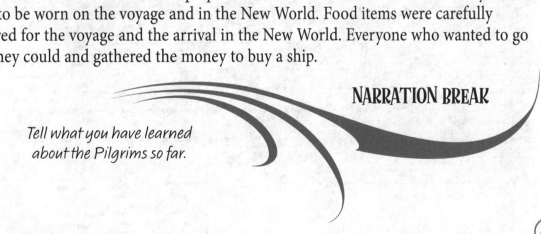

NARRATION BREAK

Tell what you have learned about the Pilgrims so far.

After buying their ship, the *Speedwell*, William Brewster went to England to gather any friends and family members that wanted to go to the New World as well. He also arranged for a ship for them to use for the voyage to America. This ship, named the *Mayflower*, was larger than the *Speedwell*. Excitement filled the air! After more than a year of preparations, the Pilgrims in Holland would be boarding the *Speedwell* and joining their families and friends in England, and then, together, they would embark on their voyage across the vast Atlantic Ocean. Together, they would be traveling to the strange new land of America. The *Mayflower* and the

The Mayflower

Speedwell had not gotten far when they had to return to England; the *Speedwell* was leaking and needed to be repaired. After the ship was patched, they set off again. They were only a short distance out at sea, when the *Speedwell* started to take on water again.

The discouraged Pilgrims sadly turned back to England once more. After a great deal of discussion, it was determined that some of them would need to remain in England until the following summer. Sadly, they said goodbye to their friends and family. The remaining Pilgrims boarded the *Mayflower* and again started on their voyage to the New World. Not all of the 102 passengers were Pilgrims. Some of them were on the voyage to reach the New World for adventure and fortune. The Pilgrims called these passengers "Strangers."

The departure was much later than had been planned. Nasty winds and storms beat against the *Mayflower*. The people were cramped, miserable, and seasick. In one storm, the ship's main beam cracked and was repaired with a large screw, which had been brought along on the voyage to be used in a house in the New World.

Christmas Day, 1620

The Mayflower Compact

In the nine-week voyage, two babies were born. Oceanus Hopkins is the somewhat unusual name of the first baby boy born on the *Mayflower*. The second was a baby boy, Peregrine White.

Finally, the horrible voyage was completed, but the hardship had just begun. Do you remember the land patent that William Brewster had secured for land in the New World? The *Mayflower* had landed far to the north of the land covered in that patent. What were the Pilgrims going to do now? It was winter, and the cold, snowy winds howled around the exhausted passengers of the ship. Many of them were ill with bad coughs and weak from months of poor nutrition.

Mr. Brewster and Mr. Bradford knew that they needed to have some sort of government in place before they left the ship to build a settlement. Together, they wrote the first governing document of what would be Plymouth Colony. The Mayflower Compact was a simple document stating that everyone would work together, sharing and helping each other. They knew that without this, they would probably all die in this harsh New World. I have heard it said that this document is thought of as the "grandfather" of our country's constitution, which we will learn about soon.

Finally, the scouting parties from the *Mayflower* found a bay a little farther south of where they had first come. They sailed into the bay and went ashore. Can you imagine what it would have been like to step off that ship into the cold, windy snow with no warm house in which to take shelter? How frightened the children must have been! When they stepped ashore, the Pilgrims did a wonderful thing; they knelt and prayed. They thanked their Heavenly Father for bringing them across the wild and stormy Atlantic Ocean to a land of freedom, where they could worship Him as they pleased.

Together the 19 Pilgrim families built their community, starting with the meetinghouse. I am sure they were thankful for the warmth of the fire in their new gathering place. Soon the meetinghouse was being used as a hospital also, for there were many people who had fallen very ill from the cold temperature and poor nutrition.

The *Mayflower* still lay anchored in Plymouth harbor; on the ship and in the small community, people lay sick and dying. Sadly, the Pilgrims buried their dead. Nearly half of the Pilgrims died that first terrible winter, but God still had a plan for Plymouth Colony. Out from the surrounding forest, God would bring help for the Pilgrims. In our next chapter, we are going to hear the amazing story of how one Indian would be saved from death to become help for the weary little group of Pilgrims.

Shoemakers petitioned for a consolidation of their craft.

"In ye name of God, Amen. We whose names are underwriten, the loyall subjects of our dread soveraigne Lord, King James, by ye grace of God, of Great Britaine, France, & Ireland, King, defender of ye faith, etc., having undertaken, for ye glorie of God, and advancement of ye Christian faith, and honour of our king & contrie, a voyage to plant ye first colonie in ye Notrherne parts of Virginia, doe by these presents solemnly & mutually in ye presence of god, and one of another, covenant & combine our selves together into a civill body politick, for our better ordering & preservation & furtherance of ye ends aforesaid; and by virtue hearof to enacte, constitute, and frame such just & equall laws, ordinances, acts, constitutions & offices, from time to time, as shall be thought most meete & convenient for ye generall good of ye Colonie, unto which we promise all due submission and obedience. In witness wherof we have hereunder subscribed our names at Cap-Codd ye 11, of November, in ye year of ye raigne or our soveraigne Lord, King James, of England, France, & Ireland ye eighteenth, and by Scotland ye fiftie fourth. Ano:Dom. 1620"

NARRATION BREAK

Retell the story of the Pilgrims crossing to the New World.

FROM SCROOBY TO AMERICA

Having arrived far north of their land near Jamestown in America, the Pilgrims faced a grim winter in Plymouth harbor.

Plymouth Harbor

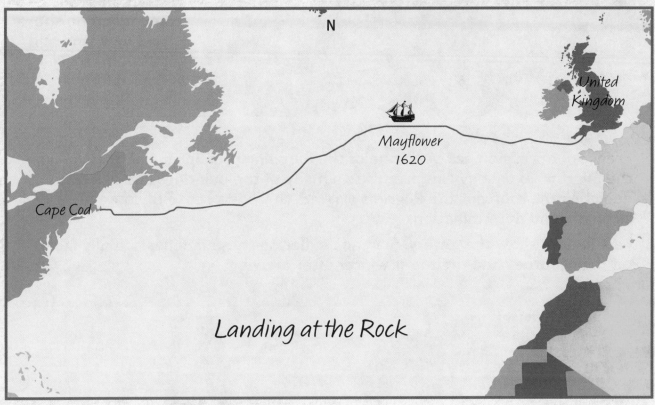

N

United Kingdom

Mayflower 1620

Cape Cod

Landing at the Rock

Plymouth Rock is traditionally associated with the Pilgrims leaving the ship having just arrived in America. The large rock, originally believed to have been around 20,000 pounds in weight, has been broken apart and relocated throughout Plymouth at various times since it was officially identified in 1741 by an elderly man who lived among the original *Mayflower* colonists.

FREEDOM FOR FAITH

It is one of the most memorable moments in American history. The brave and faithful Pilgrims leave their ships and come on shore to a new land and freedom to live their faith.

Freedom of religion has been one of the founding principles of America — and the Pilgrims exemplify this promise. In many of the paintings and illustrations depicting the moment the Pilgrims arrived, there is a sense of courage, strength, and determination.

Few images show the misery, fear, and suffering these families actually faced on their journey and their first winter after arriving.

Pilgrims going to church ▶

LIVING HISTORY

Plimoth Plantation was created in 1947 to serve as a living history museum for customs, lifestyle, and homes of the Plymouth Colony, part of which are often referred to now as Pilgrims. Taking evidence found in historical records and artifacts — the living history museum offers a glimpse of the pilgrim's daily lives and those of a neighboring Wampanoag village. Museum personnel are trained to be as authentically in character as possible as they open a window to the past, answering questions and showing how people cooked, cared for livestock, grew food, and even repaired daily tools.

Plimoth Plantation at Plymouth, Massachusetts ▼

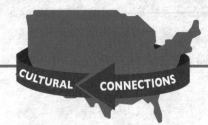
The next time you reach for your Bible, go with your family to attend a service at your church, or, if you are homeschooled or go to a Christian school, gather with your siblings or classmates to learn about God's creation, you are benefiting from what the Pilgrims did. Because this brave band of people were willing to come together with their co-passengers on the Mayflower, regardless of the differences in their beliefs, and make a government that was for them and by them, the precedence was set — this type of government would work here in this New World. Freedom of religion was a rare treasure in the world at that time. The fact that we, as Americans, have the freedom to enjoy a Christian, biblically based education from the preschool years through the collegiate level should never be taken for granted. Our entire culture is based upon the freedoms that the early settlers of our country gave everything to establish.

Woman singing in church

Freedom to worship

THOUGHTS TO REMEMBER

1. The Pilgrims thought it was worth all of the hardship to be able to worship God as they chose. They wanted to be able to raise their families in the way they chose, and they did not believe that a king or queen had the right to tell them otherwise.

2. The National Monument to the Forefathers is located in Plymouth, Massachusetts. Take a few moments to explore this amazing monument that was carefully designed to demonstrate the powerful reasons that our country was founded.

CHAPTER 6

SQUANTO
THE FRIENDLY INDIAN
AND THE FIRST THANKSGIVING

Spot Light

Starting Point: Thanksgiving is a reminder of a wonderful friendship that developed between the Pilgrims and a group of Native Americans. Sadly, this was not always the case, as Europeans came to claim the lands these tribes had called their own for generations.

The Thanksgiving Feast: Thanksgiving is one of America's favorite national holidays. Everyone loves a big turkey dinner and pumpkin pie! But what are we really celebrating?

READY TO EXPLORE?

1. How did a kind Native American help the Pilgrims survive in America?

2. How did Thanksgiving become a national holiday? Who was responsible for making it so?

We are going to pause in our story of the Pilgrims to meet someone who is very important to our country's history. You might think that this is a very sad story, and you would be right. Sometimes in life, things happen that don't make sense, or seem like they are too horrible for God to be able to use for good. This is one of those stories. Even though this story is sad, it shows us that God had His hand on what was soon going to be the United States of America.

Let's travel back in time to the year 1605. This was 2 years before Captain John Smith and the other Englishmen settled Jamestown, and 15 years before the Pilgrims came to the New World to settle Plymouth Colony.

In this year, a young Indian boy named Squanto was taken by Captain George Weymouth to England. Squanto was the nephew of an Indian chief of the Pawtuxet (paw-TUX-it) Tribe. Like many stories in history, there are different opinions of the story of Squanto. Some say that he was captured and forced to leave his home and his tribe. Others say that he agreed to go and considered the Englishmen his friends. In any case, Squanto was about 15 years old when he went to England in 1605. Can you imagine going to a strange new land where you could not speak the language? How frightened poor Squanto must have been!

While he was in England, Squanto learned to speak English very well. He learned the ways of the white man and made friends with many Englishmen, but still he longed to return to his family. Squanto was homesick. The tall buildings and noisy streets of London seemed so far from the quiet forest where he had played as a child. Here, he could not get even a minute of quiet. He longed to run barefoot through the soft grasses of his homeland and drink the ice-cold water of the streams! He missed the sounds of the birds and animals.

One day, when he had been in England for several years, Squanto met a fiery, red-haired captain who had recently been to the New World and helped build a settlement there — Captain John Smith. Squanto told the captain about how he wished to return to his home. He and the captain became good friends, and together they made plans to return Squanto to his people.

Two years later, Squanto was on board one of Captain Smith's ships heading toward America. Finally, he was going home. His heart sang! Soon he would see his parents' dear faces and hug all his friends close. Soon he would hunt and fish with his uncles. Soon the ache in his heart would be gone forever.

Welcome, Englishmen!

Imagine the excitement Squanto must have felt as he ran through the forest toward the home he had not seen in years! I'm quite certain his heart was pounding and not only from the running. Suddenly, out of nowhere, there were men! Rough hands pushed him to the ground; Squanto was being kidnapped!

Squanto and several other young Indian men were forced aboard a ship. Captain Hunt, an English captain who had a side business of slave trading, was taking Squanto away from his home yet again. Squanto's heart was breaking, his hope fading. He and the other young Indian men were tied up and left in the bottom of the ship. To Squanto, the now-familiar voyage across the Atlantic Ocean seemed to take a lifetime. How could he be going through this after everything he had already endured? Surely he would never see his home again! Squanto had no idea where he was, or where he was being taken. What was to become of him?

God knew where Squanto was, and He still had a plan for him! When Captain Hunt's ship arrived in *Europe*, Squanto and the other Indian men were herded off of the ship and taken to an auction. Do you know what an auction is? It is a sale where people try to outbid each other to buy something. At this auction, Squanto and his shipmates were to be sold as slaves. There was to be no sale that day though. Through the crowd came a priest, who demanded that the slave auction end immediately.

The priest was surprised to hear Squanto speaking fluently in English! He was a kind man who took Squanto to his monastery (a monastery is a house where monks or priests live) for shelter. The priest and Squanto became fast friends. Together they planned a way to return Squanto to his people in America once again.

NARRATION BREAK

Retell the first part of Squanto's life.

Finally, Squanto secured a ride on an English ship going to America. This time, Squanto's escorts took him close to where he knew his village was. Once again, Squanto ran through the woods. His heart kept beat with the pounding of his feet. Soon he would be home!

Squanto ran through the trees calling out the names of his mother and father. Why didn't anyone answer him? Where were the braves who had always stood guard around his village? Where were the dogs that played and nipped at the heels of frolicking children? Squanto finally slowed his pace, as he caught a glimpse of the familiar clearing through the trees.

Stepping into the clearing, Squanto finally understood why he had not seen all of the familiar activity surrounding his village. The village was gone, and the clearing was empty and silent. What could have happened to his people? Did they simply move to a better hunting ground? He had to find out! Squanto slowly turned and left the clearing, heading in the direction of the stream.

As he made his way through the forest, Squanto tried to come up with a reasonable explanation for the empty clearing. He was so deep in thought that he nearly ran into another young Indian man. This Indian was oddly dressed in an English cotton shirt and leather Indian breaches. Squanto asked the young man if he knew what had happened to the Pawtuxet Tribe. The man looked at him strangely.

"Everyone from that tribe died! A strange sickness went through and killed everyone," he replied.

Dead! Dead? His mother and father? His uncle, the great chief of the Pawtuxet? Everyone dead? Squanto could not believe it. The other young man, seeing his distress, offered to take Squanto home with him; Squanto agreed. What a sad, sad time for him. What do you think would have happened to him if he had been home with his tribe when this happened? He would have died also. God had saved Squanto's life.

Watching the Mayflower Leave

Plimoth plantation at Plymouth, Massachusetts

At the village of his new friend, Squanto met another Indian who could speak some English. Samoset and Squanto became good friends. He told Squanto about a group of strange people, who had seemed to blow in off of the ocean the winter before. These people, who called themselves Pilgrims, had suffered great hunger and sickness. They had lost many of their loved ones, including children and babies. Samoset told Squanto how he had gone to their village to see if he could help, but the people seemed to distrust him.

Squanto decided to go to the white men's village. He spoke clearly in English, telling the Pilgrims his story. They believed God had sent Squanto to them, and they trusted him. Squanto showed the Pilgrims how to hunt and fish like Indians. They did not know how to plant gardens in this new land. The vegetables and fruits that they had planted in their gardens in England would not grow in the soil here. They were very thankful for the help from their new Indian friend.

Squanto showed them how to plant corn, fertilizing it with fish remains to help it grow. He showed them how to plant squash and pumpkins, which were new foods to them. The Pilgrims planted large gardens and worked hard to bring home enough meat to dry and smoke for the winter. They finished the houses in their small village, which they had named Plymouth Colony. The warm summer and good nutrition worked wonders for them, and they grew strong and healthy.

Squanto had helped and worked alongside his new friends all summer. He was happy he could do something to help this group of kind Pilgrims. Knowing he could help save them from dying in the cold winter made him feel better. He still missed his family, but he was glad to be home in the wilderness.

They were so happy at having a good harvest that Governor Bradford appointed a day for Thanksgiving.

The Pilgrims' crops were so plentiful that they decided to hold a feast to thank God for bringing them to this New World and for providing them with a friend who had helped them so much. The air was alive with excitement. What a party this was going to be!

When you have a Thanksgiving Day feast at your house, does it last for several days? It probably doesn't, even though you may eat Thanksgiving leftovers for a week afterward. The Pilgrims' Thanksgiving feast was not just one day, though. In fact, the festivities went on for about a week. Squanto, Samoset, and many other Indians came to the feast as well. Imagine the surprise on the Pilgrims' faces when, out of the forest, came brightly painted Indian braves carrying deer and turkeys over their shoulders.

Can you just see the Pilgrim boys and girls learning the games of the Indian children? What a party they had!

I wish I could hear the prayer of thanksgiving they offered up to God that day. I can imagine it was full of gratitude for bringing them to this beautiful and bountiful land. I think it may have been very similar to the prayer that the children of Israel prayed after they entered the Promised Land.

FEAST: a large meal, usually in celebration of something.

The First Thanksgiving at Plymouth

NARRATION BREAK

Retell how God used Squanto to help save the Pilgrims.

WAMPANOAG TRIBAL GROUP

The Patuxet people were a Native American village of the Wampanoag tribal group. They are among numerous villages that died because of diseases inadvertently introduced to them by explorers.

Slavery of African Americans is well known in the history of America, but the plight of many Native American people was just as tragic. Killed over land disputes, captured, held hostage for food or information, sold as slaves, used as unwilling interpreters or guides, their stories are a tragic echo of Squanto's. While revered for helping save the Pilgrims, the loss of his family, friends, tribal heritage, and culture is a tragedy.

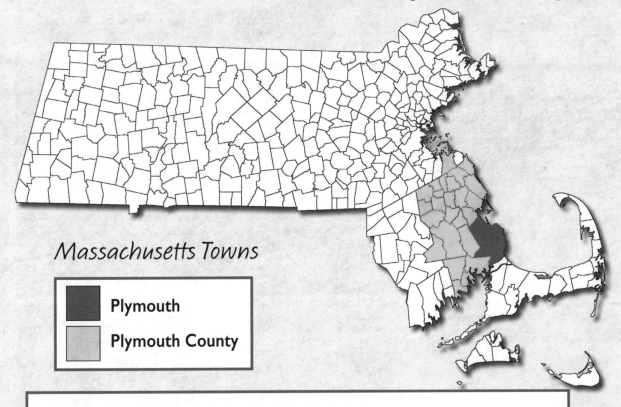

Massachusetts Towns

- **Plymouth**
- **Plymouth County**

SQUANTO'S JOURNEYS

1605 - Captured by Captain John Weymouth; taken to England

1614 - Returned to New England with Captain John Smith; kidnapped and taken to Spain

1617 - Taken to Newfoundland and tried to get to New England but was sent back to England by Thomas Dermer in 1618

1619 - He finally returned to his home on board Captain Smith's ship. Sadly, many native tribes, including his own, had died in a plague the year before. He was the last Pawtuxet.
He would work to build ties between the Wampanoag groups and the Pilgrims, and though captured at one point, he was found and returned to Plymouth by Myles Standish.

1622 - He dies in Massachusetts from either fever or poison, believed to have been 37 at the time.

▲ The first Thanksgiving 1621

Thanksgiving Day in olden time ▶

Reenactment of the first
Thanksgiving Dinner at Plymouth ▼

◄ President Harry S. Truman receives a non-pardoned Thanksgiving turkey, 1949.

President Lyndon B. Johnson receives the annual White House Thanksgiving turkey, 1967. ▼

You may see on the news each Thanksgiving that a turkey given to the President of the United States is pardoned, or set free, to live the rest of its life on a farm. It is a relatively new tradition, officially starting with President Ronald Reagan, though Presidents John F. Kennedy and Richard Nixon chose not to eat the turkey presented.

◄ President Ronald Reagan receives the annual White House Thanksgiving turkey (named Charlie), 1987.

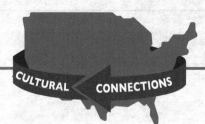

The Pilgrims celebrated their thanksgiving and thankfulness with a feast. The food they prepared was meat from the forest, vegetables from their gardens, and fruit and nuts from the land around them. For many decades, American families were responsible for providing their own food. As the centuries passed, and modern conveniences and industrialized food production became the norm, many people moved to the cities to work jobs other than farming. Think about this change. In many ways, the quality of life has risen since the early years of our country, but are there ways that the quality has gone down? Discuss this with your parents. Do you think that people know how to be self-sufficient? For example, do most women know how to sew, how to cook a meal from scratch, how to garden and raise vegetables, how to preserve those vegetables to be eaten in the winter, how to raise animals for meat or milk? How did the early citizens of our country have an advantage over us? You may want to take the time to explore this line of questions.

Pilgrim girl cooking in the kitchen

Modern corn processing plant

THOUGHTS TO REMEMBER

1. We learn in Chapter 6 about how Squanto came to Plymouth colony to help them with their crops. He also helped to negotiate good relationships between the Natives and the settlers.

2. Thanksgiving became a national holiday when Abraham Lincoln proclaimed it to be so on October 3, 1863.

CHAPTER 7

LIFE IN THE COLONIES

Spot Light

Starting Point: While the eastern coast of America was home to the first colonies, the lives of the colonists differed based on the natural resources of the areas they lived in. Whether you became a slave owner or shipbuilder, could be determined in part by the area in which you lived. These colonists sometimes faced harsh conditions and struggles defending their individual beliefs.

The Salem Witch Museum in Salem, Massachusetts

The Salem Witch Trials Remembered: The Salem Witch Trials were a dark event in America's history.

READY TO EXPLORE?

1. What was Colonial American life like?
2. What was the Great Awakening?

de la Salle
explores the
Mississippi River

The Salem
Witch Trials

The Great Awakening
sweeps the colonies

1682

1692

1740s

The years passed, and the Pilgrims' small village became a bustling, thriving community. Settlements were popping up all along the coast of North America, as more and more settlers came to the New World. These settlers were not all like the Pilgrims, who had come to the New World for religious reasons. Some of them came to get away from an oppressive government in their home country. Some wanted to make better lives for themselves, while others were "thrill seekers" looking for adventure. The one thing they had in common was their loyalty to England, for they were governed and protected by the English government.

Perhaps you live in a state that used to be one of these original 13 colonies. I am not going to fill this chapter with all kinds of dates, numbers, and statistics. However, I do want to set a backdrop of sorts for what is going to happen next in our story. Get ready to sharpen those geography skills! It will help you to look at the map in this chapter and follow along as we go through the names of the colonies.

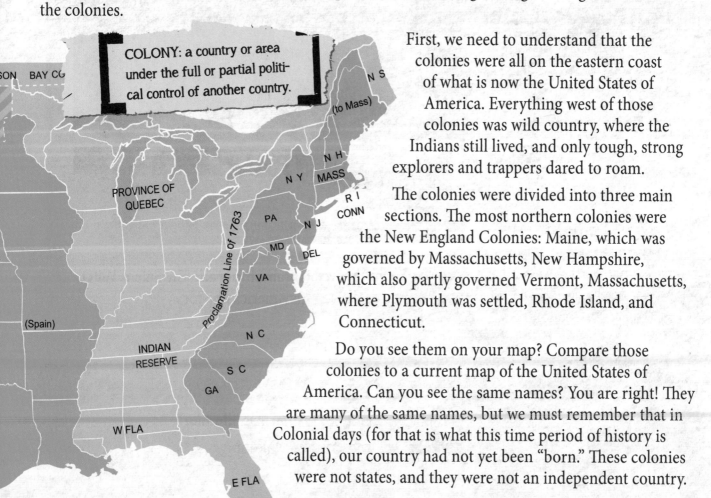

COLONY: a country or area under the full or partial political control of another country.

First, we need to understand that the colonies were all on the eastern coast of what is now the United States of America. Everything west of those colonies was wild country, where the Indians still lived, and only tough, strong explorers and trappers dared to roam.

The colonies were divided into three main sections. The most northern colonies were the New England Colonies: Maine, which was governed by Massachusetts, New Hampshire, which also partly governed Vermont, Massachusetts, where Plymouth was settled, Rhode Island, and Connecticut.

Do you see them on your map? Compare those colonies to a current map of the United States of America. Can you see the same names? You are right! They are many of the same names, but we must remember that in Colonial days (for that is what this time period of history is called), our country had not yet been "born." These colonies were not states, and they were not an independent country.

Next, were the Middle Colonies, made up of New York, Pennsylvania, New Jersey, and Delaware. These colonies were made up of the most diverse group of people. "Diverse" means different kinds and from different places. These colonists were Dutch, French, English, Irish, Swedish, Scottish, and Welsh. That is quite a variety of settlers, isn't it?

Find the Middle Colonies on your map while I tell you an interesting story about a place that I am sure you have heard of. This story is about a large city named New York City. It is one of the largest cities in the world, with millions upon millions of people living in and near it. Running through the city is the Hudson River. This river was named after an English explorer named Henry Hudson.

In 1609, only two years after Jamestown was settled, Mr. Hudson, working for the Dutch government, was on a mission to sail through the continent of North America. Doesn't that sound silly? Nobody at that time had any idea how BIG our continent really is. Henry Hudson sailed up and down the coast, looking and looking for a way to sail into the continent. Finally, he came to what seemed to be a good passageway to try.

What he had found is now the **Long Island Sound**, but he didn't know that it would not take him through the continent. He sailed along and realized that he was on a river. Now he was quite certain that he was going to sail through the great continent of North America. What do you think happened? Well, eventually he tried enough times that his men were rather tired of it all. On one of their ventures, Henry Hudson was removed from his ship and left behind on a small boat, while his men returned the way they had come.

No one knows what became of Henry Hudson, and of course, nobody ever sailed through the entire continent! Hudson did accomplish something important, though; he opened the door for the Dutch to explore that area. In 1624, the Dutch started a settlement that they named New Amsterdam. Later, the English took control of the small city and renamed it after the Duke of York. Today, we know that city as New York City.

The Last Voyage of Henry Hudson

To the south of the Middle Colonies was another group of colonies called the Southern Colonies. Maryland, Virginia, North and South Carolina, and Georgia made up this section. Look on your map of the 13 colonies; do you see these names? Virginia is the oldest of all the English colonies, because that is where Jamestown was settled in 1607.

The story of history is similar to a huge puzzle with thousands of pieces, isn't it? Have you ever worked on a jigsaw puzzle? It can be challenging but a lot of fun. I have a memory of putting together a puzzle with my dad. I was a young teenager at the time, and it took a lot of concentration. The puzzle that we built was 5,000 pieces! When it was completed, it was a beautiful picture of a sandcastle. It took us more than two months to complete that puzzle. That is the way learning history is. Seeing how all the pieces fit together is fun, but it also takes paying close attention to even the smallest details.

Do you remember earlier in our story, how the European explorers opened the door for settling the Americas? That was when slave ships started coming to America. The first was in 1503, about two hundred years back in time in our story.

By the middle of the 1700s, there were more Africans than Europeans or Native Americans living in some of the Southern Colonies. In these colonies there were many large farms, called plantations, which produced huge crops of tobacco and cotton. The taxes on these crops meant a lot of money for England. Africans were taken from their homes and brought to the Americas on slave ships, and they were treated very poorly. Slave traders in England, Spain, and Portugal were becoming very rich on the sale of humans, and England was getting rich from the crops grown with slave labor. Slavery is not a fun part of history to learn about, but just like many things in history, it is important to know about. Unless we learn about history, we can't learn from history.

As we travel down our winding path of history, we will see how slavery grew in America. We need to remember though, that even back in the 1700s, there were people who did not like slavery and were working hard to stop it. Slavery is a large puzzle piece in our country's history. In a big way, Africans, who were brought here against their wishes, helped build our country.

A slave ship in the distance

Tell why there are so many parts to and people involved in the story of how America was settled.

We are going to take our story's path from the Southern Colonies, with their huge plantations of cotton and tobacco, back north to the Northern Colonies. I want to tell you a story about something that happened in the colony of Massachusetts, the home of the Pilgrims' Plymouth settlement. The name "Massachusetts" is taken from the name of an Indian tribe that lived in that area. Many of the people who settled this colony had come to America for religious purposes.

The Puritans, as they called themselves, were strict in their religious practices. It is good to be accountable for your decisions and take responsibility for your actions, but the Puritans carried this idea a little further than most people do. Many of the villages were strictly run by the church elders and leaders. People were expected to keep track of what their neighbors were doing, and if anyone saw someone breaking the rules, they were to report them. This kind of system was bound to lead to trouble, and it did.

Have you ever said something that wasn't quite true about someone else, or had someone do that to you? I remember when I was a little girl, someone did that to me. It didn't matter how much I told the truth about it, everyone believed the other person. I remember being very angry about it when I had to take the punishment for something I had not done. I, in turn, did something back to the person who lied about me. It turned into a huge problem, with both of us getting into a lot of trouble!

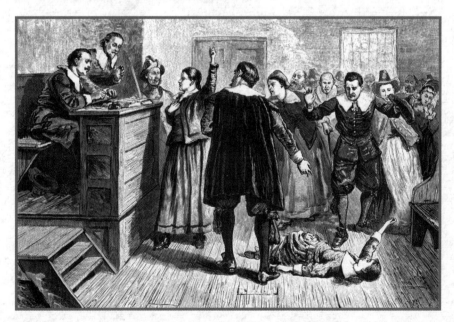

This is exactly what happened in 1692 in a town called Salem, in Massachusetts Colony. Nobody really knows why, but several young girls started accusing various people of casting spells on them. The girls even acted like they were crazy or having seizures.

This was a terrible accusation for the Puritans, and one they took very seriously. The accused people were arrested for practicing witchcraft. What

Reverend Jonathan Edwards

followed was a terrible time that would go down in history as the Salem Witch Trials. Over the next year, 19 women and 1 man, accused of witchcraft, were put to death. Fear of evil was the real enemy. Even though the girls admitted to making up the story, it was too late; no one would listen to them.

After all the sadness of slavery and witchcraft trials, I think we need to have a happy story to end our chapter, don't you? Well, I have just such a story for you. In the 1740s, about 50 years after the Salem Witch Trials, something wonderful happened in the colonies.

Do you know what a spiritual revival is? It is when an "awakening" to God moves through the hearts of thousands of people. Many of the original colonists had come to the New World looking for a place of religious freedom, but over a hundred years later, the great grandchildren of those people thought of religion and church just as something "good" people did. Many of them did not know God as the Living God that He truly is.

God always has someone to do His special work when He wants it done. At this time in history, the spotlight was on a man named Reverend Jonathan Edwards. God used Reverend Edwards to turn many colonial hearts toward Him. Edwards gathered great crowds. The crowds were so large that many times he had to hold services outside, because there were not big enough churches to hold them all! Many people were touched by the Holy Spirit and gave their hearts to Jesus.

Isn't it wonderful that God loves us so much that He sent His Son, Jesus, to be our Savior and Friend? I am enjoying our journey through history so much. Thank you for sticking with me through this chapter. So many things in life are hard to understand, and we touched on some of them today. Even though we will be revisiting the hard topic of slavery again soon, our next chapter will be a little more lighthearted. We will meet a man who brought peace between the Indians and the white settlers, and established a "City of Brotherly Love."

NARRATION BREAK

Tell about the Salem witchcraft trials, and the Great Awakening.

New Amsterdam Maps

Map of New Netherland and
New England (around 1685)

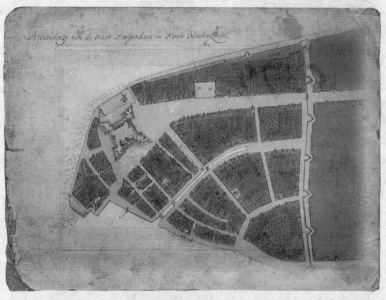

The original city map of
New Amsterdam called
Castello Plan, from 1660

Redraft of the Castello Plan,
New Amsterdam,
drawn in 1916

While many who came to the Americas sought religious freedom, sometimes these groups — for instance the Puritans in several cases — did not allow such freedom among their settlements here, leading many to leave and form communities outside of these authorities.

◀ Roger Conant is credited with founding the city of Salem, Massachusetts in 1626 with a group of other fishermen.

Salem's harbor led to fishing and trade opportunities. ▼

Memorial Park in honor of the victims of the Salem Trials ▶

The Witch House was the home of a judge during the Salem Trials of 1692, a terrible historical event that led to the deaths of men and women falsely accused with no way to prove their innocence. ▶

Salem was designated as the birthplace of the U.S. National Guard in 2013 in honor of the gathering of men in 1637 on the Salem Commons in defense of the area. ▼

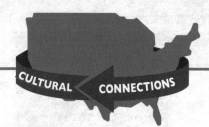
Cultural Connections: America has always been a melting pot of cultures! We have already discussed how parts of the Native American culture became part of our modern culture, as well as the words we still use that originated with the Vikings. We learned in this chapter that the original 13 colonies, which later became the first states of our country, were settled by people from a variety of countries, and with these folks came their homeland's customs. For example, the Dutch, the original settlers of New York, brought with them their customs of the celebration of the winter holidays — especially Christmas. The Northern Colonies, where the Puritans set the cultural atmosphere, did not believe in feasting and merrymaking at Christmas. It was the Dutch who brought the tradition of jolly Saint Nicholas and his Christmas Eve visit. It might be enjoyable to research the roots of other Christmas and holiday traditions.

1908 vintage German illustration of Saint Nicholas

Modern-day Santa Claus

THOUGHTS TO REMEMBER

1. We learn in Chapter 7 about the everyday aspects of colonial life. Discuss them with your child as they are brought up in the chapter.

2. We learn also about the Great Awakening, which was a powerful sweeping of the Holy Spirit in the hearts of the Colonial Americans.

CHAPTER 8

WILLIAM PENN, A MAN OF PEACE

Starting Point: The Quakers came to America to find religious freedom as well, and created a unique colony in the lands of Pennsylvania. William Penn would take a unique approach in dealing with the Native American tribes that lived on the lands that had been given to him by his king.

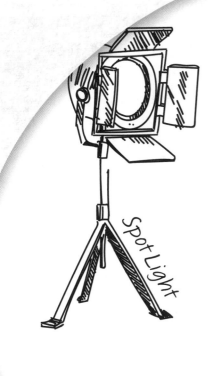

Spot Light

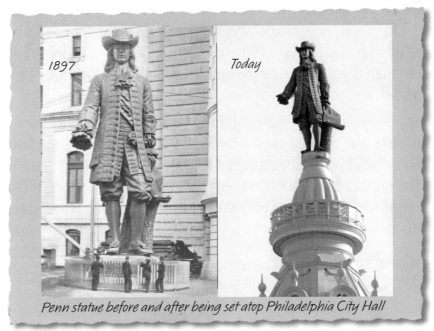

1897   Today

Penn statue before and after being set atop Philadelphia City Hall

William Penn Remembered: William Penn was a man of peace. He did everything he could to bring the love of Jesus to those around him, including the Native Americans living on the land being colonized by the British.

READY TO EXPLORE?

1. How were the Native Americans usually treated by the colonists?

2. Why is Philadelphia called "the City of Brotherly Love"?

Penn at 22

Do you remember our story of the Pilgrims, and how they suffered persecution in England because of their religious differences with King James? Today we are going to meet another group of people who suffered in the same way. You may think the name of this group is a little strange; they are called the Quakers. Sadly, this group was mistreated in America as well as in England.

Have you ever seen someone who gets picked on because they dress or act differently than others? Sometimes, when someone is different from us, it can make us feel uncomfortable. The Quakers had that effect on many people. Their clothes got a lot of attention because they were not stylish at all; instead they were plain and dark in color. More than their clothing style caused a stir though. The Quakers did not conform to the Church of England, and this made the king of England mad.

Many people did not understand the Quakers of England. They were peaceful people, who did not believe in war or any kind of violence. They were quiet and kind to their neighbors. The Quakers lived by what is sometimes called the Golden Rule. We are going to learn the story of perhaps one of the most famous Quakers there ever was, William Penn. William was the son of an English admiral who was friends with the royalty of England. He was well educated and well brought up.

QUAKERS: members of a historically Christian group of religious movements.

A meeting of Quakers

76

Charles I of England

William was first introduced to the Quaker religion when he was only 13 years old. The religion made an impression on him, for even at this young age, he was not impressed with the Church of England with all its legalism. Later, he was expelled from Oxford University for not conforming to the church's views. At his father's insistence, he attended the Inns of Court and learned about law.

In 1667, William officially joined the Quakers, or the Society of Friends, as they call themselves. He was imprisoned four times for writing and speaking about the Quakers' beliefs, but because his father was a friend to the English royalty, he was released.

King Charles of England owed William's father a large debt of money, and after his father died, William became the holder of the debt. William came up with an idea of how the king could pay it off. If the king would give him a piece of land on the west side of the Delaware River in America, Penn would consider the debt repaid.

He wanted to move to America and start a colony for the poor Quakers who suffered so much in England. He wanted to make a home where they could worship the way they chose. Penn went to King Charles with his idea.

The king thought that this was a splendid idea! In fact, he liked it so much, he gave Penn a very large piece of land. The only thing King Charles wanted from it was two beaver skins a year and one-fifth of all the gold and silver ever mined there. The king did get his beaver skins, but no gold or silver was ever mined on that land. What is one-fifth of nothing?

There was a "small" problem however — the land did not belong to the king, it belonged to the Indians, and many other groups of settlers had already claimed and settled this land. Years before the Quakers came, settlers from Sweden and Holland had settled along the *Delaware River*. After that, the English came and said that the land was theirs. This seemed to be a very popular place to claim land!

NARRATION BREAK

Retell the story so far.

William Penn knew that the land really belonged to the Indians, and shortly after arriving in America on a ship called the *Welcome*, he called a meeting of the Native Americans. Do you think this meeting was a little quiet at first? Can you imagine the Indians standing and staring at this strange white man with an English accent? They were probably glancing at each other with puzzled expressions. "Why would he want to talk to us?" their looks would say. I'm sure they were surprised to learn this man wanted to pay them for the land!

William Penn talked to the Indians for a long time. He told them about the Quakers, and how they believed in living peacefully. He told them that he was aware the land really belonged to them, and that he would pay them for the land the Quakers used. The Indians were impressed and liked William Penn. He drew up peace treaties, which are agreements between two parties to not fight, and the Indians gladly signed them.

This famous meeting between William Penn and the Indians took place under a spreading Elm tree on the Delaware River bank. This tree stood for more than a hundred years after that meeting. Today a monument marks the spot where the tree once stood. William Penn became a great friend of the Indians, and there was peace between the Quaker settlers and the Native Americans for quite some time. A settlement that quickly grew into a city was built along the river. William Penn named it *Philadelphia*. This name means "Brotherly Love," and that is exactly how these peaceful people tried to live. Philadelphia was built along the Delaware River, and its streets were built through the forest. If you went to this city today, you would see streets named after these trees. There is a Chestnut Street, a Walnut Street, a Pine Street, a Cherry Street, and other tree names as well.

The colony of Pennsylvania appealed to many people. Who wouldn't want to live in such a peaceful place? William Penn even wrote advertisements and sent them all over the colonies, telling about his wonderful colony and City of Brotherly Love. Quakers who had suffered in the other parts of America came to live there. The peace between the settlers and the Indians continued for many years. Philadelphia grew and grew, and the colony of Pennsylvania thrived.

By the year 1700, Pennsylvania was one of the richest and most populated colonies. Everyone was welcomed there, and the peace with the Indians was something rare in those times. Freedom of worship was granted to all who lived there.

The Treaty of Penn with the Indians

The Quakers finally had a place where they could live in peace.

William Penn continued to use his influence in England to help the Quakers. He went to England and secured the release of Quakers being held in prison for religious reasons. He spent all of his money and resources on the colony that he started, and his peace negotiations with the Indians ensured peace for Pennsylvania Colony.

William Penn died in 1718. He had spent his life creating something wonderful. He lived his life by the Golden Rule, the very words of Jesus in Matthew 7:12, and he had given everything he had for what he believed in most, living peacefully with his neighbor.

I hope you have enjoyed our story today. Isn't it wonderful to learn about people in history who really made a difference? Remember, you too can make a difference by living by the words of Jesus!

Friends' meeting-house at Jordans,
and the grave of William Penn

NARRATION BREAK

Retell the rest of the story. What
made Pennsylvania so special?

PENN'S PENNSYLVANIA

William Penn accomplished wonderful things in Pennsylvania, but he was not a good manager of money or legal matters. An unscrupulous business manager of his even took advantage of his habit of signing documents, but not reading them. Penn actually signed away ownership of the Province to this manager, who then demanded huge amounts of rent that Penn could not pay. Eventually the courts would rule that Penn still had ownership, though he had briefly found himself in debtor's prison at the age of 62 over the matter.

Penn faced several legal challenges, including one over the boundaries between some of the land he owned and Lord Baltimore, who also owned a huge portion of land next to his.

It wasn't just Penn who faced such challenges. Imagine the lands of the New World — and settlers and explorers from various European countries all trying to claim parts of the land, sometimes the same parts, all while the Native American's considered the land theirs. Disputes and conflicts were common.

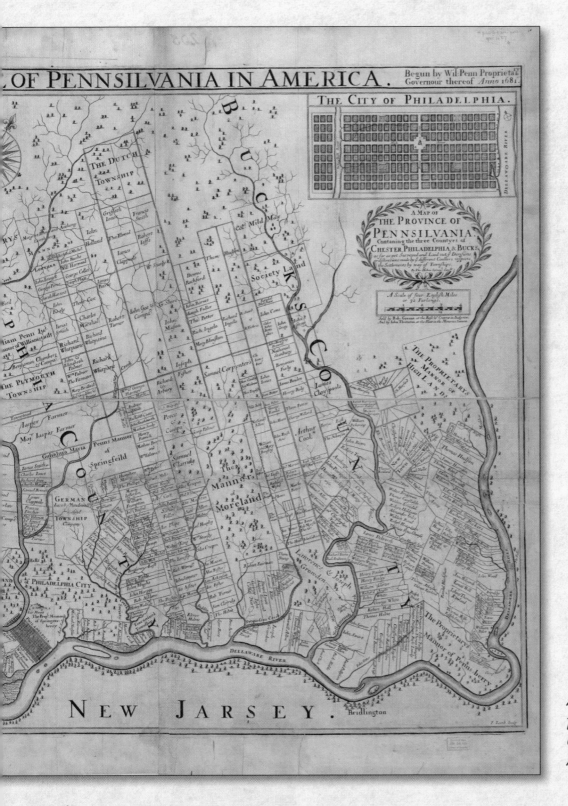

A map of the improved part of the Province of Pennsylvania in America

▲ A Religious Society of Friends (Quaker) Meeting house in New York state

Today, if you watch professional baseball, you may be aware of the Philadelphia Phillies. But you may not be aware that when the team was first formed in 1883, they were known as the "Quakers" not the "Phillies." Philadelphia in its long history had another baseball team, a hockey team, as well as a football team, all calling themselves the "Quakers." ▶

Inside a Pennsylvannia Quaker meeting house built in 1795 ▶

Many Quakers took part in efforts to outlaw slavery or helping runaway slaves. Many also refused to take part in wars or conflicts that would lead them to kill or injure others, but many have served in other ways. This is a photo of a Friends member who was a driver of their ambulance service in Germany in 1945. ▼

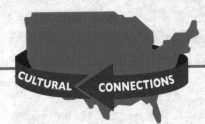
The life and work of William Penn has had an immense influence on our country. Not only did he influence our culture by showing that people could agree to live in peace, no matter what the differences in their beliefs, he is credited for setting an example of encouraging and inviting the humble folk, the average workers of America, to build their lives under better conditions, with little governmental involvement. His love for his fellow man set a precedent in a period of history where harsh judgment and punishment were common. His influence on the settling of the colonies of Pennsylvania, Delaware, and New Jersey was extremely helpful in forming the representative type of government our new country would eventually establish under our Constitution. We are still enjoying the influence of William Penn on our society.

Penn's treaty with the Indians founding Pennsylvania

Philadelphia skyline

THOUGHTS TO REMEMBER

1. We have learned through our studies of early American history that the Native Americans were often-times not treated with the utmost honesty and fairness. Peace treaties were often breached with no consequences for either side.

2. We learn in Chapter 8 that Philadelphia means "the city of Brotherly Love," a name chosen by William Penn to show the rest of the colonies and the world that everyone was welcome to live there without discrimination.

CHAPTER 9

WILLIAM WILBERFORCE, ABOLITIONIST HERO

Starting Point: The issue of slavery would be found in the early history of colonized America, but there was a growing awareness of the need for it to end. And so began the work of the abolitionists. It would not quickly be ended and continued to divide the colonies.

Spot Light

Sold for a Shell: Different types of slavery existed in Africa long before the Transatlantic Slave Trade began. Africa had also used shells as a form of money for hundreds of years. As Europeans began to purchase slaves, tribal groups fought with one another to get slaves to sell, and the Europeans used cowrie shells as a form of payment.

READY TO EXPLORE?

1. Why did the English and American colonists use slaves?

2. Who wrote the hymn, "Amazing Grace," and what did he have to do with William Wilberforce?

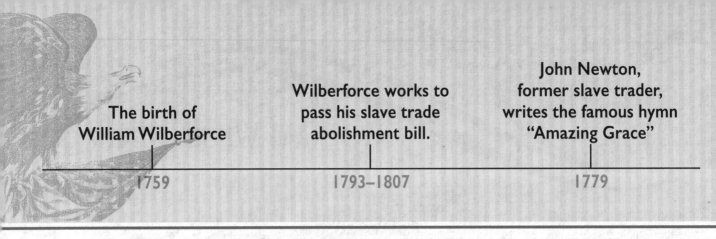

The birth of
William Wilberforce

Wilberforce works to
pass his slave trade
abolishment bill.

John Newton,
former slave trader,
writes the famous hymn
"Amazing Grace"

1759   1793–1807   1779

In this chapter, we are going to return to the rather difficult topic of slavery. I know that some of my young friends hearing this story might be very sad or even afraid to hear about this part of our history. Some of you might be wondering how this could have happened right here in America, the land where everyone is supposed to be free. Perhaps you are wondering why God even let it happen.

My young friends, so precious to me, I want you to know why I insist on writing about this in our otherwise lovely story. The answer is simple: because it happened. You see, every person living, and who has ever lived, has the capacity for good and evil.

People who love Jesus try to make doing good things their usual choice. However, there are times when greed and self-centeredness cloud the human conscience. This happens when we are not thinking or caring about Jesus' love for all humankind. When that has happened in history, there are terrible consequences that have followed. The years of slavery in our country are some of those times.

I hope my friends reading or hearing this story love Jesus and want to follow Him with all their hearts. However, it is important for us all to understand that we too have the ability to let selfishness and greed cloud our view. Jesus died for all of us, and without Him we all have the

SLAVERY: a law allowing humans to be classified as property.

evil of sin in our lives. So I tell about this part of our history to remind all of us of this. Remember, unless we learn about history, we cannot learn from history.

Another thing I want you to understand is, not all people who owned slaves were evil people. We will learn about some exceptionally godly men and women in our history who owned slaves. One of them was a man named George Washington, our first elected president. At times, people do things because it is an accepted "cultural norm." This means that because it is widely accepted in society, people think it must mean that it is justifiable to do. Of course, we all know that it is not acceptable to "own" another human being, but back in the time of the history we are studying, slavery was widely accepted.

William Wilberforce

Not all people accepted slavery as "normal" though. Today we are going to learn about just such a man. He wasn't the sort of man you would think could be a hero; it certainly wasn't his childhood dream. I want to tell you the story of this unlikely hero, because it is a wonderful example of how each and every one of us can make a difference when we stand up for what is right.

The name of our hero today is William Wilberforce. William did not live in America, but he was painfully aware of a problem that his home country of England and our country, America, shared. Slavery! Remember, slavery started in the Americas a long time before colonial times. There had been slave ships pulling up to the shores of America for more than two hundred years before William was even born.

However, before I tell you how our friend, Mr. Wilberforce, became a hero, I need to tell you about his childhood. William was born on August 29, 1759. His family was of the English upper class; this is another way of saying his family was rich. From a very young age, William had everything he could possibly want, including parties, fancy clothes, and a fine education. Poor, young William was dreadfully spoiled, I'm afraid!

When William was only 9 years old, an extremely sad thing happened; his father died. William's mother was awfully sad, and sent her young son to stay with his aunt and uncle who lived in London. His new guardians were very different from his family; they were evangelical Christians who were involved in the spiritual awakening happening in the American colonies and in England. Earlier in our story we learned that in England, people were expected to be part of the Church of England. It was not "socially acceptable" to be evangelical.

William was 12 years old when, he too, accepted the faith, and a seed was planted in his heart that would mature into a very firmly rooted tree of faith when he became a man. When William's mother and her high-class friends realized that her son was following in the footsteps of their

"radical" relatives, they did everything they could do to stop it. In a way, they succeeded, and William went back to his old ways. God was not done with our friend William, though! He became friends with a young man named Isaac Milner. Isaac was highly intelligent and a respected scientist and mathematician; he was also a strong believer in our Lord Jesus Christ. He and William had many discussions and read the Bible together. The little seed of faith, which had been planted years before, started taking root and growing. Soon William was so convicted, he renewed his commitment to Jesus.

Wilberforce

NARRATION BREAK

Retell the story so far.

During this time, William started his political career; he was elected to the British Parliament (PAR-lu-ment). The Parliament is part of the English government and could be compared to the American Congress. He had a good friend, William Pitt, who became England's prime minister at the young age of 24. Mr. Pitt would become one of William Wilberforce's best friends and strongest allies.

As William Wilberforce renewed his commitment to God, he thought of leaving his political career and becoming a minister, but William Pitt encouraged him to pray about how he could be useful to God in his place in Parliament. After much prayer and consideration, Wilberforce was convicted that God, indeed, had put him in a place of influence to be used by Him. William felt God had called him to lead the cause of abolition.

Do you know what the word "abolition" (a-bu-LI-shun) means? The root of this word is "abolish," which means "to put an end to something." What Mr. Wilberforce wanted to abolish or end was the horrible slave trade that England and her colonies in America were both involved in. Don't you just feel like standing up and cheering? I do! Finally, someone wanted to put an end to the slave trade.

William knew of the horrible conditions in which the slaves were transported from ***Africa to Europe and America***. It made him sad, as it does us, to think about the many tribes of Africa, which were completely wiped out by the slave raiders. How awful to think about the many civilizations destroyed by this dastardly practice!

For hundreds of years, slave raiders made an abundant living off of the selling of human beings. What do you think happened when these people, who ran the slave trade business, heard what

Depiction of a slave ship

Mr. Wilberforce was trying to do? Most people don't like it when someone else says they are going to get rid of their way of making money, and this is the incredible stronghold that our friend, William, was up against.

After William made his cause known, he soon found out who his real friends were. Poor William! He was threatened and hated by many people; he received death threats and was on the receiving end of terrible rumors. William did not let this get to him though. He worked tirelessly to put together a bill promoting abolition. In 1793, he brought his first bill before the House of Commons. (The House of Commons could be compared to our Senate.) He lost by eight votes — was all his work for nothing? No! William kept going; he would not give up on the cause of freedom. He continued to put together bills demanding the end of the slave trade.

William Wilberforce

Every time he came with another bill, William was voted down. How discouraging! Time after time, he presented another bill. Slowly, something began to happen. Little by little, he was starting to gain support for his cause of abolition. The tide was turning; slowly but surely he was moving forward.

William Wilberforce and his supporters worked for nearly 20 years. Finally, in 1807, the vote was in his favor, a resounding win of 283 in favor of abolishing the slave trade, to only 16 who opposed it. He had done it! It had taken 20 years and 11 proposed bills, but he had finally succeeded.

William did not stop there; he spent the next 25 years working to completely abolish slavery. He wanted all the slaves in England to be set free. In 1833, three days before he died, William heard the wonderful news: the House of Parliament had passed the bill abolishing slavery in the entire

The House of Commons in Wilberforce's day

British Empire. I love stories of the faithfulness of God's servants!

So that is the true story of how a spoiled rich boy grew up to be an extremely important person in history. William Wilberforce, who married a lady named Barbra Spooner, was the father of six children. He is also considered to be the father of abolition. He was an active member of the British Parliament for 26 years. God had a great plan for him, and I am happy to tell you, he listened! Isn't it simply amazing how one person can have such an impact on history?

Have you ever tossed a small pebble into a pond or even a puddle of water? When I was a child, we had a small stock pond in a back pasture where the cows would come to drink. I used to lie on my stomach on a log that was hanging out over the water, and drop small sticks and pebbles into the water so I could watch the ripple effect. It always amazed me how wide and far-reaching the circles would get from the tiniest stone. It didn't matter how small the stone was, if I dropped it hard enough, it would cause a big ripple. This is exactly what happens in life.

Speech in the House of Commons

Since the creation of man, all human life has had a ripple effect. Some cause a big enough ripple to be felt for a long time afterward, while others are barely noticeable. And just like the stones I used to drop in the pond, size doesn't matter. Even small people can cause a big effect. We have learned that greed can make humans do bad things, but, if we follow the words of the apostle Paul in 1 Corinthians 13:4–7, we can cause a positive ripple effect.

NARRATION BREAK

What is your favorite part of our story today?

Slaves in Colonial America

As colonists arrived in the Americas, they would sometimes become indentured servants — agreeing to work for a set number of years for a person if that person would pay their passage to the colonies or pay off a debt.

But the cases of John Casor and John Punch would hint at the dark future of slavery. Punch, an African, ran away with two other indentured servants, though they were European. When caught in 1640, Punch was punished by being legally required to serve the remainder of his life for having run away. The other two men had their indenture time lengthened, but did not face a lifetime of service.

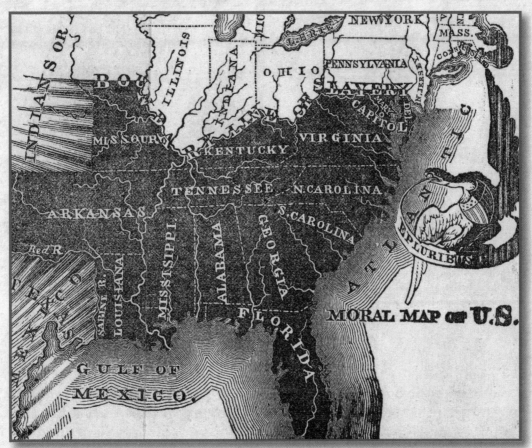

This anti-slavery map was first published before the annexation of Texas and republished several times up to 1857. Slave states are shown in black, with black-and-white shading to represent the threatened spread of slavery into Texas and western territories.

Casor would face a similar fate. He was indentured to Anthony Johnson, a free black man and property owner. Casor said that Johnson forced him to work beyond the legal length of time, and went to work for another man as an indentured servant. Johnson sued the other man in 1655, and the court declared Casor a slave and said that free black men could own slaves.

By 1770, over 273,000 slaves were living in colonies in America. They were part of a vast economy in which slaves would be transported from Africa to Europe and the Americas, then trade goods like sugar would then be transported and sold.

From the very beginning of America, the question of slavery was one that hovered over its future. It would remain a point of division as America started on the path to becoming a fledgling nation.

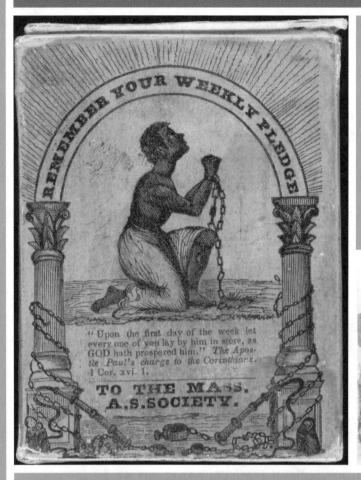

◀ A collection box for the Massachusetts Anti-Slavery Society in the 1850s

Celebrating the end of slavery in the District of Columbia in 1866 ▼

A Mix of Laws

The word "abolitionism" refers to the effort to end slavery, and the word is still used today. As the split widened between the northern and southern American states over the issue of slavery in the years after the Revolutionary War, the country was left with a wide assortment of laws and legal opinions on the issue that were often in direct conflict. For example, in 1777 Vermont outlawed slavery, yet in Virginia there were laws in support of the institution and regulation of slavery.

Sometimes laws were enacted that restricted or ended the commerce and industry of transporting and selling slaves but did not offer freedom to those already enslaved. Some places had no laws regarding slavery, and so slaves in those areas were stuck with no legal status or rights.
Slaves didn't always wait for their freedom to be granted to them. Sometimes they chose to rebel, to fight for their freedom. Some revolts occurred before the Revolutionary War, such as the Stono Rebellion, the New York Slave Revolt of 1712, and the New York Conspiracy of 1741. These and other efforts often failed, leading to the death of many.

Rev. ELIJAH PARISH LOVEJOY
Was born at Albion, Maine, 1802,
And MURDERED at Alton, Ill. Nov. 7, 1837,
A MARTYR to LIBERTY.

▲ Memorial card
for Elijah Parish
Lovejoy

The Death of An Abolitionist

Reverend Elijah Parish Lovejoy was a minister,
newspaper editor, and relentless opponent of
slavery. Lovejoy was not popular for the stances
he took on slavery in Missouri, a state that was
already at odds within itself and with its "free
state" status of its neighbors over the issue. Facing
controversy and thefts and vandalism designed
to prevent the publication of his paper, Lovejoy
moved to Alton, Illinois. After his printing press
was destroyed several times, Lovejoy became
even more determined to press the issue of abolitionism. While trying to protect the printing press
and his newspaper, Lovejoy was killed by a mob in
1837 and buried in an unmarked grave, without a
service, while no one was found guilty of his mur-
der. Yet to others in his family and the abolitionist
movement, he served as a powerful example to do
more and give everything to cause of freedom for
those still denied it.

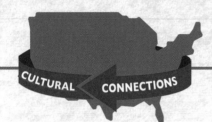

Parent/teacher, please pre-read this to decide if it is appropriate for your students.

Although William Wilberforce did not live in America, he has had an immense effect on our country and indeed the entire world. Since the earliest civilizations, the world has struggled through tremendous battles of social justice issues. Issues of slavery, cruelty to children (many civilizations even sacrificed their children to their gods), inequality of women, and harsh treatment of animals, just to name a few, were front and center in many cultures across the globe. The settling of America brought these world cultural elements here, to a new arena. Would they be allowed to continue? Or would there be enough voices raised, calling for the abolition of the enslaving cultural norms that victimized the downcast and downtrodden? Brave heroes like William Wilberforce can be thanked wholeheartedly for being those brave voices.

Slaves crushing coffee

A girl carrying an ABOLISH CHILD SLAVERY! sign at a New York City May Day celebration, 1909.

THOUGHTS TO REMEMBER

1. There are a number of reasons that the British and Americans used slaves. One is tradition. The use of slaves and menially paid servants was deeply engrained in the fiber of the world's cultures almost from the beginning of civilization. Of course this doesn't make it acceptable, but at this time in history, it was simply an accepted part of life.

2. William Wilberforce and John Newton (author of "Amazing Grace") were fast friends. John Newton was a former slave trader who had a foundational change of heart. This would be a fascinating "bunny trail" if your children are interested.

CHAPTER 10

YOUNG GEORGE WASHINGTON AND THE HORRIBLE WAR

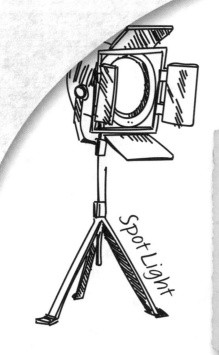

Spot Light

Starting Point: There was only so much new land available, and a number of countries laid claim to parts of it. This inevitably led to conflicts such as the French and Indian War. Ironically, it would be soon after the war's end, that Americans would have to fight for their freedom.

Reconstructed Fort Necessity, southern Pennsylvania

Fort Necessity: Fort Necessity was a small, circular wooden fort that George Washington and his 400 men built in the center of a clearing in late June of 1754.

READY TO EXPLORE?

1. Why was Washington called the "Bulletproof George Washington"?

2. Why were the French and Indians fighting with the British and American colonists?

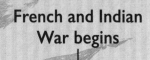

French and Indian War begins	Relocation of the French Acadians by the English	French and Indian War ends
1754	1760	1763

Today, I would like to tell you the story of one of my very favorite people in history. I am quite certain that you have heard the name of this famous American, for George Washington is often called the Father of our Country.

Did you know that George Washington was also an extremely knowledgeable woodsman? He loved the forest and was known to spend weeks exploring the wilderness on the western border of the British (English) colonies. He was also familiar with the Native Americans and their ways. George Washington was quite the fellow, wasn't he?

Washington

There are stories of how George became a land surveyor at the age of 16. Do you know what a surveyor is? It is someone who measures land. To be a surveyor, you have to have a good head for numbers and mathematics. You also have to be trustworthy; George was both of these. People trusted him to correctly measure the land, which they wanted to sell. At 21 years of age, George was hired by the British government to "keep an eye on" what the French were doing.

SURVEYOR: a profession in which boundary lines of property are decided.

Did I just say the French? Yes, you heard me right! Do you remember our chapter about Christopher Columbus and the other European explorers? *France* had claimed large portions of land covering a huge area of what is now the middle of our country, all the way up into *Canada*, our neighbor to the north. I know all of this can be very confusing, so I want you to stop here, and let's go take a look in your Teacher Guide at the map for this chapter. Do you see the large area of land claimed by France? Compare it to a modern map of North America. That's a lot of land, isn't it? Remember, England had the 13 colonies, but they were really quite a narrow strip on the east coast of North America. The French had more land, but the English had more people. Back when George Washington was a young man (and remember, this was still before the 13 colonies became the United States of America), the French and the English were bickering over land.

Washington the Surveyor

This bickering between England and France was nothing new; it had been going on for years and years in Europe, and now it had carried over the ocean to the New World. Even though George Washington lived in the British Colonies and was on the English side, many of the American Indians were not. They would rather have the French on their land than all of those British colonists.

George volunteered to help the British army, which had been sent from England to confront the French army after they had taken over several English forts on the frontier. The British General Braddock was not very educated on the American frontier or the ways of the Indians. Unfortunately, he was not very teachable either.

On one march, George Washington was with General Braddock on the way to an English fort that had been taken by the French. All of a sudden, bullets came raining down on the terrified British troops. General Braddock, who had scoffed at George's warnings about the sneakiness of the Indians, did not know what to do. George and his militiamen from Virginia darted behind trees to hide, but the bright red coats of the British officers and soldiers made perfect targets. Many of the soldiers were killed or wounded. General Braddock was badly hurt and died a few days later.

General Braddock

All of these terrible quarrels between the French and the English were just the beginning of a long and bloody war. We call this war the French and Indian War because there were many Indians on the French side fighting against the British. Sadly, this was an extremely horrible war in which many innocent people died. Families of settlers were killed and their homes destroyed.

Do you remember what we talked about in our last chapter — how greed can cause people to do awful things that they would otherwise never dream of doing? The love of money can cause this type of insanity, but sometimes greed for land or power can be another cause.

Let's take another look at the map in the Teacher Guide. Do you see the area just west of the 13 colonies? It is a long strip of land starting at the most southern border, down by the state of *Louisiana*, and stretching all the way up into *Canada*. This is the land that the quarrel was about, for it is land that both France and England claimed.

General Braddock and armed settlers

The Death of General Braddock

Isn't it amazing that two kings, who lived more than three thousand miles away across the ocean, were causing all of this trouble? They were fighting over land that belonged to neither one of them. I am quite sure that if those two kings had been made to come to America and actually do the fighting themselves, the war would have lasted nine minutes instead of nine years.

NARRATION BREAK

Retell what you have learned so far.

I must tell you a very old story about some of the French settlers who came to North America. These people came from France three years before Jamestown was settled in Virginia by the English. This French settlement was well to the north of Jamestown. If we were to find the location of this French settlement on a modern map, it would be called *Nova Scotia*, Canada. However, back in 1604, it was called Acadia (u-KAY-dee-u).

The settlers of Acadia were peaceful farmers who were loyal to their motherland of France. Even back in those days, England and France were arguing and bickering about this and that. Like two naughty children, they carried on back and forth. Whenever there was trouble between England and France, English forces were sent to pick on the poor people of Acadia.

By and by, the fort at Acadia was taken over by the British. There are many stories of how badly the English treated the residents of Acadia. They stayed in control there for almost ten years but ended up giving it back to the French in a peace settlement. Again, several years later, the English took over the fort, and this time, they did not give it back.

Acadia became Nova Scotia and a province of England. The people of Nova Scotia were still Acadians in their hearts, though! Most of them still held fierce loyalty to their beloved France. This is how it was when the bloody French and Indian War began.

The war had been raging for almost nine long years, and once again, Acadia was in the spotlight. You see, the inhabitants of Acadia, or Nova Scotia as it was now called, were not fond of the British rule they had been under. Many of them became spies for the French army stationed in nearby New Brunswick. They constantly informed the French of the English whereabouts. This made the English very angry, and they responded with cruelty. When it became known that there were many Acadian informers, the British decided to do something drastic and quite terrible. British soldiers stormed into the province of Acadia, to round up all the population — men, women, and children. The soldiers spread out over the countryside, gathering everyone they could find. It would be nearly impossible to find out who the spies were; therefore everyone was removed.

Young and old were herded together with barely enough time to gather scant provisions for their journey. How terrified they must have been, as they were forced into ships and taken away from their homes. Sadly, families were often separated, and children lost track of their parents, because they were put on different ships.

Many of these people were sent to French settlements in Louisiana, while others were scattered throughout settlements in America. The British were not finished yet; they burned the people's homes so that they would have nothing to come back to, even if they tried.

Perhaps someday you will have a chance to read an unabridged version of a famous poem, which was written about what happened to the Acadians. The poem, "Evangeline," was written by a man

Evangeline Discovering Her Fiance in the Hospital

Silent a moment they stood in speechless wonder, and then rose
Louder and ever louder a wail of sorrow and anger,
And, by one impulse moved, they madly rushed to the door-way.
Vain was the hope of escape; and cries and fierce imprecations
Rang through the house of prayer; and high o'er the heads of the others
Rose, with his arms uplifted, the figure of Basil the blacksmith,
As, on a stormy sea, a spar is tossed by the billows.
Flushed was his face and distorted with passion; and wildly he shouted,
"Down with the tyrants of England! we never have sworn them allegiance!
Death to these foreign soldiers, who seize on our homes and our harvests!"
More he fain would have said, but the merciless hand of a soldier
Smote him upon the mouth, and dragged him down to the pavement.
In the midst of the strife and tumult of angry contention,
Lo! the door of the chancel opened, and Father Felician
Entered, with serious mien, and ascended the steps of the altar.
Raising his reverend hand, with a gesture he awed into silence
All that clamorous throng; and thus he spake to his people;
Deep were his tones and solemn; in accents measured and mournful
Spake he, as, after the tocsin's alarum, distinctly the clock strikes.
"What is this that ye do, my children? what madness has seized you?
Forty years of my life have I labored among you, and taught you,
Not in word alone, but in deed, to love one another!
Is this the fruit of my toils, of my vigils and prayers and privations?
Have you so soon forgotten all lessons of love and forgiveness?
This is the house of the Prince of Peace, and would you profane it
Lo! where the crucified Christ from his cross is gazing upon you!
See! in those sorrowful eyes what meekness and holy compassion!
Hark! how those lips still repeat the prayer, 'O Father, forgive them!'
Let us repeat that prayer in the hour when the wicked assail us,
Let us repeat it now, and say, 'O Father, forgive them!'"
Few were his words of rebuke, but deep in the hearts of his people
Sank they, and sobs of contrition succeeded the passionate outbreak,
While they repeated his prayer, and said, "O Father, forgive them!"

—Taken from "Evangeline," written by Henry W. Longfellow (1847)

named Henry Wadsworth Longfellow. Here is a short passage from this wonderful epic poem. This selection was copied without editing from the original poem.

The French and Indian war finally came to an end in 1763. The English were triumphant and drove the French farther west. George Washington resigned his commission from the Virginia militia and returned to his home at Mount Vernon. He married a pretty, young widow named Martha, who had two young children. We will hear more about George Washington in our coming chapters, for he has a very important role in our story.

The ride through history is a bit bumpy sometimes, isn't it? We are about to hit a sharp curve in the road. The 13 colonies are about to unite into one nation. You might want to pull down your hat; in our next chapter, the wind is going to be a little colder.

NARRATION BREAK

Retell the story of Acadia.

Claiming the New World

Since so many countries wanted the lands of the Americas, conflict was inevitable. These maps show just how much of the lands were disputed between two or more countries.

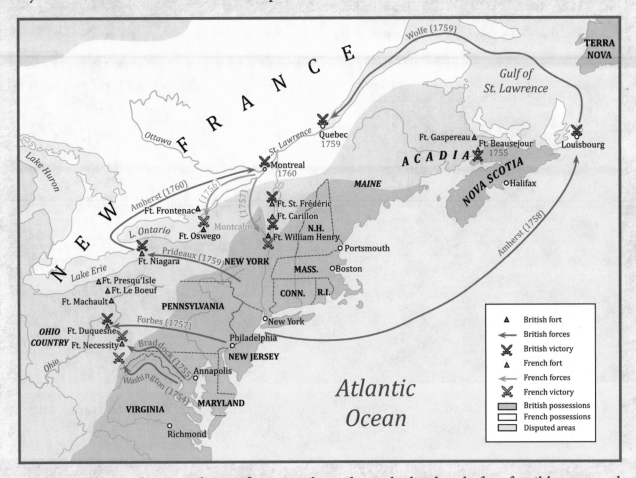

As always, those who won the conflict won the right to the land and often forcibly removed those already living on it. Soon, however, an unexpected series of conflicts would pit one of the largest empires in the world against 13 small colonies in America in a fight for freedom.

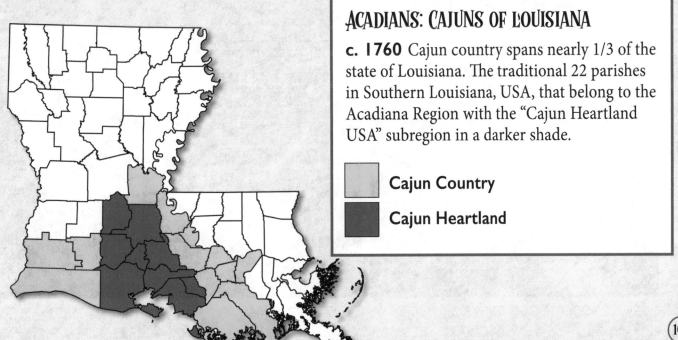

Acadians: Cajuns of Louisiana

c. 1760 Cajun country spans nearly 1/3 of the state of Louisiana. The traditional 22 parishes in Southern Louisiana, USA, that belong to the Acadiana Region with the "Cajun Heartland USA" subregion in a darker shade.

Cajun Country

Cajun Heartland

▲ The Cajuns settled in the bayous of southern Louisiana. A white egret and a turtle share a log in a Louisiana Bayou Swamp.

Cajuns are well known for their delicious dishes, including gumbo. ▶

The Acadians in the Atchafalaya, "Evangeline," by Joseph Rusling Meeker, 1871 ▼

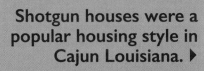

▲ Many Acadians were expelled from Canada during the French and Indian War.

▲ Boiled crawfish is also a popular Cajun dish.

Shotgun houses were a popular housing style in Cajun Louisiana. ▶

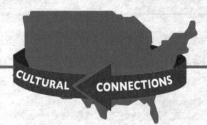

CULTURAL CONNECTIONS

Cultural Connections: Way up at the northern border of the state of Maine and our northern neighbor, Canada, in the beautiful, fertile St. John Valley, is a small area of Maine with a big history. In 1838–39, Great Britain and the United States were disputing the boundary between the state of Maine, in the United States, and New Brunswick, Canada. In 1842, this dispute was settled, and a boundary was drawn. The people in this area consider themselves to be Maine Acadians, and they work hard to preserve their Acadian heritage and culture, as well as their historic treasures. Among these historic treasures is a fort, with a military blockhouse, which was used during the 1838 boundary disagreement. You may find it a fascinating topic to research and read about the Acadian culture in Maine.

Memorial of the Acadians of Nantes

The cliffs of Fort Amherst in St. John's Newfoundland

THOUGHTS TO REMEMBER

1. Washington earned his nickname because of an instance, during the early years of the French and Indian War, when he should have been killed by gun fire. Instead, he came away completely untouched and unharmed, with bullet holes in various parts of his uniform and hat. He even had a horse or two shot out from underneath him.

2. We learned the French and Indians teamed up to fight the American colonists and the British over land west of the thirteen colonies. Other reasons for fighting included broken treaties and violence between the Indians and the colonists.

CHAPTER 11

WINDS OF CHANGE IN THE ENGLISH COLONIES

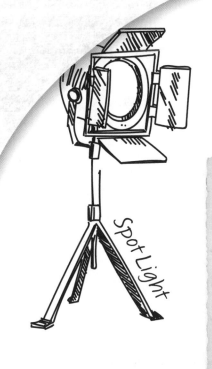

Spot Light

Starting Point: Inequality was at the heart of the conflicts that would lead to the Revolutionary War. Despite the American's being British citizens, they began to be taxed specifically on goods they needed, like tea and sugar. They had no representatives to fight for their rights.

Brick of Tea

Totally Tea-Time: Tea was a staple in the colonists' life. Because of their roots in Europe, tea was considered a necessity of life. The unjust tax on tea was meant to hurt everyday life for the colonists. The tea that was used at the time was not nicely boxed teabags like what we have today; it was pressed into hard bricks that were shaved into boiling water.

READY TO EXPLORE?

1. What was the Boston Tea Party?
2. Why did the Americans get so angry about the taxes on tea and stamps?

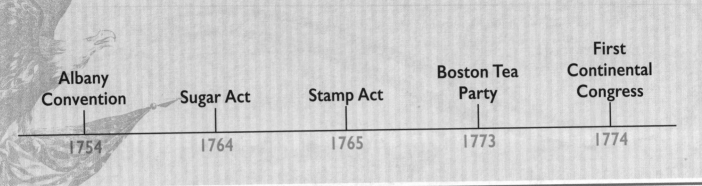

Albany Convention	Sugar Act	Stamp Act	Boston Tea Party	First Continental Congress
1754	1764	1765	1773	1774

Are you ready to start a new adventure in our history story? Today, we are going to hear how the winds of change started to blow into the 13 British colonies stretched out along the eastern coast of North America. This wind would start as a small breeze and end as a gale-force wind.

To understand the background for our story, we need to rewind time to the year the French and Indian War started — 1754.

The colonists were becoming concerned about the possibility of the French trying to come into the colonies. It was in the year 1754 that each colony sent its best men to *Albany, New York*, to discuss the possibility of uniting into one nation. This historic gathering is called the Albany Convention.

Among the men who gathered there was a man that you may have heard of. Benjamin Franklin was a printer from Philadelphia who was considered one of the finest minds in America. We will learn more about him later, but for now, I want to tell you about something Mr. Franklin wrote to show the men at the convention in Albany.

Below, is a picture of what Mr. Franklin drew. Do you understand what he meant when he drew this? Do you see the letters by each "piece" of the snake? These letters are the abbreviations for the names of the 13 colonies.

Mr. Franklin was trying to make everyone understand that the colonies, all separate and spread out, were like this snake, chopped up and harmless. He wanted to encourage all of the colonies to work together and be united. He believed that if they would do this, they could be strong and deadly, like some healthy snakes.

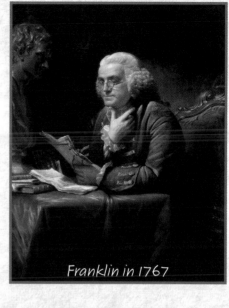

Franklin in 1767

To understand the atmosphere in America during this time, we need to remember that each colony, though they were ruled by England, was its own separate entity. Each one operated as its own little nation. The men at the convention did not agree with Mr. Franklin's idea of uniting, however, and for 30 more years, the colonies remained disconnected.

As we know, England won the French and Indian War, but there was still unrest in America. There were a lot of people who did not care for the rules or taxes of the British. The Indians, who did not like the way the English built forts and cut down the forest, were retaliating by murdering settlers and burning down their homes. The French settlers, who had lived somewhat peaceably under French rule, were angry at being taxed by a government to which they held no loyalty. There were a lot of unhappy people!

Many colonists still considered themselves loyal British subjects, and up until now, they had been taxed the same as the British citizens in England. But something happened in 1764 that made many colonists change their minds — King George came up with a tax specifically for the British colonists in America. This tax, called the Sugar Act, was followed by another tax, the Stamp Act, in 1765.

BOYCOTT: to stop buying or using goods or services as a protest.

Mocked in this British print, Society of Patriotic Ladies of Edenton, a group of women sign a petition to boycott English tea.

Have you ever heard the term, "no taxation without representation"? This means that unless people have a voice in their own government, that government has no right to tax the people. This is exactly how the colonists answered the Sugar Act and the Stamp Act. How angry they were with King George! This kind of government is called tyranny, and they would have none of it. The colonists refused to pay the tax, and King George was forced to repeal it.

Obviously, the king did not learn very easily that the colonists would not be bullied. In 1767, he tried again, this time taxing several imported items. Among the items was tea. Again, the colonists rebelled, and again the king was forced to drop most of the taxes. However, he kept the tax on the tea. I'm sure he thought that the colonists, being "good English folk," would pay the tax so they could have their tea.

Many of the colonists boycotted tea drinking. When you boycott something, it means that you refuse to have anything to do with it, usually because you

Destruction of Tea at Boston Harbor

believe it is wrong. King George still thought he would win this argument, so he sent several ships full of tea to America. He was wrong again. The ships' cargo was not even allowed to be unloaded, and the full ships sat in the harbor.

Maybe you have heard about something that happened on board one of these ships, the one that docked in *Boston Harbor*, in December of 1773. This is one of my favorite stories of our country's history, and I am quite sure you will enjoy it also.

Though the air in Boston was thick with tension, the evening was calm and quiet.

The cold, December moon hung in the sky, reflecting on the dark water of the Boston harbor. A ship, silently bobbing in the water, lay docked at the end of a wharf. Nothing on board was stirring, except an occasional movement and a flash of red from a patrolling British officer making his rounds of inspection.

Suddenly, this calm scene was interrupted by a flurry of activity. Footsteps pounded through the streets. Peaceful citizens of Boston ran for their lives, for out of the night came painted faces and scantily clad bodies of . . . Indians?

At first glance, you would have thought that a mob of Indian warriors, decorated in warpaint, had invaded the streets of Boston! But look again. Does that "Indian" have a ribbon tying his long hair back? And look there; that one has black, leather colonial-style shoes. What about that younger one over there? He has a white cotton shirt.

These strange figures swarmed onto the quiet ship in the harbor. Wild war whoops echoed down the streets where a few curious faces peeked from the shadows. What were they doing on the ship? Axes rang through the air mingling with the whooping and stomping. The ship's cargo of precious English tea was sent flying through the air! The "Indians" are really brave colonial fathers, brothers, and sons. "We will send a message loud and clear! We will not pay the taxes, and we will not drink the tea!" was what they were saying.

By the time they were finished that evening, thousands of pounds of expensive, English tea lay on the bottom of the harbor. This demonstration of resistance is known as "The Boston Tea Party." When news of the Tea Party reached the ears of King George, he was not smiling. He stamped his foot and decreed that the Americans would pay for the tea that lay at the bottom of Boston Harbor.

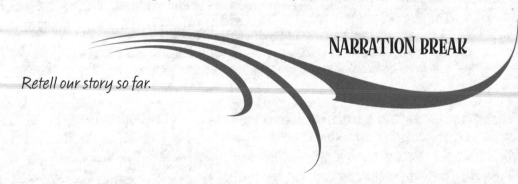

NARRATION BREAK

Retell our story so far.

John Hancock at his desk

How was this to end for the colonists? There were a great many of them who were tired of being pushed around by an unfair king from across an ocean. The king was as stubborn as he was unfair, and when his demands for repayment for the tea were met with the colonists' defiant refusal, he sent ships to the Boston Harbor to make sure no ships could go in or out. This was meant to shut down business in Boston, and it worked. Business slowed, but the colonists stuck to their refusal.

It seemed the time had come for the colonies to unite. Just as in every cause that has ever existed, there were people for and against uniting as one against England. There were some people who remained loyal to England. They had the attitude that the king had a right to do anything he pleased; after all, he was the king! However, most saw the necessity to become a country, independent from England.

So while King George's ships lay guarding the Boston Harbor, meetings were being held all over the colonies to discuss the next step in fighting for their rights. These meetings were open to those who were interested in having their opinions heard. There is one meeting in particular that might be of interest to us. It is being held in a church in Richmond, Virginia.

The year is 1775.

Come with me, let's slip into this meeting; perhaps we will see the faces of some of the freedom fighters who will go down in the history of our country. Look, I see Thomas Jefferson and George Washington! Over there is John Hancock, and another man named Patrick Henry. These men speak strongly about our rights as human beings. They say that no man, whether he is a king or peasant, has the right to rule over others with tyranny.

The atmosphere in the meeting is charged! We can feel the tension as one after another, the men get up and give their opinion about what should be done next. Some of them think that they would be foolish to go up against the English army, the mightiest army in the world.

Patrick Henry addressing the House of Burgesses

Others say that this can and should be resolved diplomatically. After all, it has only been in the last ten years or so that it has gotten bad; maybe a more diplomatic king will soon come to power.

The discussion continues on and on, and we look at each other and tap on our watches. Maybe we should slip out the back door, the same way we came in. It doesn't look like anything is going to be resolved tonight. These men seem like they could debate the subject of fighting for freedom for at least another four hours. We are both yawning; we must be in another time zone!

Suddenly, we both sit up straight and lean forward; neither of us is sleepy anymore. Standing straight and speaking clearly, Mr. Patrick Henry has the floor. We find ourselves leaning forward to catch his words. Our hearts pound with excitement, for here is a man that we can agree with! All thought of slipping out the door is gone from us. This is a speech that will be quoted throughout history. Dramatically, Mr. Henry paces the floor, his words building with intensity.

"Give me liberty or give me death!" These words seem to hang in the air. Slowly, throughout the meeting hall, the sound of agreement rises to a crescendo, and we find ourselves on our feet, cheering along with everyone else. "Give me liberty!" "Give me liberty!" "To arms!"

Aren't you glad you decided to come with me today? Grab a hold of my hand, because we are getting ready to jump into one of the most exciting times in the history of our country. A new country, our country, is about to be born! In our next chapter, we are going to meet some very important men. One is a wise printer who came up with many riddles and sayings still repeated today. The other is someone that made an everlasting imprint on our history by writing one of the most important documents ever written. I hope you rest up because we have a war to fight — "Give me liberty, or give me death!"

Gentlemen may cry, peace, peace — but there is no peace. The war is actually begun! The next gale that sweeps from the north will bring to our ears the clash of resounding arms! Our brethren are already in the field! Why stand we here idle? What is it the gentlemen wish? What would they have? Is life so dear, or peace so sweet, as to be purchased at the price of chains and slavery? Forbid it, Almighty God — I know not what course others may take; but as for me, give me liberty or give me death!

NARRATION BREAK

Retell what we "saw" at our meeting.

IMPORTANCE OF THE COLONIES FOR TRADE GOODS

The colonies in America didn't just trade goods overseas — they also traded goods among themselves. The climate, geography, and natural resources of the colonies were different. Some had harbors that helped to make them centers of trade, while others focused more on agricultural crops or timber because of forests.

This map shows the location and the trade goods of the original 13 colonies.

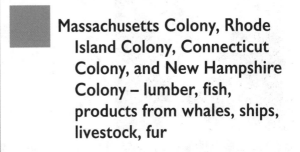
Massachusetts Colony, Rhode Island Colony, Connecticut Colony, and New Hampshire Colony – lumber, fish, products from whales, ships, livestock, fur

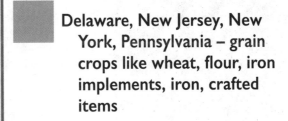
Delaware, New Jersey, New York, Pennsylvania – grain crops like wheat, flour, iron implements, iron, crafted items

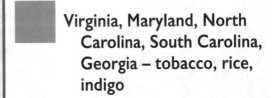
Virginia, Maryland, North Carolina, South Carolina, Georgia – tobacco, rice, indigo

Trading with the Indians

◀ Patrick Henry led Virginia's opposition to the Stamp Act (1765) and was an outspoken critic of the Intolerable Acts (1774).

Samuel Adams organized the Boston chapter of the Sons of Liberty in response to the Stamp Act (1765). ▶

◀ Paul Revere participated in multiple protests against the Tea Act (1773), including the Boston Tea Party.

Thomas Jefferson referenced the Quartering Act (1774) as a reason for rebellion in the Declaration of Independence. Thomas Jefferson Memorial at Missouri History Museum in St. Louis, Missouri. ▼

◀ James Otis Jr. popularized the phrase "no taxation without representation" because of the Currency and Sugar Acts (1764). Bronze statue of James Otis, Jr stands in front of the Barnstable County Courthouse, Massachusetts.

James Madison wrote the Constitution's Third Amendment to prevent the Quartering Act (1774) from happening again. ▶

Benjamin Franklin's testimony helped repeal the Stamp Act (1765). ▶

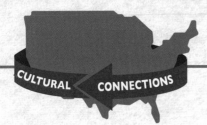

Any country that wishes to remain independent and unconquered must have a way to protect itself. When the colonies were being terrorized by their mother country, England, they did not have an official army; instead, they had militias, which up to this time operated under the authority of the English rule. In coming lessons, you will learn how this militia became the beginning of the Continental Army, the first American army. In modern times, our armed forces consists of these five branches: the Air Force, the Army, the Coast Guard, the Marine Corps, and the Navy. Each branch is responsible for specific areas of protection. Ask your parent if anyone in your family has served in any of the branches of the American Armed Forces.

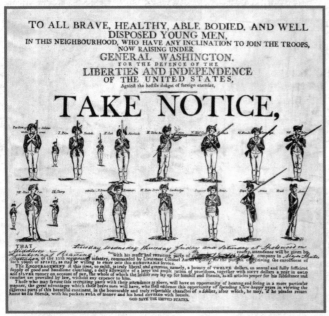

Continental Army recruitment broadside, 1776

Army Recruitment poster
from World War I, c.1917

THOUGHTS TO REMEMBER

1. and 2: We learn in Chapter 11 that the Boston Tea Party was a demonstration of resistance against the British taxes imposed on the American colonists. It wasn't only the high taxes that angered the colonists; it was the fact that the taxes came with no rights of representation in their government. This type of taxation without representation is a mark of a tyrannical government. It was because of the Americans' indignation toward such a government that thousands of pounds of expensive English tea found its way to the bottom of the Boston Harbor.

CHAPTER 12

THE POWER OF WORDS

Starting Point: Some ideas are very powerful, such as concepts like freedom, fairness, and justice. While they are just words, for the American colonies fighting back against injustice, they were at the heart of a dream for a better world that still draws people today.

Spot Light

The Very Intelligent Benjamin Franklin: Benjamin Franklin was an extremely intelligent man! He was, among other accomplishments, an inventor. We still use many of his inventions today, such as lightning rods, bifocal glasses, and the glass harmonica!

READY TO EXPLORE?

1. What is a printing press?
2. What is a declaration of independence?

Young Ben Franklin improving his language skills

Perhaps my young friends hearing this story have heard the names of the two men who are the subjects of today's story. These two men are well known in our country's history, for they helped in many ways to bring liberty to the colonies.

Back in the time we are speaking of, when the 13 colonies had not yet become a nation, there seemed to be a great number of people who did amazing and wonderful things. However, there is something that I want all of us to remember: all of these people started out as children. That's right, they were not always big and "powerful." Most of them never dreamed that they would become known throughout history as our founding fathers.

The first person that I would very much like to tell you about is a man named Benjamin Franklin. You heard about Mr. Franklin in our last chapter, and many of you have probably read stories about him. When you hear his name, what comes to your mind? I suppose many of you might think of his experiment with the kite and the key; but that was much later in his life. Benjamin did a lot before he decided to test the electricity of that storm; which, by the way, was a very dangerous thing to do!

Let's start at the beginning. Benjamin was born in Boston in 1706, one of 17 children. Of those 17 children, 10 of them were boys, and Ben was the youngest son. Do you have brothers or sisters? I do, but not nearly as many as Ben had! That must have been a very busy household indeed.

Ben only went to two years of formal school, before he had to come home to help his family. His father was a candle and soap maker, and he needed help running his shop, but Benjamin did not like making candles and soap. Nevertheless, he worked hard dipping candles and stirring the tallow for the soap. He was a bright boy who loved to read and write, so he filled the long hours of work with daydreams of having adventures at sea.

When he was 12, Ben's father sent him to work for his older brother, James, as an apprentice. Do you know what an apprentice is? Back in early America, an apprentice usually worked for a relative or a friend of the family who owned a business. The business owner trained the apprentice in whatever trade it took to run the business. The apprentice, usually a young boy, in turn signed a contract promising to work for a certain length of time, usually ten years. They were paid in room and board, but most of the time, they did not get a salary.

Benjamin's brother was a printer and owned his own shop. Ben and his brother

Benjamin Franklin at work on a printing press

did not get along very well. Benjamin liked being a printer, but did not like the fact that he had to work without pay for nine years, until he was 21 years old. I am sure they had quite the quarrels, as brothers sometimes do.

Ben decided that he was going to learn how to write well, so that he would have a fine education by the time he was free from his apprenticeship. He could not go to school, so Ben came up with a plan. To accomplish his goal, he read articles, speeches, and documents. After thinking about what he had read for several days, he would write what he had read from memory. After he was satisfied with his writing, he would very carefully compare and correct his work against the original. Benjamin became an exceptionally good writer this way. This is still a good way to learn to write well.

Benjamin's brother started a newspaper called the *New England Courant*, and Benjamin worked for him. He learned how to edit, set type, and run the printing presses. Ben loved working on the newspaper! He thought the articles and advertisements were very interesting. In fact, he thought they were so interesting, that he decided to write some articles of his own!

Ben, knowing that his brother would not print something that he had written, wrote his article the way he wanted and signed his name "Silence Dogood." I am beginning to think that our young friend Ben was quite the prankster, aren't you?

The articles Ben wrote poked fun at the Puritan Church for being so strict. Most people thought they were funny, so he wrote 13 more! Ben enjoyed writing for the newspaper, and making people laugh and think.

Not everyone in Boston thought his articles were funny, and his brother, James, got into a lot of trouble for printing articles poking fun at the Puritan Church. He was told that he could not run his printing shop anymore, so he made Ben run it instead. Benjamin enjoyed being the editor of his brother's newspaper, but this change did not help his relationship with his brother.

After his apprenticeship, Ben decided to go look for a job in another printing shop, so he left Boston and went to Philadelphia, the City of Brotherly Love. Ben loved Philadelphia, and always considered it his hometown.

Benjamin Franklin

He spent many years working in a printing shop, and eventually he owned his own. Ben was becoming a very well-known character throughout the colonies. People liked him for his charming smile and quick wittiness, which made them think. He was always coming up with riddles and sayings. Some of these sayings are still said today. Have you ever heard these?

"Early to bed, early to rise, makes a man healthy, wealthy and wise," or, "A penny saved, is a penny earned"? These are both Ben's sayings!

Benjamin married a lady named Deborah, and they had three children. He loved his family, and spent hours playing with his children, and commonly referred to Deborah as "my beloved wife." I could fill an entire book with stories of what Benjamin Franklin did; he has so many accomplishments attributed to him. He was on several different political boards representing Pennsylvania. Did you know that he was the very first United States Postmaster? Well, he was! In fact he is the person who decided that we needed a postal service.

He was so well known for his witty comments that he wrote a book called *Poor Richard's Almanac*, which sold like "hotcakes" in the colonies. This book was not only full of humor, it predicted the weather and told farmers when it would be best to plant their crops. Yes, Ben was a pretty smart fellow!

Besides writing books and starting the Postal Service, Benjamin was also an inventor. Ben loved science, and he was very curious by nature. He wasn't satisfied in knowing that something worked; he wanted to know WHY it worked! He also wanted to invent things that made life easier for people, like bifocal glasses, lightning rods to keep houses safer during lightning storms, and a stove that was more efficient and warmer.

I could go on and on about the accomplishments of Mr. Benjamin Franklin. However, I will close our story of this interesting man by telling you that in his later years, Ben joined the cause of abolition. He tried hard to keep peace between England and the colonies, but when he knew that it was hopeless, he staunchly supported the colonies. Benjamin Franklin was quite a man, wasn't he?

Franklin and Electricity

NARRATION BREAK

*Tell your favorite part of the story
of Benjamin Franklin.*

Now, I want to tell you about one of my favorite people in the history of our country. Please meet Mr. Thomas Jefferson. Thomas was born in 1743, in the colony of Virginia, and he grew up to do something very important!

Thomas Jefferson

Thomas grew up in a large family of eight children, which by now you probably understand was common in those days. He was a bright boy who loved to read, write, and learn. He was always popular at the parties for his dancing, singing, and playing the violin. At the young age of 16, Thomas went to college to become a lawyer.

When he grew up, Thomas Jefferson did become a lawyer. He was also a horticulturist (hor-ti-CULT-tur-ist), someone who knows a lot about growing plants; an architect (ARK-it-tect), someone who designs buildings; an archaeologist (ar-kee-OL-o-jist), someone who digs up and studies ancient ruins; and a paleontologist (pa-lee-on-TOL-o-jist), someone who studies fossils to find out about history from a long time ago. He also designed and built his own house, which he called Monticello. Can you imagine how busy Thomas was? I have never met anyone who does as many things as he did!

In 1776, Thomas was called on to do something very important. At a meeting of the Continental Congress (that's what the leaders of the colonies called themselves), it was decided that Thomas would write the Declaration of Independence. Do you know what a declaration is? It is a proclaimed decision. The decision the colonies had made was to become independent from the British Empire.

Can you imagine what it would feel like to have this kind of assignment? At that very moment, the future of what would become the great country of the United States of America rested squarely on the shoulders of Mr. Thomas Jefferson. The words he wrote would tell England and the world what kind of country we were going to be. These are the words that flowed from his heart into the Declaration of Independence:

NATION: a large group of people with common characteristics and customs.

We hold these truths to be self-evident, that all men are created equal, that they are endowed by their Creator with certain unalienable Rights that among these are Life, Liberty and the pursuit of Happiness. That to secure these rights, Governments are instituted among Men, deriving their just powers from the consent of the governed. That whenever any Form of Government becomes destructive of these ends, it is the Right of the People to alter or to abolish it, and to institute new Government, laying its foundation on such principles and organizing its powers in such form, as to them shall seem most likely to effect their Safety and Happiness.

These are powerful words, aren't they? I would like very much for all of my young friends to someday read the whole Declaration of Independence. But even more than that, I pray that all Americans, young and old, not forget why and how our country was founded; for no other nation has ever been founded on such principles as these.

Thomas Jefferson went on to hold some pretty important offices, including becoming our third president of the United States. However, I am not going to spend a great deal of time telling you all about them; instead, I am going to show you some of the literary works that came from his pen.

I believe that Mr. Jefferson himself is able to show you what kind of person he was far better than I can by writing my own words about him. Following are some quotes taken from Thomas Jefferson's own writing. I encourage all my young friends to carefully consider the words of Mr. Jefferson, for they are important pieces that fit snugly into the jigsaw puzzle of history we are constructing.

"That government is best which governs the least, because its people discipline themselves."

"Do not bite at the bait of pleasure till you know there is no hook."

"On matters of style, swim with the current, on matters of principle, stand like a rock."

"Honesty is the first chapter of wisdom."

"All tyranny needs to gain a foothold is for people of good conscience to remain silent."

"A nation ceases to be republican only when the will of the majority ceases to be law."

It is important to know the power of words. In this lesson, we have learned about two men who used their words for the cause of freedom. I would like to end our chapter with one of my favorite "word Scriptures" from Psalm 21:14:

Let the words of my mouth, and the meditation of my heart, be acceptable in Thy sight, O Lord, my strength, and my redeemer.

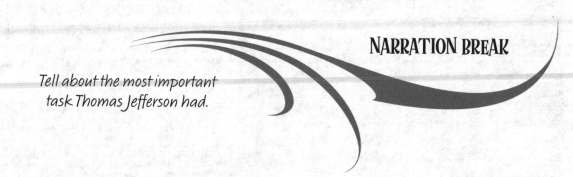

NARRATION BREAK

Tell about the most important task Thomas Jefferson had.

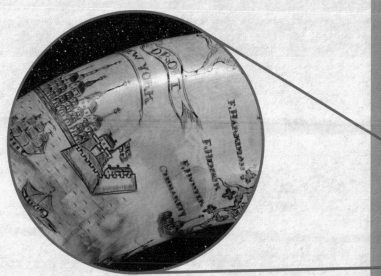

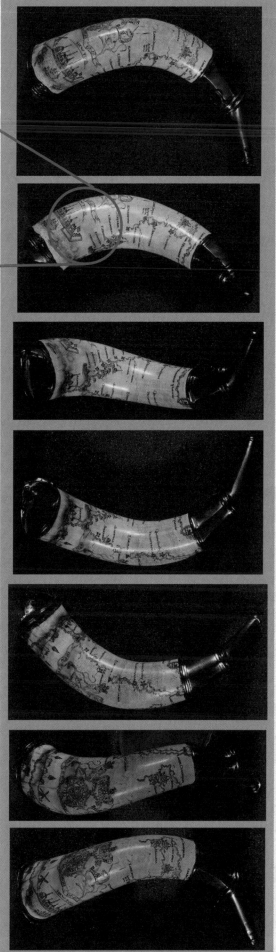

POWDER HORN MAPS

"One of the most fascinating cartographic formats represented in the Library's holdings is a collection of eight powder horns inscribed with maps, dating from the time of the French and Indian War and the American Revolutionary War. For soldiers, hunters, or frontiersmen in the late colonial period, powder horns were indispensable companions to their muskets. Fashioned out of cow or ox horns, they made convenient containers for carrying and protecting gunpowder. Usually handmade, these horns were often inscribed with rhymes, references to particular campaigns, names of forts or towns, diary entries, or maps. Because maps were scarce at the time, it is possible that map-inscribed powder horns served as guides for their owners, but it is more likely that the map images provided records or mementos of the areas that the owners traversed or the campaigns in which they were involved."*

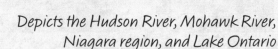

Depicts the Hudson River, Mohawk River, Niagara region, and Lake Ontario

*(http://www.loc.gov/exhibits/treasures/tr11a.html#obj1)

◄ Jefferson provided over 6400 of his own books to the Library of Congress when their collection was destroyed in 1814.

◄ Jefferson served as an ambassador to France and as America's first Secretary of State.

Jefferson not only founded the University of Virginia but also designed the school's Rotunda building (above) and the state's capitol building. ▶

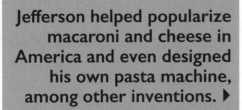

▲ Franklin helped found several institutions that still operate in Philadelphia today, including a hospital, library, and university.

▲ Franklin's many inventions included a musical instrument — the glass harmonica.

▲ In response to a devastating fire, Franklin helped found the first volunteer fire department and insurance company in America.

Jefferson helped popularize macaroni and cheese in America and even designed his own pasta machine, among other inventions. ▶

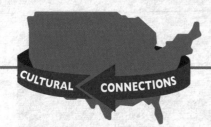
Apprenticeships have been around since the beginning of civilizations! We read in the New Testament of the Bible that James and John, the sons of Zebedee, were with their father in his boat, learning the trade of fishing. In our chapter, we learned that Benjamin Franklin was an apprentice to his brother, James — this is how he learned the trade of printing. But are there still apprentices today? The answer is yes! There are still many occupations that are passed from one skilled worker to the next. This learn-on-the-job approach is a great way to receive an education and a skill at the same time. Apprenticeship programs, which are operated from a county and state level, make this type of occupation training a legitimate option for higher education and occupational training.

A shoe repairman and his young apprentice

Apprentice learning ironworks with a professional teacher

THOUGHTS TO REMEMBER

1. A printing press in the colonies was manually operated. The printer lined up small letter stamps to form the words that he wanted to print. The stamps would be brushed with just the right amount of ink. A large sheet of paper was placed over the entire set of stamps, put into a clamping device, pressing the paper down on the inked letters!

2. A declaration of independence is a formal document, in which one country declares complete sovereignty from what is currently a ruling power.

CHAPTER 13

THE BRITISH ARE COMING!

Starting Point: With such powerful ideals in the hearts of some colonists and a stubborn king who ruled an empire, it was inevitable that liberty in America would have to be won in a difficult fight.

Paul Revere Statue at the Old North Church in Boston, Massachusetts

Historical Landmark: You can still visit the Old North Church. Not only is it a historical landmark, it is still an active church with a congregation.

READY TO EXPLORE?

1. Who wrote a poem about that famous ride of Paul Revere?
2. Who were the Minute Men?

**Battles of
Lexington
and Concord**

**Second Continental
Congress meets**

**Fort Ticonderoga
is captured**

April 18–19, 1775   May 10,1775   May 10,1775

Listen my children, and you shall hear,
Of the midnight ride of Paul Revere,
On the eighteenth of April, in Seventy-five;
Hardly a man is now alive
Who remembers that famous day and year.

These words from the famous poem, ***The Ride of Paul Revere***, by Henry Wadsworth Longfellow, ring through my childhood memories. I was probably right around your age when I learned this epic poem about the famous ride of Paul Revere. I hope you are ready for a fast ride through the cool night air, because that is exactly where you and I are going! Are you ready to ride?

Have you been feeling the rising tension in the 13 Colonies over the last few chapters? The relationship had not been going very well between the colonies and their "mother" country of England. In fact, the relationship was going from bad to worse, and we are going to see it completely disintegrate in this chapter of our story.

Today, I would like you to meet a man who, like Thomas Jefferson and Benjamin Franklin, wanted freedom for the colonies stretched out along the Atlantic coast. This man's name was Paul Revere. Mr. Revere lived in Boston, the town where the famous "tea party" demonstration took place. Our story today takes place not quite two years after the tea party. The brave group of men, who had organized the tea party, were called "the Sons of Liberty." These men knew they had to stand together for their rights, and the people of the colonies looked to them for leadership and guidance.

All over the colonies, men and boys were gathering guns and any kind of weapons they could. Gunpowder was being made and stored in warehouses at carefully guarded locations around the colonies. The Sons of Liberty held secret meetings to plan for an attack from the British, and they had riders ready at a minute's notice to jump on their horses and ride to warn the others of the enemy's approach.

There were British solders stationed in the colonies, so these plans had to be carried out as secretly as possible. If anyone who was loyal to the British found out where these stores of weapons and gunpowder were, there would be big trouble! If anyone was caught making plans to rebel against the British, they would be hanged for treason against the king of England. Messages between the Sons of Liberty were in code, so others did not know what they said.

And so, there was a great "spy system" throughout Boston and the surrounding towns. Trust was a hard thing to come by, for there were friends turning against friends and brother against brother. Those who remained loyal to England were called Tories. Patriot against Tory; Tory against Patriot — tension was high.

After the Boston Tea Party, King George sent many more soldiers to patrol the colonies. The hostility between the people and the soldiers was rising every day. There were fights and arrests happening on a regular basis. Something was going to happen . . . and soon.

Have you ever been in a situation where you knew something bad was going to happen, like a really terrible storm? I remember one time when I was nine years old, the weather was very stormy above the farm where I lived. The clouds were swirling and had a strange green hue. It seemed like the wind did not know which way to blow, and the trees looked like they were going to break right off and fly away! I was dreadfully afraid; so afraid, in fact, that I hid under my bed.

As I watched from my "safe spot," I saw a funnel cloud come out of the sky. I gasped in horror as it roared right down through the cow pasture, ripped the roof completely off of the barn and tossed it into the field! I will never forget the noise of that storm. Even more than the noise, I will never forget the feeling I experienced right before the twister came. The air seemed like it was trying to push me right through the floor.

I tell you this story because I want you to imagine what it would have been like to be a child, just as you are now, but living in the colonial era at the time of the Boston Tea Party. Imagine that you see the red coats of the British soldiers every day. You see the fights, and you feel the fear. What would it have been like? Just like I felt as a child when the storm came through, you would have probably wanted to hide until it was over! Everyone around you would have been talking quietly, and most of the time stopped when you came in the room.

Perhaps your family doesn't want war between the colonies and England. Tories. You would hear that word behind your back at church, and turning around, you would see a child who used to be your friend, sticking their tongue out at you. "My father says your father is a coward!" or "Are you afraid to fight for freedom?" These taunts, and others, would come flying at you all day long.

There are four other children in your neighborhood who are "Tories," and you choose to play with them. "What is going to happen next?" would be the question in the front of your mind all day long, day after day. Just like the feeling I felt before that twister, you would feel the air pushing down on you.

Maybe it is the other way around, and your family is on the Patriot side. You have heard your parents talking quietly after they think you and your brothers and sisters are asleep. You hear your mother's worried voice asking about your older brother — will he have to fight? Your father's deep voice answers, but you cannot make out the words.

Redcoats back from a raid

Your father spends many evenings away from home, for he is a member of the Sons of Liberty. He and your older brother were in Boston on the night of the Tea Party. You are not sure, but you think that they were probably involved with it; your mother spent the day wringing her hands. You know something is going to happen soon. There's that feeling in the air, a pressure that is a constant presence.

NARRATION BREAK

Tell how it would feel to live at this time in the colonies.

The storm, which had been brewing for several years, was about to break loose. Dr. Joseph Warren, one of the leaders of the Sons of Liberty, had received word, through the spy network, that the British Army was on the move, marching from Boston to Lexington. Dr. Warren was concerned they might be on the way to Concord to seize the weapons and gunpowder stored there.

"The British are coming!"

John Hancock and Samuel Adams, two other Sons of Liberty leaders, were in Lexington, and Dr. Warren wanted them to be aware. Paul Revere and William Dawes were called upon to spread the alarm.

Mr. Revere was sent across the Charles River to take an inland route to Lexington, while Mr. Dawes traveled up the Boston Neck toward Lexington. Paul Revere had made arrangements with the sexton of the Old North Church to set up a signal in the church tower; one lantern in the steeple to signal the British approach by land, and two lanterns to signal approach by sea. This signal could be seen across the Charles River in Charlestown, and it would warn the Sons of Liberty stationed there which way the British were coming. Two lights are glowing from high in the steeple window; they are coming by sea!

You and I are going to ride along with Mr. Revere, but we need to stop and look at our map. Mr. Revere might be familiar with this route, but we need to make sure we know where we are going in case we get separated. There is a map for us at the end of this chapter. Let's take a few minutes and acquaint ourselves with our journey. It's almost 11 o'clock at night, so it is very dark indeed. And with all the British soldiers stationed around Boston, we do not want to get lost!

Are you ready to go? Come; let's stay close to Mr. Revere. He has reached the shores of the Charles River and is talking to two men. These must be his friends that he has arranged to take him across the river. As we get in the boat, Mr. Revere signals to us with his hand. He warns us that we must be quiet and not call attention to our group. Mr. Revere's friends steer the boat across the river, carefully staying clear of the British war ship anchored not far away. It is very dark, and the mid-April air is chilly. We are shivering in excitement!

Paul Revere

Once we are on the other side, Mr. Revere is onto the horse that is awaiting him, and we mount our horses also. Cries of "God speed!" from our friends in the Sons of Liberty follow us through the night. As we ride along, Mr. Revere calls out to the darkened houses that we pass, "The British are coming! The British are coming!" Suddenly, Paul Revere holds up his hand; he sees two soldiers on patrol about a quarter of a mile down a side road.

Quietly and quickly, we choose another direction and ride until we are safe from the sight of the British regulars. Our hearts are pounding! Our next stop is the house of Isaac Hall, the leader of the Minute Men. The Minute Men are the Patriots that form a great network through the colonies. These men are ready to fight at a moment's notice. Mr. Revere rides up into the yard of the Hall house, "The British are coming! The British are coming! They are coming by sea!" We wait for Mr. Revere to give the leader the message of the approaching soldiers, and then we are on our way again.

On we ride, and at the town of Medford, we turn onto another road. As we ride along, we help Mr. Revere warn all the colonists in their dark houses. "The British are coming!" The cry rings through the cool night air over and over again, and with it comes the certainty that something big is about to happen. Lights are burning in the windows as faces appear at the door. Men and boys spill out into the night, heading for the guns and horses that are waiting in the nearby barns. Dogs yap with excitement, as wives and mothers rush to prepare food for their husbands and sons.

As we ride on toward the town of Lexington, we pray that we are not too late to warn John Hancock and Samuel Adams. We know Mr. Revere shares our concerns, for he spurs his horse on faster. Finally we gallop into the yard of the home of Reverend Clark, where Mr. Hancock and Mr. Adams are staying. We are much relieved to see our friends are safe and sound.

We know that in the quiet woods and farmlands behind us, men and boys, farmers, merchants, tailors, and blacksmiths are scrambling to spread the word, "The British are coming!" There are hundreds of men gathering from every direction, waiting for further instructions. Mr. Dawes, the other messenger who had taken another route, rides into the yard, and Mr. Revere is thankful to see him. After they exchange accounts of their journeys, they tell us to stay in Lexington; they are going on to Concord, which could prove to be too dangerous for us.

Mr. Revere and Mr. Dawes, along with another friend, a young doctor, continued on their way to Concord to warn the Sons of Liberty posted there of the coming trouble. It is good that we decided to stay in Lexington, for the three men were stopped by a group of British regulars. Mr. Dawes and the doctor got away, but Mr. Revere was stopped and brought back to Lexington.

All morning, Minute Men and English soldiers gathered on the town green. It was just a short time later that a skirmish between the two groups turned into a fight. Emotions were running high, and both sides were in the mood for a fight.

Mr. Revere, who had been released, and Mr. Hancock watched as the disagreement grew. Suddenly, a shot was fired! Nobody knew who had fired, and it didn't seem to matter. This shot is called the "shot heard around the world," and it was the shot that started the American Revolution. The soft wind of change that had started blowing many years before had turned into a powerful, raging storm.

PATRIOT: someone who feels a strong support for their country.

NARRATION BREAK

Tell what you thought of our ride with Mr. Revere.

THE MIDNIGHT RIDES

The adventurous ride of Paul Revere was actually more dangerous than exciting. At the time, it was very difficult to send messages, and the events of this night were among the initial sparks of conflict for the Revolutionary War. Colonial forces had been gathering supplies in locations in anticipation of possible conflict. One such spot was at Concord, Massachusetts.

British soldiers were sent to take the supplies, but they were not aware that the colonials had already moved them. In an effort to warn communities along the path of the attack, Revere rode on horseback warning other patriots and towns along the way. He was joined by many others who also rode throughout the night to give the warning to others.

Revere's ride was part of a simple communication system put in place to give enough warning for colonials to gather their militias in defense of their communities. Events of this night include the Battles of Lexington and Concord. While the colonials initially were driven back near Lexington, the colonials held their ground with a group of the British on the Concord bridge. As the British forces regrouped and headed back to Boston, they were attacked by different groups of colonials during the day until they could reach additional forces.

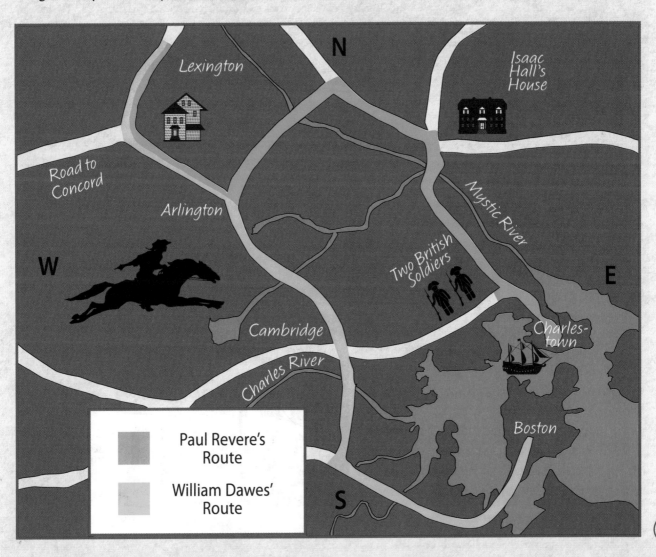

▲ 2. His first stop was the nearby Old North Church, where he told men to raise lanterns to warn neighboring Charlestown.

▲ 1. Revere's House still stands in North Boston today. His midnight ride started here around 10 P.M.

3. At about 11 P.M., ▲ Revere was rowed across the Charles River to Charlestown while a British ship lurked nearby.

4. Revere then rode a few miles to Medford, where he stopped at 11:30 P.M. at the Isaac Hall House to wake the leader of the local militia. ▶

▲ 5. Next, Revere rode several more miles to Lexington, getting there shortly after midnight. He stopped at the Hancock-Clarke House to warn John Hancock and Samuel Adams.

▲ 6. Revere then tried to ride to Concord but was captured a few miles outside of Lexington near Lincoln around 1 A.M.

▲ 7. Revere was released after an hour and returned to Lexington. He went to the Buckman Tavern at 4:30 A.M. to help Hancock move a trunk.

From here, Revere was an eyewitness to the war's first battle as it unfolded at 5 A.M. on the Lexington Common. ▶

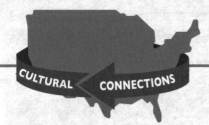

The poetry of Henry Wadsworth Longfellow is mostly centered on the daily life of America. We have learned about his poems depicting the happenings of the French and Indian War and the famous ride of Paul Revere. The art, music, and writings of our country's early years were affected greatly by what was happening — the battle for independence from England, the exploration of the wilderness, the hardships and triumphs of everyday life. It is an important part of our cultural history and can still be enjoyed today! Take a few minutes to study the work of some of these great early American artists and sculptors: Jeremiah Theus, Patience Wright, William Rush, and John Hesselius.

Drawing of young Longfellow, 1852

Photo of Henry Wadsworth Longfellow, 1868

THOUGHTS TO REMEMBER

1. We learn in Chapter 13 that Henry W. Longfellow (the same man who wrote "Evangeline") wrote "The Ride of Paul Revere."

2. We also learn that the Minute Men were the Colonial American militia, who were trained to be ready in a matter of minutes when called upon to defend their colony. These men would become the American Continental Army.

CHAPTER 14

STORIES OF THE AMERICAN REVOLUTION

Spot Light

Starting Point: The American Revolutionary War is an inspiring collection of experiences and history by regular people who believed in the goals of liberty and gave all they had, some even their lives, to see the dream realized.

The stone walls of Fort Ticonderoga

Fort Ticonderoga: Fort Ticonderoga is located near to the south end of Lake Champlain in the state of New York. The fort is star-shaped.

READY TO EXPLORE?

1. What kinds of men fought in the Revolutionary War?

2. What roles did women and children have in the war?

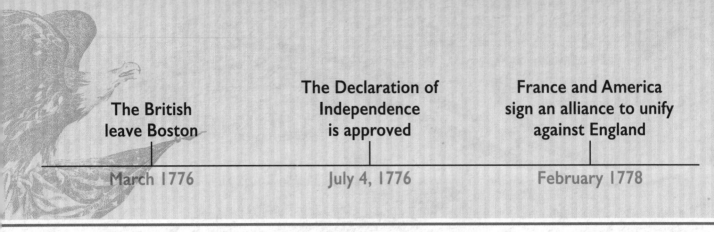

The British leave Boston	The Declaration of Independence is approved	France and America sign an alliance to unify against England
March 1776	July 4, 1776	February 1778

In this chapter, we are going to learn about the war that the colonies fought for their freedom from England — the American Revolution. This was a long war, full of heroes and tales of bravery, and it would take me a great deal longer than one or two chapters to tell you about it all. Instead of giving you a large number of names, dates, and battle information, I am going to tell you the story of only a few of the most important people and their brave deeds.

As you remember from our last chapter, the first shot of the Revolution was fired in Lexington. The British had gone there to capture the stores of ammunition gathered by the Patriots. They did not succeed, for the brave Patriots held them off, forcing them out of Lexington.

After the battle at Lexington, the English army marched on to Concord. Again, they planned to capture the stockpile of ammunitions there, and again they failed, for the American soldiers, who had beaten them there had hidden most of the ammunition in the woods. From all over the colonies, men laid down their tools of trade and picked up their weapons, ready to fight for freedom. The British, who had thought they would have an easy time, were surprised by the fighting spirit of these colonists!

The English soldiers, who had marched on Lexington and Concord, now turned to march back to *Boston*. They had a hard time of it though, for along the way American soldiers hid and ambushed them, "Indian style." By the time the remaining British troops reached Boston, they were being chased by twenty thousand American militiamen. I wonder if those British soldiers felt like bear cubs that had awakened a giant nest of swarming bees!

It was during this time that the leaders of the colonies, the Continental Congress, were meeting to appoint a commander in chief for what was now being called the Continental Army. They chose George Washington. Brave Mr. Washington is a bit older than he was in our last encounter; he had spent the last 17 years running his plantation and helping the Sons of Liberty. Shortly afterward, the American spy network learned the British were trying to fortify their control in Boston by sending troops out into the hills around the city. The Americans beat them to it and set up battle lines throughout the hills.

What followed was to become the famous Battle of Bunker Hill. It took three attacks from the British to knock the Continental Army back, and it would never

136   *The Battle of Lexington*

The Death of General Warren at the Battle of Bunker Hill

have happened at all except the Americans ran out of gunpowder. Many more British soldiers than American soldiers were killed that day. Even though they won the Battle of Bunker Hill, the British were starting to understand that this war was not going to be as easy as they had thought it would be to win.

General George Washington was busy training his men. The farmers and other tradesmen who had filled the ranks of the voluntary colonial militia, were now fitted for uniforms and being trained in ways of battle. General Washington was a fine man who loved God and his country, and he was a great general. He put a plan into action to regain control of Boston and its harbor.

One night, he ordered his men to quietly station themselves and their cannons on the hills looking down on Boston. The unsuspecting British, who were occupying the city, awoke to a rather unpleasant surprise! It would be rather unsettling to wake up to an army and cannons surrounding your town. The British had the battle of Bunker Hill fresh in their memories and decided to leave Boston without a fight.

After leaving Boston, the British came with a bigger army to New York. Their plan was to seize the northern colonies along with the bigger cities of New York and Philadelphia. They thought if they could do this, the other colonies' resistance would crumble.

General Washington met the British army at New York, but the smaller American army could not hold off the determined English forces, and Washington and his army were forced to flee through New Jersey. This was very discouraging for the American army. The year after that, the British again defeated the American army and took control of Philadelphia. The king of England was thrilled to see the American front crumbling to his soldiers. Surely these stubborn colonists would not be able to withstand for long and would soon give up!

What was the American response to this? Mr. Thomas Jefferson was appointed to write something very important. Do you remember what it was? Yes, the Declaration of Independence was written in 1776. It was July 4, 1776, when the Congress adopted the declaration. The Americans may not have won those battles, but the war was not over yet. Determination and celebration filled the streets of Boston and other towns throughout the colonies. People came together to celebrate the freedom they knew was worth fighting for. The Liberty Bell rang strong and clear as the people celebrated together.

Are you starting to see how the puzzle pieces are fitting together now? Let's take a few minutes to look at the "American Revolution Timeline" in your Student's Journal. Take the time right now to review what has happened so far in our "Fight for Freedom" story.

NARRATION BREAK

Use your American Revolution Timeline to retell what has happened so far in our story of the Revolution.

After the Declaration of Independence was written and celebrated, the Americans took heart, and little by little started winning battles. The first major victory for the colonists came when General Washington and his troops secretly crossed the Delaware River into New Jersey on the day after Christmas 1776. There they surprised the enemy and won the battle at Trenton.

Another battle was fought and won in the upper part of New York near Saratoga. With great determination, the American army drove back the British that had marched down from Canada. A while later, Ethan Allen and Benedict Arnold, the brave commanders of the "Green Mountain Boys," and militia from Massachusetts and Connecticut, took control of Fort Ticonderoga in New York.

General Washington was having a rough time of it, though, and was encamped in Valley Forge in Pennsylvania. It was a bitter winter, and the men did not have enough clothes, coats, or boots to keep them warm.

Throughout that terrible winter of 1777, many men died of frostbite and disease. The dwellings they had were ramshackle and did not keep the wind from blowing through. Spirits sagged as winter dragged on and on. General Washington prayed for his men and for the cause of freedom.

Finally, after months of starving and freezing conditions, something good happened!

Our old friend Benjamin Franklin, who was in France at the time of these battles, heard the news about how his fellow colonists were having a hard go of it. He decided to go talk with the king of France. Of course, as we know, France and England did not get along.

Washington Crossing the Delaware

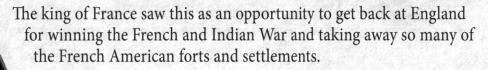
John Paul Jones

The king of France saw this as an opportunity to get back at England for winning the French and Indian War and taking away so many of the French American forts and settlements.

It wasn't long before there were French reinforcements sent to General George Washington. Among the new faces were several officers from other countries besides France. It seemed that this revolution was catching the attention of the world. Finally, spring came and with it better health. The days were filled with training, and the men's spirits lifted. By early summer, the group at Valley Forge looked like different men. Clothes and shoes had been gathered from all over the colonies to replace the ragged uniforms the men had been wearing. The new training gave the men a new-found confidence. All over the colonies, hope was rising, and the fight for freedom continued on.

Now I would like to tell you the story of another brave hero of the Revolution. This man did not fight his battles on the rolling hills or in the forest of America. His battleground was the sea. Even though America did not have a navy, John Paul Jones used whatever ships he could find to fight the British in the Atlantic Ocean. Many of the ships were pitiful indeed! It would take great courage to face the highly trained, world-renowned, English navy with its huge man-o-war fighting ships fitted with heavy guns and cannons. Courage was one thing these men had!

The American Navy, if that is what you could call it, was made up mostly of sailing men who used their own ships to attack the British ships bringing ammunitions and food to their army fighting in America. These men were called privateers. However, they did not just capture the English shipping vessels; they captured many fighting ships also.

Commodore John Paul Jones was known for his bravery and knowledge of the sea and ships. It was well known that John Paul Jones would not back down from a fight easily. He was Scottish by birth and had the typical Scottish temperament, but had come to America when he was young, and considered it to be his homeland.

One could fill up an entire book with stories of John Paul Jones' adventures, for there are many! Since I cannot do that, I will tell you my favorite story of his courage and determination. I have often heard it said that courage is not the lack of fear, but the overcoming of it. If you never face fear, you never need courage. Our stout-hearted lads of the sea certainly had their courage tested, for time and time again they were faced with odds that were very much against them. This particular story about John Paul Jones certainly shows us that he faced fear with great courage.

Commodore Jones was on the flagship of his fleet. The ship was a rotten tub of a ship that had most certainly seen its better days! John Paul had named this ship the *Bonhomme Richard* or the *Poor Richard*, after Benjamin Franklin's *Poor Richard's Almanac*. The fleet sailed back and forth looking for an English warship to fight, but only found

The Bonhomme Richard

unarmed merchant ships. They soon lost interest in waylaying and capturing the goods intended for the British army stationed in America.

Finally, a large fleet of merchant ships was spotted, and John Paul Jones gave the orders to get closer. As they approached, the American saw that the fleet of vessels was being guarded by two frigates. The larger of the two had more than 40 guns on it. Of course, this is the one that John Paul went for! Can you just see it? The sight of the junky, old, rotten ship chasing the strong, well-fortified British warship must have brought laughter to the captain of the English ship.

The English warship, the *Serapis*, was soon shooting holes all up and down the sides of the *Bonhomme Richard*. The old ship was leaking like a sieve, but John Paul was not giving up. When the captain of the English warship called out, "Have you surrendered?" John Paul gave this response, "I have not yet begun to fight!" Why would a leaking ship make John Paul surrender? He would rather go to the bottom of the sea with his ship.

Jones commanded that his ship be brought so close to the enemy ship that the English gunners could not open the gun ports. He also ordered that his ship be lashed to the English ship! The *Bonhomme Richard* was on fire, and water was pouring into her sides. One of the officers on board the ship thought for sure they were on their way down, so he freed the English prisoners they had captured earlier. Of course, the prisoners saw that they were fighting one of their own ships, and did everything possible to help the English warship.

One of John Paul Jones' men who was fighting on the rigging threw a hand grenade into an open hatch of the English warship. The explosion cleared the deck of the English ship, and only the English captain was left standing there. Jones took control of the English frigate, and transferred his crew onto it. The *Bonhomme Richard* sank to the bottom of the sea with its flag still waving.

There were many heroes and amazing battles in the American Revolution. In our next chapter, we are going to hear the sad tale of a hero turned traitor, discover what kind of life an American soldier had, and meet some very interesting women who bravely served our country. I hope you have enjoyed today's story of heroism. Our America is well on its way to becoming an independent country.

FLEET: largest group of naval vessels under one commander, organized for specific purposes.

Battle between the Bonhomme Richard and the Serapis

NARRATION BREAK

Retell your favorite part of the story.

AN HISTORIC HARBOR: BOSTON

The natural harbor at Boston has led to the city being a center of trade since the colonial period, and it remains a popular port today. It also served as the site for the Boston Tea Party, though that was not the only resistance to the Tea Act.

The Philadelphia Tea Party took place after the townspeople had met and presented a list of resolutions in opposition to the Act. They met in what we now call Independence Hall. Their resolutions were adopted by the people of Boston a few weeks later, which would be followed by the Boston Tea Party in December 1773.

Just days later, a British ship, the *Polly*, tried to make it to Philadelphia to unload its cargo of tea. Stopped in the town of Chester, the townspeople made clear the consequences to the captain should he attempt to unload his cargo. He chose to take on supplies and leave without unloading his cargo.

Boston Harbor

(CC BY-SA 3.0)

A chart of the harbor of Boston

▲ Though the war continued for a couple of more years, Cornwallis' surrender at Yorktown, Virginia, in 1781 ended the war on land in America.

Charleston, South Carolina, was attacked twice before the British seized it — residents painted the steeple of this church black to make it harder for the British to see it and target it. ▶

▲ The Battle of Moore's Creek in February 1776 was an early Patriot victory that featured colonists fighting and defeating Scottish Loyalists wielding broadswords.

▲ British Colonel Banastre Tarleton was noted for his ruthlessness, which caused many Southerners to side with the Patriots.

Dunmore's Proclamation (1775) promised freedom for any slave who fought for the British. Thousands of African Americans served on both sides during the war. ▶

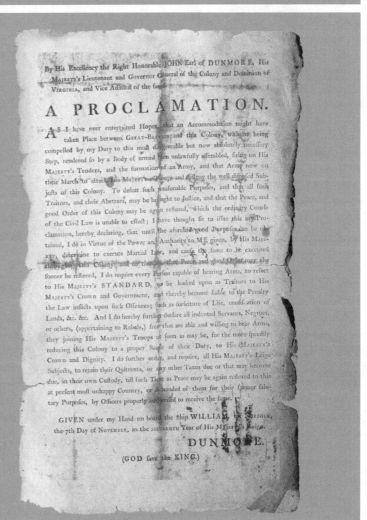

By His Excellency the Right Honorable JOHN Earl of DUNMORE, His Majesty's Lieutenant and Governor General of the Colony and Dominion of VIRGINIA, and Vice Admiral of the same.

A PROCLAMATION.

AS I have ever entertained Hopes, that an Accommodation might have taken Place between GREAT-BRITAIN and this Colony, without being compelled by my Duty to this most disagreeable but now absolutely necessary Step, rendered so by a Body of armed Men unlawfully assembled, firing on His Majesty's Tenders, and the formation of an Army, and that Army now on their March to attack His Majesty's Troops and destroy the well disposed Subjects of this Colony. To defeat such treasonable Purposes, and that all such Traitors, and their Abettors, may be brought to Justice, and that the Peace, and good Order of this Colony may be again restored, which the ordinary Course of the Civil Law is unable to effect; I have thought fit to issue this my Proclamation, hereby declaring, that until the aforesaid good Purposes can be obtained, I do in Virtue of the Power and Authority to ME given, by His Majesty, determine to execute Martial Law, and cause the same to be executed throughout this Colony; and for that so that Peace, and good Order may the sooner be restored, I do require every Person capable of bearing Arms, to resort to His Majesty's STANDARD, or be looked upon as Traitors to His Majesty's Crown and Government, and thereby become liable to the Penalty the Law inflicts upon such Offences; such as forfeiture of Life, confiscation of Lands, &c. &c. And I do hereby further declare all indented Servants, Negroes, or others, (appertaining to Rebels,) free that are able and willing to bear Arms, they joining His Majesty's Troops as soon as may be, for the more speedily reducing this Colony to a proper Sense of their Duty, to His Majesty's Crown and Dignity. I do further order, and require, all His Majesty's Liege Subjects, to retain their Quitrents, or any other Taxes due or that may become due, in their own Custody, till such Time as Peace may be again restored to this at present most unhappy Country, or demanded of them for their former salutary Purposes, by Officers properly authorised to receive the same.

GIVEN under my Hand on board the Ship WILLIAM, off NORFOLK, the 7th Day of NOVEMBER, in the SIXTEENTH Year of His Majesty's Reign.

DUNMORE.

(GOD save the KING.)

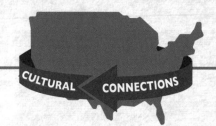

It is interesting to note that although the United States of America, which was originally 13 English colonies, eventually won the War for Independence, the two nations have maintained a mostly friendly relationship with each other since the mid-1800s. In fact, since the 1940s, the two nations have shared a "special relationship" — a bond forged as allies against the tyrants who tried to take over the world during World War 2, which you will learn more about in a later volume. England and America share the bond of a common heritage, language, and, in many ways, a common culture.

Lancaster bombers from the
Battle of Britain, World War II

Royal Air Force Aerobatic Team
the Red Arrows, 2011

THOUGHTS TO REMEMBER

1. All kinds of men fought in the Revolutionary War. From grandpas to young boys, the male population of the colonies were considered soldiers.

2. Women and children took care of farms and plantations while men and boys were away fighting. Women were part of spy rings that helped give information to the Continental Army. They also sewed uniforms, provided food for the army, sheltered groups of traveling soldiers, and were nurses for the wounded. Some women and girls even cut their hair, dressed like men, and fought in actual battles.

CHAPTER 15

MORE STORIES OF THE REVOLUTION

Starting Point: During the Revolution, whole families and communities stood for and lost much for the cause of freedom. Spies, prisoners, injustice, and even having enough food and supplies for the small Continental army was a challenge!

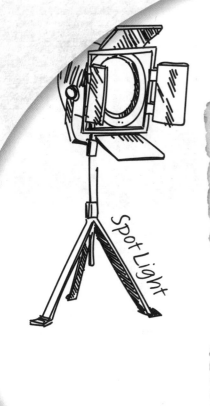

Spot Light

The Culper Spy Ring: The Culper Spy Ring was the colonial spy network that operated during the War for Independence. The spy ring gathered information and kept Washington and his men informed about what was happening in the British camps.

A page from the code book of the Culper Spy Ring

READY TO EXPLORE?

1. Who acted as spies for General George Washington?

2. What role did spies play in the great War for Independence?

Spies! What do you think of when you hear that word? Not all spies are bad; in fact, the American victory over the British was largely due to the spies that worked during the Revolution. The American army depended heavily on their spy network to let them know where and when the British were moving their troops.

At the time of the American Revolution, there were no cell phones or email, but the communication system had to be able to quickly communicate important messages to the right people at the right time! This was accomplished by the spy rings that General Washington had all over New York and Philadelphia.

Benedict Arnold

There were many men and women who worked as spies. These people were usually in positions to hear news, such as an innkeeper or a store clerk, and they used many ways to communicate that there was something important for the general to know. Anna Strong, one of General Washington's main spies, used her laundry line as her form of communication. Different-colored clothing items hung on certain lines held different meanings.

Some spies wrote in invisible ink or in coded messages that no one else could understand as an army code. Spying was a dangerous job; some of the American spies were found out by the British and killed. We will never know the names of all of the colonists who acted as spies.

The British had their spies, also. As we learned before, not all of the colonists felt that they should be a separate country from England. Some of them were afraid that the British would win the war and then make the colonists' lives miserable as punishment for the rebellion. There were many British spies, but none so well known as Benedict Arnold. Perhaps you have heard the expression, "he/she is a Benedict Arnold." This means a person surprised everyone by turning against something or someone in a traitorous way.

I want to tell you the story of the real Benedict Arnold. In our earlier chapter, we read about the battles of Ticonderoga and Saratoga. Both of these important battles ended in American victories, for which General Benedict Arnold was largely responsible.

Benedict was not happy for several reasons, though. First, he was passed over for a promotion, even though he was wounded in battle. Second, he did not get the recognition he felt was due him for his heroism. I don't know if this lack of recognition was real, but it truly bothered Benedict Arnold.

He became very angry with the colonies' new friendship with France. He was so angry, in fact, that he decided to change sides. He asked George Washington for the position of commander of the West Point Fort, fully intending to deliver it over to the British. One of America's finest had turned traitor and was now a spy for the British! Thankfully, his plotting was to no avail, for his plan was uncovered in time.

I would like to pause in our story here and consider the difference between the life of a Continental (American) soldier and the life of a British soldier. You might not realize that there was a very big difference, indeed! A British soldier was well trained and schooled in the ways of war. When a British soldier was sent to war, he was provided with a warm woolen uniform, a pair of warm leather boots, a rifle with a bayonet, and plenty of food provisions. Even though the life of a British soldier was not easy, for they, too, were away from loved ones and surrounded by fighting and death much of the time, the British army had sturdy tents, warm winter clothes, and plenty more when all of those wore out.

In contrast to this, there was no American army before George Washington became the first Commander in Chief. Each colony had its own militia, which was only a group of ordinary men who would stand together to protect their colony. Washington decided there was no way the colonial militia that existed before the war would be able to defend and beat the well-trained British army. It was a well-known fact that the British army was the best in the world!

General Washington took the groups of men and made them into one military — the Continental Army. The colonists did not have the money to supply everyone in their army with quality uniforms and guns. If a soldier was lucky enough to get a uniform, or at least part of one, the name of the colonial woman who had hand-sewn it would be embroidered on the inside of the jacket. As for weapons, men who joined the army were expected to bring their own.

Many of the "men" were really boys. Some of them were not even teenagers yet. There were many boys who were probably no older than you! Can you imagine being a soldier? Many of these children were drummer boys or flag carriers, but many of them actually did the fighting, also.

A British officer

NARRATION BREAK

Retell what you have learned so far.

This war for freedom, which we call the American Revolution, was truly a family matter. Fathers and sons were fighting, and sometimes even grandfathers, while many of the daughters, mothers, and grandmothers sewed and cooked for the army if it was anywhere near their home.

Fighting, sewing uniforms, sharing food, and spying…all of these jobs could have been done by the people in one family! There are many documented cases of women and girls who cut their hair, disguised themselves as men, and fought alongside the men in battle. I think these brave colonists knew they were fighting for something that was as precious as life itself — freedom!

It is easy to think that life here in America has always been the way it is now, but when we are learning about history, it is important to not think about what happened then in the light of what life is like right now. What does this mean?

As you are reading this story, are you in a warm room? Do you have on enough clothes to keep you comfortable? Did you eat breakfast this morning, and if it is afternoon, did you have lunch? Will you take a warm bath or a shower tonight or sometime soon? If you live someplace cold, do you own a pair of boots that will keep your feet warm and dry when you walk outside? If you live in a warm location, do you have fans or even air conditioning? Do you have a comfortable bed to sleep in at night?

The American Revolutionary soldiers did not have all of this. They were cold and hungry most of the time in the winter. In the summer, they still fought, sleeping on the ground at night. Can you just hear the mosquitoes whining in their ears? Food was not plentiful, either! They had to have hunting parties to get meat, and it was dangerous to go hunting when there were British soldiers everywhere.

Now add to this picture, you are a young person who hasn't seen your parents in a very long time. You are not sure where your father is because he was put in a different battalion and has been fighting in different locations than you. Your mother and younger siblings were left at home, and you certainly hope they have more food than you have had to keep you going.

You are not sure who you can trust because you are never quite sure who is on what side. Every day you see British soldiers, and some of them look just as young and scared as you are. It was because of these brave young Americans that the 13 separate colonies, spread out along the East Coast, became a united and free country.

Yes, this American Revolution was a family matter, and there were women who fought alongside the men or made uniforms for the army. There were also women and children who followed the army from battlefield to battlefield for protection. During the war, many homes were utterly destroyed, and there were many families torn apart by death on the battlefield.

General Washington understood the value of these scattered groups of families. He allowed these women and children to follow the army in return for their help in cooking and caring for the army. Many of these women acted as nurses for the wounded men on the battlefields and brought food and water to the men between battles.

Knitting Stockings for the Soldiers

There are many tales of heroic women during the Revolution. I would like very much to tell you the story of two of them. The first account is of a young lady named Sybil Ludington. Sybil was the 16-year-old daughter of a commander in the militia. She volunteered to ride and warn the countryside that the British were marching on Danbury, Connecticut. Through her brave actions, the militia gathered and was prepared to fight by the time the British had assembled their troops. Sybil became known as the "girl Paul Revere," who rode 40 miles in the rain to warn of a British attack. What a brave girl!

Molly Pitcher at the Battle of Monmouth

HEROIC: having the characteristics of a hero or heroine; very brave.

Have you heard the story of Mary Ludwig Hayes, better known as Molly Pitcher? Why in the world would someone named Mary Ludwig Hayes be nicknamed Molly Pitcher? First, Molly was a common nickname for women named Mary during the Revolution era. Mary received her nickname, "Molly Pitcher," by bringing water to the men on the battlefield where her husband, William, was fighting.

When William Hayes fell on the battlefield, Mary (Molly) saw that he had been killed and took his place at the cannon. She bravely finished the battle, stationed at that cannon. Even though a British cannon ball went right between her legs, blowing away half of her petticoat and skirt, she was unhurt and received great honor for her heroic act.

How do you like our story of heroism, spies, and traitors? History is so full of interesting tales of every kind, isn't it? I would like to finish our story today with another story of a woman during the Revolution. This woman did not fight on a battlefield or ride with a warning of the impending British attack; she sewed instead.

Betsy Ross was a seamstress whose story, much like those of Christopher Columbus and Leif Ericson, has become somewhat of a legend through the years. Even though Betsy may not have sewn the very first flag for our

The Birth of Old Glory

country, the story is worth hearing. Betsy was a young widow at the time. Her husband of only two years had been killed in an explosion. It is said that General Washington went to Betsy and asked her to sew a flag from a design that he brought her. Betsy is credited for changing the original six-pointed star to a five-pointed star.

Can you imagine sewing the first American flag? Many people do not believe that Betsy Ross actually sewed the very first flag, but many others do. At any rate, she did make many of the early flags and was paid well by the American government to do so. Have you ever seen a Betsy Ross flag? There are 13 stripes of red and white, and in the upper left corner, there is a dark blue panel with a circle of 13 stars. What do you suppose the 13 stripes and stars stand for? If you guessed the 13 colonies, you would be right. The circle of stars signifies the equal strength of the colonies, large and small. Someday you may be able to go visit the Betsy Ross House, where it still stands in Philadelphia.

We have come to the end of our story of the American Revolution. There are many, many other stories that were not in our story, stories of heroism and traitors. Maybe you will learn more about them as you get older; I hope you do, for stories of how our country gained its freedom from England are among my favorites of all times.

In our next chapters, we are going to learn how the 13 colonies became one nation, with one government and one president. You will recognize the name and face of this very important man because he is a familiar friend in our story of history.

13-star flag sewn by Betsy Ross

NARRATION BREAK

Retell your favorite part of our story today.

REDRAWING THE MAP – THE LOSS OF TERRITORY

Remember when French settlers were removed from their lands when France lost the war with Britain?

The victory over the French in the French-Indian War led to French concessions of lands to the British. This included an enlarged area of the British Province of Quebec to the north and west.

The Proclamation of 1763 also ceded a large portion of land to the Native American tribes in a landmark agreement, which included access to the Great Lakes region. Another benefit of the agreement for Native Americans was the temporary ban on new non-Native American settlements in the area, marked as the Proclamation Line.

Further south, the British also gained the lands of West and East Florida in the proclamation. It was to these British-owned areas that many still loyal to Britain fled after the Revolutionary War rather than remain in the newly formed United States.

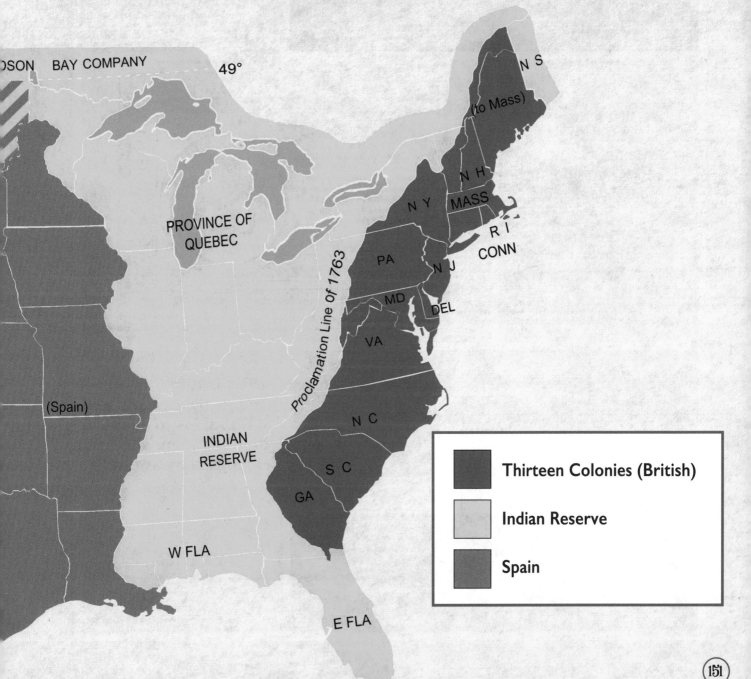

◀ Captured Americans were considered traitors, not enemy soldiers, until 1782, so they were not treated according to established rules for military prisoners.

Prisoners (or their governments) were expected to pay for or supply their own food and lodgings, which was difficult for the newly formed American government. ▶

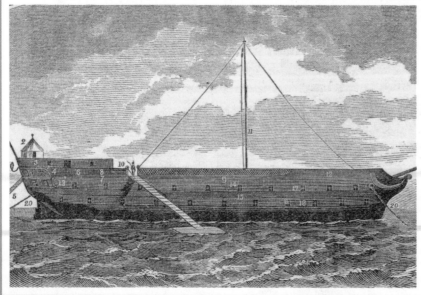

◀ The British frequently used prison ships to house captured men. The HMS *Jersey* was the most infamous.

At Trenton, George Washington captured a thousand German mercenaries (Hessians) as prisoners. He ordered his men to "treat them with humanity." ▶

Prisoner exchanges were an accepted practice at this time. British General John Burgoyne was exchanged for over one thousand men. ▶

◀ Ethan Allen was captured and spent time in both American and English prisons, as well as on a prison ship, before being released in an exchange.

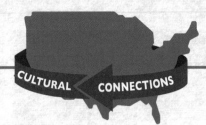

In our chapter about the Revolutionary War, we learned that there are documented cases where girls and women cut their hair, dressed like men, and bravely fought right alongside their brothers in arms. Why did they have to do that? Now, in modern America, women can join any branch of the armed services if they want to help protect our country, but back in the time period that we are studying, women did not have the same rights as men. In fact, in certain colonies, women could not own land, vote, earn certain college degrees, or enter into a legal agreement. Interestingly, single women had more rights than married women. Unmarried women could work in any occupation that did not require a college degree that was restricted to the male population, whereas the occupation of married women was extremely restricted. You will learn later about how women have gained the rights of equality.

Molly Pitcher Brigade was formed a year before the U.S. entered World War II, 1940.

Young female US soldier

THOUGHTS TO REMEMBER

1. We are still discovering how intricate and widespread Washington's spy rings truly were! His "spies" could be anyone from an old man or woman to a young housewife hanging certain colored clothing on a certain clothesline on a certain day! Anyone could be a spy!

2. These spies played a huge role in the War for Independence! Without them, our young country would not have won the war. So crucial were their roles, that Washington kept their identity completely secret and coded.

CHAPTER 16

13 COLONIES BECOME ONE NATION

Starting Point: Fighting for freedom drew the colonies together. They united under the Articles of Confederation, but that wasn't working. These principled men knew things had to change, but how did they cement their hard-won rights into a governing document?

Spot Light

The Constitution of the United States of America: The Constitution of our great country is a precious piece of our country's history. Many men and women have died to protect it and the country it was written to govern.

READY TO EXPLORE?

1. How many men were part of writing the Constitution?

2. How is our government different than any other country's government?

The American Revolution had finally come to an end, and our new country was now independent from England. In many ways, the fight to become a real country had just started, for the colonies had not yet learned how to govern themselves.

The colonies were now states, struggling to become part of a whole new country. Under the Articles of Confederation, the states were allied together but still very independent from each other. Therefore, each state had its own money, and one state's money could not be used in the other states. For example, if you lived in New Jersey, you could not use your 'New Jersey money' in Massachusetts.

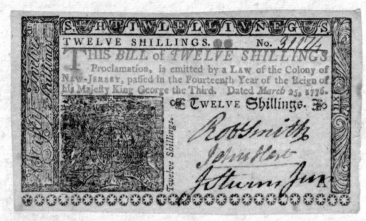

Currency from the Province of New Jersey — front side

The new country was poor and could not even afford to pay the soldiers who had fought for so long for freedom. No one was sure who had the power to do what, and no one knew who had the right to make "national money." England had always made the rules and enforced them; now nobody knew who was boss! Confusion was the general atmosphere throughout our new country. Within a few years after the Revolution was over, the country was in shambles.

People started rebelling, and things were not going well. Even though each state had its own leadership, they were not cooperating with the new central, or federal, government that had been put into place. There was a lot of arguing going on because this government did not have much power to accomplish anything.

Finally, in the spring of 1787, a convention was called. The leading patriots who had helped guide the colonies through the Revolution were called together to try to find a solution to the growing problems.

George Washington, who had been in retirement for several years, came back to help set up the country. I can imagine he really needed that rest! Delegates from the new states came together to discuss the future of their new country. The men gathered for the

Currency from the Province of New Jersey — back side

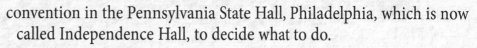
John Hancock

convention in the Pennsylvania State Hall, Philadelphia, which is now called Independence Hall, to decide what to do.

George Washington was chosen to be president of this convention, which became known as the Constitutional Convention. At this gathering, it was decided that a set of laws that applied to all Americans should be written. Many familiar faces were in that meeting hall: John Hancock, Benjamin Franklin, and George Washington were there, along with James Madison and Alexander Hamilton. The group of men gathered there were of varying ages and backgrounds. The youngest of them was 27 years old, while the oldest, Benjamin Franklin, was 81!

So, you may be asking, "What did these men decide, and what does the Constitution say? What are the principles upon which it is based? What would be so different about it than the governments of other nations?"

The biggest difference was this new government would be "by the people, for the people." In other words, the people would have a voice in their governmental decisions. To do this, there had to be some kind of voting system put into place. Up until now, each state had its own government, but there had to be a central government to take care of matters that concerned everyone, country-wide. Do you think these men had any idea that what they were doing was extremely important to the whole world?

Carriage ride by Independence Hall

I think that the best way to really get an idea of what this convention was like is to go there ourselves. Are you ready to be time travelers again? I hope you brought your umbrella and rain boots because the streets of Philadelphia are extremely muddy due to all the rain they've been receiving. The spring of 1787 was the wettest spring they have had in a very long time.

Let's quietly slip in the back door of Independence Hall. We will need to be very quiet and careful not to disturb the men working here. It is stuffy and uncomfortably warm here, and the light coming in the tall windows flanking the room is dim due to the rainy sky.

The men look tired and grumpy; some of them look downright worried. Remember, we are learning the history of our country from the viewpoint of the present. We know that we have a wonderful country, different than any other

Benjamin Franklin was 81 when he signed.

country in the world, but these men do not know that this new "baby" country of theirs is going to be a great and powerful nation one day. All they know is what they have been through for the last 20 years to become free. What if they cannot pull the country together? Will they be able to stand up to a bigger, stronger country if need be? This is a very serious task, indeed.

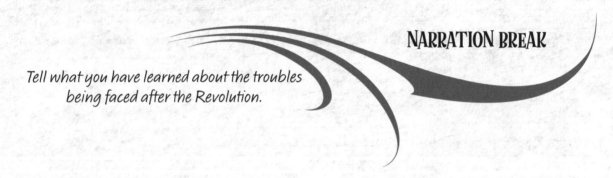

NARRATION BREAK

Tell what you have learned about the troubles being faced after the Revolution.

As we find a table in the corner, we look around for a familiar face — maybe one that was at the meeting when Patrick Henry made his rousing speech. We smile at each other when we see the tall form of George Washington sitting at the front of the room. He looks quite a bit older than the last time we saw him, but he has the same kind eyes and strong features.

As we watch, a small, well-dressed man steps forward. James Madison, a young man from Virginia, begins to speak. This is the man who will become known as the "Father of our Constitution." He explains that he has been studying government for over a year and has come up with some ideas that he believes will help the states be more equal and unified.

Instead of each state having one vote, James Madison explains, the more-populated states have more votes. That way, the actual voices of the people are being heard. The right to make federal laws, declare war, and print money would belong to the federal government, which would be made up of elected representatives from each state. This plan, presented by Mr. Madison, became known as the Virginia Plan.

We can see that there are plenty of men here who do not agree with James Madison's plan. The representatives from the smaller states of New Jersey and Delaware are downright angry! They believe that the larger, more-populated states are going to be able to "squish" the smaller states. The debate is on!

Back and forth the argument goes. We are beginning to think that nothing is going to be accomplished today. Finally, a compromise is reached. Instead of having one house of government representatives based on the population of the state, there will be two houses of Congress. The House of Representatives will be based on population, and its members will be elected every two years. In the Senate, every state is equal, each one having two votes.

James Madison

You and I look at each other, for we know that we are both thinking the same thing. "What about the slaves? Don't they count as part of the population?" As if reading our minds, the representatives from the southern states ask this very question.

Another debate ensues. The southern representatives are convinced they should be able to count the slaves as population while the northern representatives disagree. The northern representatives say the slaves do not hold any other rights as citizens — why should they be counted? Finally, it is agreed upon that every five slaves will count as three white people. We shake our heads; how sad this makes us! We stand up to leave the Hall. We know from history that slavery is a problem that is going to cause a lot of trouble for our country. We also know that history is sometimes made in a

Scene at the Signing of the Constitution of the United States

day and other times started in a day. Today we have witnessed both; the writing of our constitution is a history showstopper. The compromising on the horrible issue of slavery is something that will have to be worked on.

As we slip out into the cool rain, the air feels fresh and welcoming. Once outside, we turn to look through the tall windows of Independence Hall. The men inside are gathering around the table at the front of the room. As George Washington leans forward, we see carved on the back of his chair a sun on the horizon. Is it a sunset or a sunrise? It is most certainly a sunrise, for what we have just witnessed is the beginning of a new day for our new country.

The United States Constitution is a very unique document. Never before in history has a country been founded on such principles. Following is the preamble, or beginning part, of the constitution:

> *We the People of the United States, in Order to form a more perfect Union, establish Justice, insure domestic Tranquility, provide for the common defence, promote the general Welfare, and secure the Blessings of Liberty to ourselves and our Posterity, do ordain and establish this Constitution for the United States of America.*

The words "slave" or "slavery" do not appear in the Constitution because there were plenty of people by this time who did not like slavery. Unfortunately, they did not know how to address the issue, and so the uncomfortable topic of slavery remained in the corner.

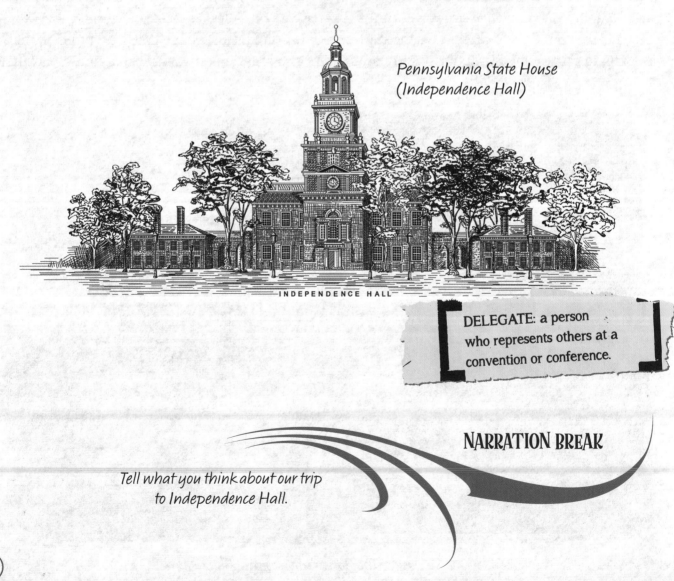

Pennsylvania State House
(Independence Hall)

— INDEPENDENCE HALL —

DELEGATE: a person who represents others at a convention or conference.

NARRATION BREAK

Tell what you think about our trip to Independence Hall.

OLD PHILADELPHIA

Philadelphia hosts a number of interesting and unique sites from the earliest history of America. From the Liberty Bell to Independence Hall, you can see and explore history all around you. Having served as the capital of the Pennsylvania Colony, it also hosted the gatherings for the Declaration of Independence and the Constitution.

Betsy Ross House in Philadelphia

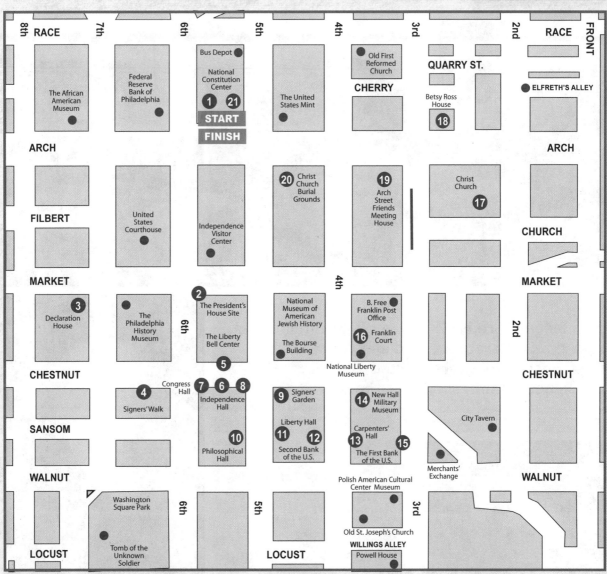

1. **National Constitution Center**
2. **The President's House Site**
3. **Declaration House**
4. **Signers' Walk**
5. **The Liberty Bell**
6. **Independence Hall**
7. **Congress Hall**
8. **Old City Hall**
9. **Signers' Garden**
10. **Philosophical Hall**
11. **Liberty Hall**
12. **Second Bank of the U.S.**
13. **Carpenters' Hall**
14. **New Hall Military Museum**
15. **The First Bank of the U.S.**
16. **Franklin Court & B. Free Franklin Post Office**
17. **Christ Church**
18. **Betsy Ross House**
19. **Arch Street Friends Meeting House**
20. **Christ Church Burial Ground**
21. **National Constitution Center**

▲ Independence Hall's Assembly Room in which both the Declaration of Independence and Constitution were drafted and signed by the founding fathers.

◄ John Langdon had to pay his and another delegate's own way because his state didn't support sending representatives. He served on the committee that developed the slavery compromise.

▲ Elbridge Gerry refused to sign the Constitution because he didn't like the final version; he wanted a Bill of Rights.

◄ Gunning Bedford Jr. was suspicious of the delegates from larger states and infamously told them, "I do not, gentlemen, trust you."

Roger Sherman wrote the compromise between large and small states that allowed the convention to go forward. ▶

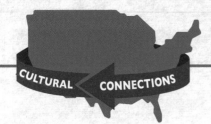

Have you ever studied the printing on a one, five, ten, twenty, fifty, or one hundred dollar bill? Money is a big part of everyday life in America. You can hardly go anywhere or do anything without paying something for it! Even if your mom drove you to the park, a few miles down the road, it cost something — the cost of gasoline to fuel your family's vehicle! But what is money, anyway? You may really enjoy exploring how money is made!

Coin press built for the
San Francisco Mint, 1873

The US Treasury Department in Washington D.C.

THOUGHTS TO REMEMBER

1. Fifty-five men were at most of the meetings concerning the Constitution (although there were never more than 46 men together at one time), and 39 signed the Constitution.

2. Our government is unique because it is a representative government. It is FOR the people, BY the people.

CHAPTER 17

FIRST IN THE HEARTS OF HIS COUNTRYMEN

Spot Light

Starting Point: When it came time to choose the first president for the nation, George Washington was a natural choice because of his courage and integrity. He could have been a king, but chose instead to be a servant of the people!

Mount Vernon is situated on the banks of the Potomac River.

Mount Vernon: Mount Vernon is George Washington's home. He inherited the plantation when his older brother, Laurence's widow, Ann, died in 1761. Approximately one million people tour Mount Vernon each year.

READY TO EXPLORE?

1. Who was the first president to live in the White House?

2. What caused George Washington's death?

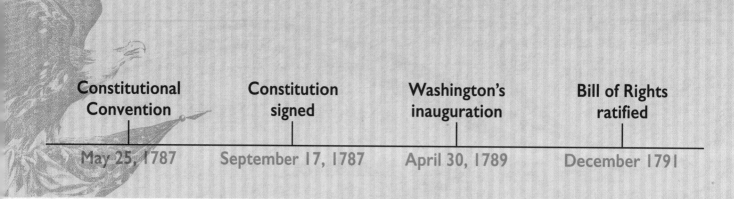

Constitutional Convention	Constitution signed	Washington's inauguration	Bill of Rights ratified
May 25, 1787	September 17, 1787	April 30, 1789	December 1791

After our exciting visit to Independence Hall in *Philadelphia*, we are all probably wondering, "What will happen next?" The Constitution, the cornerstone of our new government, was written and agreed upon, but the country still did not have a leader. Who would it be?

People from all over the country argued about many issues concerning how the nation should be set up, but what everyone seemed to agree on was who our first elected president should be. George Washington was everyone's favorite; he had proven himself to be trustworthy and courageous.

During the Revolution, he had taken the untrained farmers and tradesmen who had made up the militia and patiently turned them into a united army worthy of recognition. Everyone knew him as a fair and honest man who loved his family and his country. Through the hard winter of Valley Forge, he had prayed for his men. Everyone respected him as a leader and because his words were full of wisdom.

We have gotten to know George Washington well, for we have followed him from the backwoods of Virginia through the Revolution. We watched him reside over the Constitutional Convention, and we saw the respect everyone present had for him.

Today, we are going to see him in a different role. Many of you already know that George Washington was our first elected president, but did you know that he was not the first official president? After the Revolution but before the Constitution was written, there was a stretch of time when somebody needed to be at least mostly the boss. The man who got that job was named John Hanson. Mr. Hanson was in office for only three years. Our country's government is set up in a way that says only the person who wins the people's votes can be president. This is called being elected. John Hanson might have been chosen for the job by the Continental Congress, but he had not been elected by the people of the country.

INAUGURATION: a ceremony celebrating the beginning of a leader's term of office.

Inauguration of George Washington

When it came time to have an elected leader, George Washington was chosen. People everywhere hailed him as a hero. I think they would have made him king if he would have let them! But George Washington did not want to be king; he wanted to remain a servant of the people.

On his ride to New York to be sworn into office, people lined the roads and streets to celebrate and cheer. "Long live George Washington, our President!" rang through the streets. George Washington was sworn into the office of president in 1789. The following year, Congress and President Washington moved to *Philadelphia*. The city of *Washington, D.C.,* was not yet built, so the government center was based in *Philadelphia* for ten years.

President Washington

Since no one had ever been the real president of the United States of America before, no one really knew what the job involved. There was an outline of sorts if you used the Constitution to know what you could or couldn't do, but the particulars were left up to the individual to do his best. This is exactly what George Washington was known for — doing his best in everything he did. President Washington was not the kind of man who felt that he needed to do everything by himself, therefore taking the glory for all accomplishments. Instead, he surrounded himself with men he trusted, and he listened to their advice. One such man was Alexander Hamilton, a young man whom George Washington had made an officer during the Revolution. Now President Washington made him the first Secretary of the Treasury. Alexander Hamilton was wise when it came to money, and he had a plan to help the new nation get off to a better start financially. By taxing certain liquors and all imported goods, Hamilton was able to pay debt and regain credit for the nation.

The Washington Family

George Washington served two terms in office. There were many people who wanted him to remain in office, but he refused; he wanted to go home to Mount Vernon. Throughout his eight years as president, George did many good things to get our country off to a good start. He signed treaties with the Indians to keep peace, and he kept our new country out of a war that had started in Europe. When farmers in Pennsylvania tried to start a revolt against the whiskey tax, he called in the army to keep things under control.

After he served as president, George enjoyed his retirement at home. He had served his country well and deserved some rest! He spent his time riding around his large estate, sometimes going 15 miles north to watch the building of the new city, Washington, D.C., which was to be the new capital city. George Washington died in 1799, at the age of 67 years old. He is still revered as a great leader. George Washington is sometimes called the "Father of Our Country" and "First in war, first in peace, and first in the hearts of his countrymen."

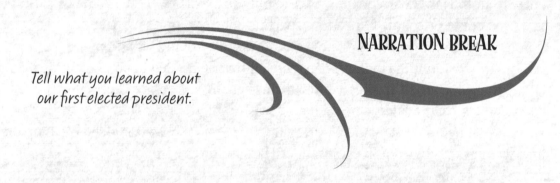

NARRATION BREAK

Tell what you learned about our first elected president.

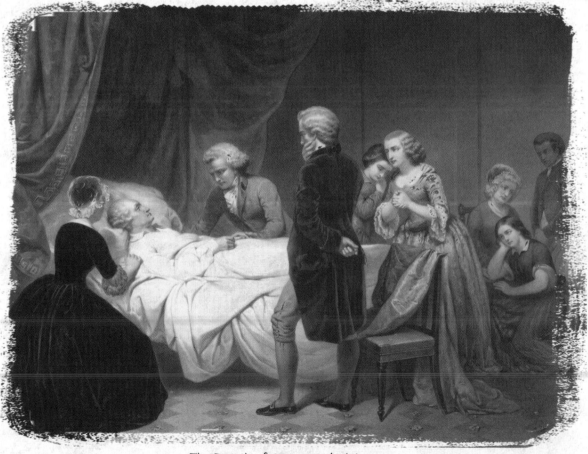

The Death of George Washington.

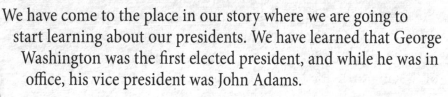
John Adams

We have come to the place in our story where we are going to start learning about our presidents. We have learned that George Washington was the first elected president, and while he was in office, his vice president was John Adams.

John Adams is recognized as one of the leading founding fathers of our country. Born in 1735, he went to Harvard College at the age of 16 and became a well-known lawyer. Before he was vice president, John Adams was a delegate from his home colony, Massachusetts. He became more well-known throughout the colonies for his outspoken opposition to the taxes on tea and stamps, which led to the Boston Tea Party.

Mr. Adams was present at the Continental Congress Convention when Patrick Henry declared dramatically, "Give me liberty or give me death!" John Adams also helped appoint George Washington as Commander in Chief of the army during the Revolution.

When Mr. Adams became the second elected president of the United States of America in 1797, he was filling some pretty big shoes; George Washington had been an immensely popular leader! There were also other issues that faced John Adams. The war that was raging between England and France (who else!) was affecting the waterways for the American ships.

Something needed to be done, and it was up to the president of the United States to do it. The poor American merchants were losing many of their shipments to pirates and French privateers. President Adams authorized the building up of the American Navy. Soon the American ships were sailing in peace because the pirates and privateers were just a little afraid to bother them now!

Harvard College

John Adams was the first president to live in the new White House in Washington, D.C., the new capital city. These are the words he penned to his beloved wife, Abigail, "I pray Heaven to bestow the best of Blessings on this House and all that shall hereafter inhabit it. May none but honest and wise Men ever rule under this roof." John Adams was president for only four years from 1797–1801. After his time in office, he retired to his home in Massachusetts.

Abigail Adams

Mr. Adams was good friends with our next president, Thomas Jefferson. He wrote many letters to Jefferson from his retirement, encouraging and advising him. Our country was still very young, and it had many issues to settle. Slavery was one of them, and settling the wilderness west of the states was another. In our coming chapters, we will revisit our friend, Thomas Jefferson, who became our third president.

Our story's path has wound through the years, from the Bering Land Bridge to the Presidential Suite in the White House. We have met many important people and experienced many heroic acts. I hope you know where your hiking boots are — in our next chapter, we are going to meet a very interesting man who is going to take us on an expedition like we've never been on before!

White House, Washington, D.C.

NARRATION BREAK

Tell what you learned about our second president.

A WORKING FARM

When George Washington inherited Mount Vernon, it was and remained a working farm on lands owned by the family since 1674 and called first Epsewasson and then Little Hunting Creek Plantation. Washington had made efforts to improve the home and add to the surrounding lands.

Washington as farmer at Mount Vernon

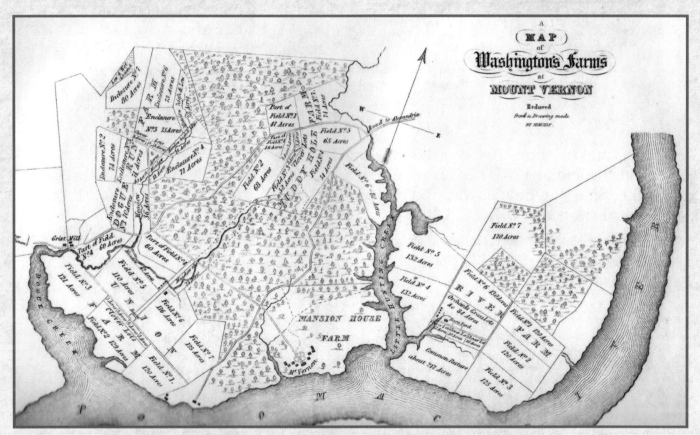

A Map of George Washington's Farms at Mt. Vernon, reduced from a drawing made by himself.

While tobacco at the plantation meant slaves were needed, by 1766 Washington was experimenting with other crops, grinding grain, fishing, and other needed services. Though he owned the slaves that were inherited with the plantation, Washington is said to have refused to break up families and hired skilled indentured people to teach the slaves skills that they could use.

Washington made provisions for the slaves in his will — at least those he could legally free — upon the death of his wife Martha. Not all the slaves of Mount Vernon would see freedom because some were inherited by Martha from the estate of her first husband — and were legally bound to remain attached to that other estate.

◀ Massachusetts Governor James Bowdoin enforced tax collection and raised taxes in the mid-1780s to help pay for the debt incurred from the American Revolution.

◀ The people of western Massachusetts could not afford the tax increases, and the dissatisfied people organized around former Revolutionary war commanders Daniel Shays and Job Shattuck.

Shays and his men tried to seize the armory in Springfield in 1787, but his rebellion failed. Shays' Rebellion was one reason the Constitution was written. ▼

In 1798, the government raised taxes on land and slaves to fund a war with France. John Fries organized tax protests among German Pennsylvanians. ▶

As the first Secretary of the Treasury, Alexander Hamilton instituted a tax on whiskey in 1791 to pay for the country's debt from the Revolutionary War. ▶

◀ Many rural Pennsylvanians believed this tax was similar to British taxes on the colonies, and they revolted. President Washington called on the army to suppress the rebellion.

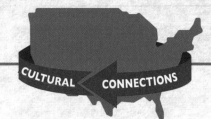
We learned in our chapter that George Washington was elected as our first true president. How does someone become the president? As I am writing this, we are less than two months away from the presidential election of 2016. As you are reading this, that election has happened, and the United States has chosen a new leader. Our government was set up to be "for the people, by the people." Our free election process is truly the bedrock of our American culture.

Voting machines are coming into use in some states, 1908.

Modern-day voting booths

THOUGHTS TO REMEMBER

1. John Adams was the first president to live in the White House, although it wasn't finished when he moved in.

2. Technically, George Washington bled to death. Bleeding was a technique used to try to remove infection from a person's body. In Washington's case, they removed too much blood for him to survive.

CHAPTER 18

LOOKING WEST

Starting Point: The spirit of exploration and adventure didn't stop at the boundaries of the original colonies. Fearless men and women braved the frontiers, building communities and expanding the footprint of the nation!

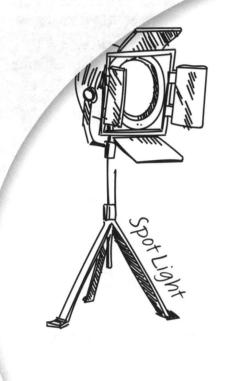
Spot Light

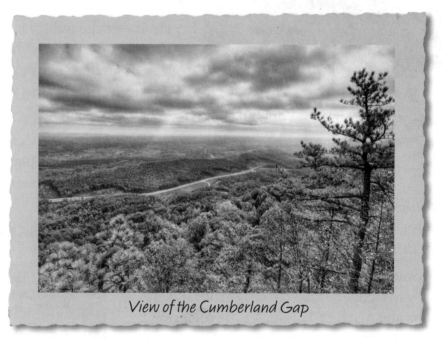
View of the Cumberland Gap

Daniel Boone: Daniel Boone is one of America's most famous explorers. He discovered the Cumberland Gap, a passageway through the Appalachian Mountains.

READY TO EXPLORE?

1. What was Daniel Boone's job during the French and Indian War?

2. What kinds of weapons were available in Daniel Boone's time?

Are you ready for a grand adventure? We are about to embark on one of the best in American history. We are going to go roaming into the wilderness where there are Indians and wild animals, but don't be afraid; we are going to have an adventure guide who knows these trails and forests well.

I would like very much to introduce you to Daniel Boone. He knows the forest like the back of his hand, and he knows how to deal with wild animals and Indians. Daniel grew up in the woods on the western border of the colony of *Pennsylvania*. He was number 6 of . . . you guessed it . . . a large number of children — 11 to be exact!

Daniel was born in 1734, before the 13 colonies became a country. His parents, Squire and Sarah Boone, were Quakers. Daniel grew up playing with the friendly Indians who lived in the forest around his family's home. As we learned earlier, William Penn had made peace treaties with the Indians, which were kept for many years by the people living in *Pennsylvania*.

We are going to take the a few minutes right now to study the map back in chapter 7. Let's look at it together. Do you see the colony of *Pennsylvania*? Did you notice that the western border of the colony is wilderness? That is where young Daniel played with his young Indian pals. I can almost hear the laughter and yelling of the children as they climbed the trees.

Do you like to play in the woods? I remember as a child, I loved to play "capture the flag" with my brother. We lived on a farm, which had a strip of forest spreading out about a quarter of a mile wide behind it. On the other side of the forest ran a good-sized river. We used to play for hours in those woods! What a fun time we had. I used to imagine that I was a

Daniel Boone

grand adventurer who knew everything about the woods and the river. Of course I really didn't, but it was great fun to pretend.

Let's look at our map again and find the vast wilderness covering huge amounts of land west of the 13 British colonies. Remember, those are still colonies on your map, for we have gone back in time to learn about Daniel's childhood. Can you see the area called *Kentucky*? This is the land that Daniel would be the most interested in as a grownup. Now, find the colony of *North Carolina*. This is where Daniel's family moved when he was 15 or 16 years old.

Boone in early manhood

Daniel liked living in *North Carolina* very much, for there were fewer people living there than in crowded *Pennsylvania*, and there was more wilderness in which to hunt. This made Daniel very happy, and he spent the next three years hunting and exploring the forest and wilderness near their home. He even went on longer adventures deep into the woods. Daniel was becoming more and more at home in the forest, and he was also learning that not all of the Indians were as friendly as when he was a child.

In 1755, 19-year-old Daniel enlisted in the North Carolina militia to fight in the French and Indian War. He was quite an asset to the army because he was very knowledgeable about the forest and the Indians. Daniel was given the job of driving supplies to the groups of militia men stationed in the forest. He knew all the secret paths and was able to get through the forest even though there were French soldiers everywhere.

Soon after Daniel returned home after his time in the French and Indian War, he met the girl who would become his wife. Rebecca Ryan was a tall girl with dark hair and calm eyes. Daniel liked her calmness and her sense of humor. He had courted Rebecca for a year when he decided that he wanted to see if she really was the one he wanted to spend his life with.

One day, as they were sitting together under a tree, Daniel reached over and cut a hole in her clean, white apron with his big knife! Why do you think he did this? He wanted to see if she would get upset; he did not want to marry a girl who would upset easily. If she got upset about a hole in her apron, she would probably get upset about things like Indians and wild animals. Rebecca did not get angry, and when she just said mildly, "Now what did you do that for, Daniel?", he knew that she would make the perfect wife for him.

NARRATION BREAK

Tell what you have learned about Daniel Boone so far.

Daniel and Rebecca were married soon after. I am sure that Rebecca knew him well enough to know that he was not going to settle down and farm, and he didn't. He still loved to explore and roam about looking for adventure.

Even though Daniel and Rebecca had ten children, he still kept exploring. He traveled way down south to *Florida*, and he even bought some land there. Rebecca was not willing to leave their home in *North Carolina*, so they never lived in *Florida*.

In 1767, Daniel went on an exploring expedition with several other men to explore *Kentucky*. Not many people had explored that far west of *Virginia* because the king of England had told the colonists not to go that far. Daniel had a mind of his own, though, and while he was on the expedition, he decided to explore some of the Native American trails.

It was by following one of these trails that Daniel found the *Cumberland Gap*. The Gap lies between what are now the states of *Virginia, Kentucky*, and *Tennessee*. This amazing geographic formation makes a natural path, which the Indians and the wild animals used to travel through the Appalachian Mountains.

On the other side of the *Cumberland Gap*, Daniel found the most beautiful country he had ever seen! The wild animals were so abundant he could hunt something different every night for dinner. Daniel wanted to bring his family here, for he knew that the rich land would make wonderful farmland.

He and the other men were on the expedition seven months. Can you just imagine the fun Daniel had? He loved exploring so much that I'm sure he would have stayed there, roaming about and hunting, if he had not had a family to care for. Finally, Daniel and the other men decided to return to civilization; they were just finishing up with their fun when . . . Daniel and one of his friends were captured by Indians! The Native Americans did not hurt Daniel or his friend, and within a week, Daniel had figured out a way to escape. They stole some of the Indians' horses and escaped into the night, but were recaptured two days later. Finally, the two men managed to get away without getting caught.

ESCORT: accompanying another for protection, security, or as a mark of rank.

Daniel Boone escorting settlers through the Cumberland Gap

When Daniel Boone and his friends returned from this beautiful new land, everyone was talking about his adventures. The news of the rich farmland and bountiful wildlife in *Kentucky* grabbed the attention of many. Eventually, Daniel went back to *Kentucky*. He wanted to make it easier for settlers to get to *Kentucky*, so he helped plan a "road" though the wilderness.

This road, which was called the Wilderness Road, was really nothing more than wagon tracks through the trees and thick vegetation. After the road was completed, a settlement, named Boonesborough after Daniel Boone, was started in the *Kentucky* wilderness. Daniel moved his family there in 1775.

When you have finished reading this chapter, ask your teacher to help you find a picture of the *Cumberland Gap* in an encyclopedia or online. The Appalachian Mountains run a long way down the East Coast. They are very beautiful, but they are also very high and rugged.

People in Daniel Boone's day did not have airplanes to fly over the mountains or four-wheel-drive vehicles to drive through them. There were no roads, and there were no highways. There was nothing but trees, miles and miles and miles of trees, and in those trees lived many wild animals — bears and mountain lions, wolves, and many other kinds of creatures. There are rivers and streams cutting through the mountains, and there are cliffs from which you can fall if you are not very cautious! If you were going to travel through the wilderness, you needed to have an accomplished and knowledgeable guide. Daniel Boone was just such a guide, and he made many difficult journeys through the mountains, escorting settlers to the settlements in *Kentucky*.

Daniel Boone had a life full of excitement. He was captured by Indians several times; one of those times, he was captured by the Shawnee Indians. He was so brave that the Indians adopted him as one of their own. Daniel learned that the Shawnee were planning on capturing Boonesborough; he escaped and managed to get home in time to defend the settlers from the unfriendly Indians.

There are many adventure stories about Daniel Boone, but there is one in particular that I want to tell you. Shortly after moving to Boonesborough, Daniel's daughter Jemima and two of her friends, Betsy and Fanny Callaway, were kidnapped by Shawnee Indian braves. Of course, Daniel and the Callaway girls' father went after them!

The girls tried their hardest to slow the braves down by acting like they could not ride the horses well. They continually "fell" off of their horses and left bits and pieces of their clothing along the way, which made a clear path for their fathers to follow. Three days later, the men caught up with the kidnappers. Daniel was able to kill one of the braves from a distance and make a distraction, so the other men could go in to rescue the girls.

Capture of the Boone and Callaway Girls

While they were getting away, one of the Shawnee braves sent a tomahawk sailing after the girls, and Betsy Callaway bent down and picked it up. If you would like to see that tomahawk, you can. It has been passed down through Betsy's family ever since and is now on display at the Nathan Boone Home in St. Charles County, Missouri. I am quite sure if one of us had been captured by Shawnee Indians and then rescued by Daniel Boone, we would have kept that tomahawk as a souvenir, too.

Daniel Boone lived to be an old man and died in 1820, at the age of almost 86. He has been remembered throughout history as an amazing man — one who loved adventure and was alive with the American spirit. He was a husband, father, explorer, colonizer, and soldier in both the French and Indian War and the American Revolution.

I hope you have enjoyed our story of Daniel Boone. We have learned a lot about our great country, and we are about to learn a lot more! The many puzzle pieces are beginning to create a bigger picture, aren't they? In our next chapter, we are going to see our country double in size!

NARRATION BREAK

Tell your favorite part of our story. How did Daniel Boone help our country grow?

KENTUCKY AND THE STORY OF JOHN FILSON

This map of Kentucky is by landholder, surveyor, schoolteacher, author, and historian John Filson. It notes, "This map of Kentucke, drawn from actual Observations is inscribed with the most perfect respect, to the Honorable the Congress of the United States of America, and to His Excellency George Washington late Commander in Chief of their army, by their Humble Servant, John Filson." The small key at the top shows stations/forts, salt springs/licks, towns, dwelling-houses/mills, wigwams. The dotted lines represent roads, some cleared; others not. It was published in combination with Filson's book, *The Discovery, Settlement and Present State of Kentucke.*

Having served in the War for Independence, Filson helped bring the exciting adventures of Daniel Boone to readers in the book, as well as telling of the natural beauty and opportunities found in the lands of Kentucky. He vanished in 1788 on a surveying trip after an attack by the Shawnee, and is also known as one of the founders of Cincinnati.

John Filson

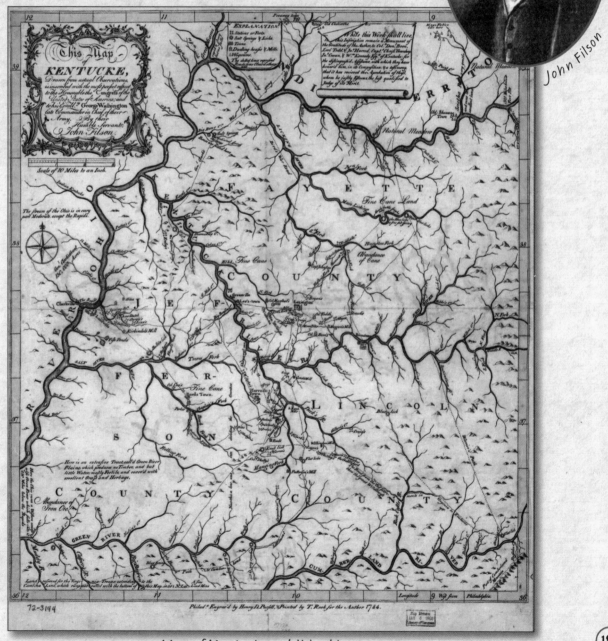

Map of Kentucke published in 1784

181

▲ Increased settlement in Kentucky caused tension with the local Indians. Daniel Boone's teen-aged son James was killed by Indians when the family tried to move there in 1773.

One of Daniel Boone's North Carolina neighbors was Christopher Gist. He explored Kentucky in the 1750s and twice saved George Washington's life while working as a scout. ▶

▲ Southeast Kentucky near the Cumberland Gap. View where three states meet: Virginia, Tennessee, and Kentucky

Simon Kenton was a noted frontiersman who served as a Boonesborough scout and once saved Daniel Boone's life. He later helped explore and settle Ohio. ▶

The Shawnee were a prominent Indian tribe in Kentucky in the 1700s. In the early 1800s, Shawnee leader Tecumseh formed an Indian Confederacy to resist further settlement. ▼

Dr. Thomas Walker crossed the Cumberland Gap nearly twenty years before Daniel Boone. He also built the first cabin in Kentucky in 1750. (Replica depicted) ▼

REPLICA OF
FIRST HOUSE
IN KENTUCKY

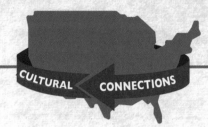
In our chapter, we learned about how Daniel Boone helped cut paths through the wilderness for pioneers to use in their travels to the West. In our modern times, the road systems of our country are quite amazing! Ask your parent or teacher if you can look at a current atlas of our road systems. It is this national road system that allows us to have our neighborhood stores stocked with all types of products, from toys to food. Large shipments of agricultural goods, boxed goods, and canned items are shipped to fill the sections of our local grocery stores. Huge tankers full of refined fuel travel from coast to coast, filling large underground storage gas tanks that pump through the gas stations' pumps into your family's vehicle.

Many settlers headed westward and help to expand American territory.

You might say that our road systems support our everyday life!

THOUGHTS TO REMEMBER

1. Daniel Boone was a member of the North Carolina Militia during the French and Indian War. His job was driving supplies to the groups of soldiers stationed deep in the forest. He was good at his job!

2. The weapons available at Boone's time included muskets, knives, swords, and the Indian tomahawk.

CHAPTER 19

THE LOUISIANA PURCHASE, WHAT A DEAL!

Starting Point: Did you know that wars were not the only way that a nation could grow? It was a good business deal with France that landed America a huge chunk of land in the middle of the country!

Spot Light

City of St. Louis skyline

The Gateway Arch: The Gateway Arch marks the beginning of Lewis and Clark's Expedition. The Museum of Westward Expansion is commemorative of what they discovered on their journey through the vast wilderness of the west.

READY TO EXPLORE?

1. What do you know about Thomas Jefferson's war with some pirates?

2. What kinds of wild beasts were thought to have lived in the great unknown west?

Our country was growing! With the settlement of Boonesborough in *Kentucky*, and the "roads" leading through the wilderness, the West seemed to be opening up for settlement. The United States of America was like a gangly teenager that seemed to be outgrowing its borders.

The year was 1800, and our third president had just been sworn into office. Thomas Jefferson, our friend who wrote the Declaration of Independence, was now president. He lived in the not-yet-finished White House in the not-yet-finished city of *Washington, D.C.* There was nothing glamorous about *Washington, D.C.* yet! The streets were dirt, and when it rained, they got very muddy.

By this time, our country had doubled its size from when it was the British colonies. Settlers had pressed westward into

Portrait of Thomas Jefferson

the land that the 1783 treaties with England and France had opened up. I don't want you to think that this land was tame, though, for it was far from that! It was still vastly unsettled and teeming with wild animals. Also, many Native Americans lived there. There was often trouble between the Indians and settlers, for the Indians knew the ever-widening borders of the states were taking more and more of their hunting grounds.

America was also becoming involved with international issues; Jefferson made the decision to fight in the Barbary Wars because American merchant ships were being attacked by pirates and American sailors were being held for ransom. However, the majority of the nation's focus was on the growth of its national territory from the original colonies.

Look at the map at the end of this chapter. You can see the area of land west of that. They are now states. Now look at the area of land west of that, starting down at the *Gulf of Mexico* and stretching all the way up to the *Great Lakes.* This is the land that the United States received from England through the Treaty of 1783. Now look further west. Do you see the big strip of land starting down in *New Orleans* and stretching all the way up to the border of Canada? This area was still owned by France and was called the Louisiana Territory. It's a very large area, isn't it?

President Jefferson decided to see if the United States could buy some of this land from France. At this time in France, the ruler was named Napoleon Bonaparte; he was also a general and sometimes not a very nice man. He was on a mission to conquer as much of the world as he possibly could. At first, he turned down President Jefferson's offer to buy some of the Louisiana Territory. He had plans for that land, which included building forts and fortifying them with his army. This doesn't sound like a good thing for our young country, does it? Fortunately, things did not go as Napoleon Bonaparte had planned, and his conquests were cut short in Europe.

By 1803, Napoleon desperately needed money to maintain his army in France, so he sold the Louisiana Territory to the United States of America. Do you think that much land would cost a lot of money? I suppose that the sum of $15 million does sound like quite a lot, but when you consider that the land included in that purchase was eventually "cut up" into more than ten states, it really does not sound like much!

After Thomas Jefferson bought the Louisiana Territory, he realized that Americans did not know much about this part of our continent. He set about

Hoisting of American Colors over Louisiana

finding someone willing to explore the new territory. Mr. Jefferson did not have any idea what laid out in this vast, unknown land. Perhaps there were woolly mammoths and other strange beasts!

The third signing of the Louisiana Treaty

Let's pretend we are explorers of the Louisiana Territory. Have you ever been on an exploration expedition? We will need a map, hiking gear (we are going to be traveling through some pretty rough terrain), a canoe, and some kind of weapon to hunt food and to protect ourselves from the wild animals (not to mention hostile Natives). If we are packed and ready, let's begin.*

We will also use the map in this chapter and a map of the United States of America as it looks now. We need to do some exploring ourselves before we read the story of the men President Jefferson found to explore the Louisiana Territory. If you have your scavenger hunt list ready, its almost time. Check off each location and item on your list as we come to it.

Napoleon Crossing the Alps

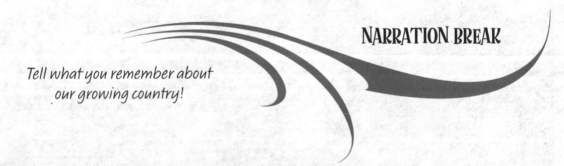

NARRATION BREAK

Tell what you remember about our growing country!

We are going to start our journey down in the French settlement of *New Orleans*. (Do you remember the story of Acadia in Chapter 10? Many of the people who were forced to leave their homes there were moved to *New Orleans*.) This town is right on the *Gulf of Mexico*. Do you see it on your map of the Louisiana Territory and on the modern map? We are going to be traveling north, up the *Mississippi River*, which is the next item on our list. The Mississippi River runs all the way from *Minnesota* down to *New Orleans*.

As we travel up this vast river, we see beautiful vegetation all along its banks. Huge oak trees, with moss growing from their branches, remind us of tall, stately ladies in long, flowing evening dresses. The native flowers are breathtaking; their fragrance fills the air. Delicate, yellow deer pea flowers grow in clumps along the water's edge, and the lovely pink and white marshmallow flowers seem to nod their heads at us from their long, graceful stems.

We check our maps to see how far we have come. We will be stopping soon, and tomorrow, we will continue up to the settlement of *St. Louis*. There, we will be turning west onto the *Missouri River*. We had better get our rest; we are going to be heading into some pretty wild territory!

As we head out, we notice that the morning air is significantly cooler here than it was in *New Orleans*. We are quite a bit farther north today than when we left on our journey yesterday. The land through which we will travel today is quite beautiful. We will need to keep our eyes open for Native Americans, though. I understand that there are quite a few tribes that inhabit this part of the continent. We must remember that in the year 1803, there were no highways, bridges, airplanes, or cars. We are going to have to either take our canoe up the rough waters of the rivers or we are going to have to hike, carrying our gear and canoes with us.

This part of our trip is through the area that is now the states that make up the center part of our country. Let's look at our modern map and find the states of *Missouri, Nebraska, Kansas, Colorado, Iowa, Wyoming, Montana,* and *Washington*. These are not all the states the Louisiana Territory covered, but these are the ones we will look at today.

There are many types of terrain in this territory. We have seen mighty rivers, bug-infested swamps (down near *New Orleans*), seemingly non-ending rolling hills, vast forests, and gorgeous vegetation. We are amazed at the beauty of this country!

As we travel up the *Missouri River*, the land gets flatter, and there are fewer trees. We are entering the *Great Plains*, which now makes up the states of *South Dakota* and *North Dakota*. If we keep our eyes open (for we are getting very tired!), there is an excellent chance that we will see at least one herd of buffalo. This area is known for them.

Our journey has been quiet so far, and we have not encountered any unfriendly Natives. This is good, because we have never had to deal with hostile Indians before. The plains stretch out as far as we can see, and the bluffs coming down to the *Missouri River* are the only thing resembling a hill. Our guide tells us that soon we will be coming into *Montana*, which has plenty of mountains. When we do get to the mountains, we are going to have to leave our canoes behind. These are the *Rocky Mountains,* and they are just as their name suggests — rocky!

We have traveled hundreds of miles in our explorations, and we still have many left to cover before we reach our destination, the Pacific Ocean. For now, we are going to stop and rest for

the night. I certainly hope there is something good for supper tonight; I'm starved! I suppose pizza would be out of the question?

CANYON: a deep valley with very steep sides

After a good night's sleep, we are on our way again. We are going to be moving up into the *Rocky Mountains* today. As we climb, our guide tells us about how the *Missouri River* has its headwaters in these mountains. The Missouri is one of the longest rivers in North America at over 2,300 miles long.

As we look down from a high ledge, we see gorgeous waterfalls. This truly is beautiful country. Aren't you glad that you came along on this exploration trip? The animals, birds, vegetation, and yes, even the insects are amazing! We are stopping early tonight, for everyone is tired from the climb. I am glad because I want to add to my journal all of the beautiful things we have seen today.

Tomorrow, we are going to be heading down the other side of the mountains and finishing our last leg of the journey. The *Pacific Ocean,* the biggest ocean in the world, is on the west side of where we

Expedition on the Columbia River

are tonight. We will be catching a ride on the *Columbia River* toward the Pacific tomorrow. I've heard that this river can be quite rough, with rapids shooting through canyons in the mountains. We are in for an exciting trip — sleep well!

NARRATION BREAK

Let's look back and review what we have learned today about the part of our country that was included in the Louisiana Purchase.

JEFFERSON'S CHOICE: WAR OR NEGOTIATION?

It was 1802, and President Thomas Jefferson had a big problem. Spain was ceding lands to France, and included was the city of New Orleans, the port of which was critical to American economic interests and shipping, which France had closed.

Jefferson sent a letter to the U.S. Minister to France Robert Livingston stating "every eye in the US. is now fixed on this affair of Louisiana. Perhaps nothing since the revolutionary war has produced more uneasy sensations through the body of the nation."*

After initial moves that could have led to war, France makes known that they are willing to sell Louisiana to the Americans. Negotiations begin and at the end the deal a price was reached. It would be $15 million for 827,000 square miles of land, and as you can see on the map, land that would become many of the Midwestern states we know today.

The city of New Orleans, and the Mississippi River

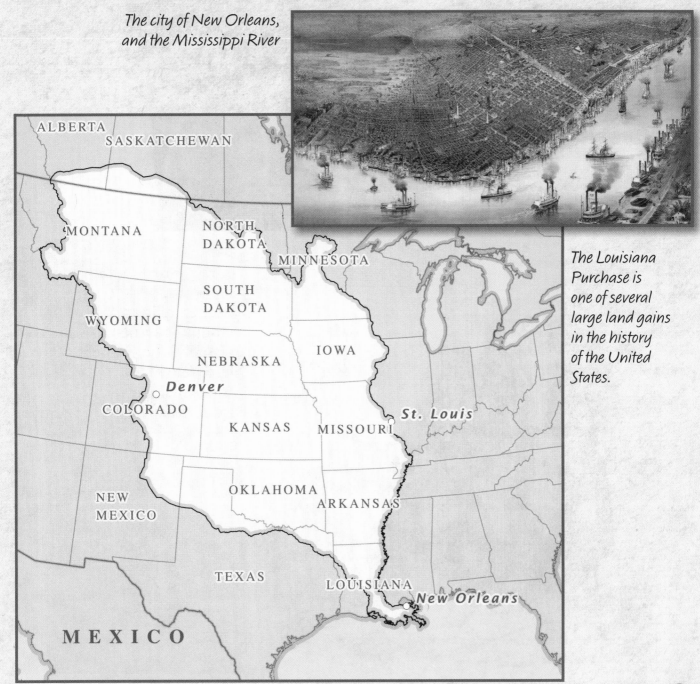

The Louisiana Purchase is one of several large land gains in the history of the United States.

* The writings of Thomas Jefferson. v.10. Jefferson, Thomas, 1743-1826. page 311, http://hdl.handle.net/2027/uva.x000275544

In 1608, Samuel de Champlain founded the city of Quebec on the lands Cartier had claimed several decades earlier, opening up New France for settlement. ▶

◀ The Huron tribe were important French allies and trading partners. Usually, the French had peaceful relationships with local Indians.

French explorers Jacques Marquette and Louis Joliet floated down the Mississippi River and explored the surrounding areas in the 1670s (Re-enactment depicted). ▶

▲ In 1534, Jacques Cartier claimed France's first land in modern-day Canada.

The descendants of New French settlers still live in Canada today. French Is the official language of the province of Québec. ▶

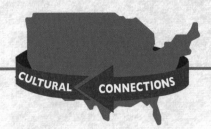

CULTURAL CONNECTIONS

The Mississippi River, which has its headwaters in my home state, Minnesota, and runs the entire width of our country, is one of our most impressive natural resources. The "Mighty Mississip" has played a crucial role in almost every aspect of our country's growth, and over the last century, many state and national parks have been established to preserve its natural beauty. Millions of families enjoy visits to wildlife refuges and protected nature areas for indigenous plants that are open to the public. Maybe you have one of these parks near enough to visit!

Steamers on the Mississippi River

Mississippi River at New Orleans

THOUGHTS TO REMEMBER

1. Thomas Jefferson had two wars with a group of North African states (known as the Barbary States). These states (ruled by Muslim kings and warlords) were attacking American merchant ships, demanding ransom for their safe return. Jefferson refused, and instead gathered the newly formed American Navy and cleaned house!

2. No one was sure what lived in the unexplored west! They thought there might even be woolly mammoths out there.

CHAPTER 20

THE ADVENTURES OF LEWIS AND CLARK

Starting Point: Imagine being brave explorers who are gathering supplies to travel across the country – documenting scientific discoveries and meeting new Native American tribes as you map the vast, unknown wilderness.

Spot Light

1803 Lewis and Clark map

Lewis and Clark: The great explorers, Lewis and Clark, made detailed drawings and wrote concise descriptions of the flora and fauna they discovered on their exploration.

READY TO EXPLORE?

1. What does "flora and fauna" mean?

2. What modes of transportation did Lewis and Clark use on their trip to the Pacific Ocean?

Captain Meriwether Lewis

Now that we have had a grand exploration of our own, we are going to hear the story of the men President Jefferson found to explore the Louisiana Territory in 1804. This territory was vast, stretching for thousands of uncharted and unmapped miles. Nobody was even sure how much land there was! As we learned on our own expedition, it was beautiful but rough country.

In 1804, there had only been two other explorers who had ever crossed the great continent of North America; one was a man named Cabeza de Vaca in 1536, and the other was a Canadian trapper who had explored in the late 1700s. This wasn't good enough for Thomas Jefferson, though; he wanted details! President Jefferson needed someone to study the botany (plant life) and geology (types of land forms) of the territory. He also needed to know what Indian tribes lived there and if they were friendly or hostile. The land was wild; it been inhabited only by French Canadians and British hunters and trappers for many years. Who knew if these groups were going to be friendly or not?

The explorers who traversed the Louisiana Territory would have to be excellent at keeping journals because Thomas Jefferson wanted detailed drawings and specimens of as many wild creatures and plants as possible. They would also have to be brave, handy with a gun, and diplomatic, for they were sure to run into Indians, who were not always very welcoming.

President Jefferson had just the person for the job — his good friend, Meriwether Lewis, a captain in the United States Army. President Jefferson had known Captain Lewis for a long time, and he knew Lewis was a man whom he could trust.

Captain Meriwether Lewis chose as his aide his friend, Second Lieutenant William Clark. Lewis called his

Second Lieutenant William Clark

friend Captain Clark and treated him as an equal partner on the expedition. Preparing for such a long voyage took some doing! What should they take? They would be gone for far too long to actually take enough provisions to last the entire expedition. They would have to hunt for their meat, which meant they would need to bring weapons and gunpowder. They would be traveling up the *Missouri River* just as we did on our imagined expedition in our last chapter, so they would need sturdy boats of some kind.

Finally, on May 14, 1804, they were ready to start. The men had spent the last few months organizing and planning the trip. The official starting point for the expedition was the mouth of the river Dubois, near present-day *Hartford, Illinois.*

At the end of this chapter is a map of the Lewis and Clark Expedition. Follow along as we follow their route to the Pacific Ocean. This expedition took a lot longer than our recent fanciful journey. They faced real Indians, crossed real mountains, and spent two whole years on the trail!

Sacajawea Guides the Lewis and Clark Expedition

EXPEDITION: a journey taken by a group of people with a particular purpose.

I can only imagine the going was slow, as they made their way up the *Missouri River*. Lewis and Clark kept carefully-detailed journal entries of all the wildlife they encountered. Botanical (plant) samples were taken and carefully preserved to show scientists back home, and pictures of new wildlife species were carefully drawn and described. Pages from these journals are still available to be seen in museums today.

A few months later, one of the men in the expedition party became very ill. On August 20, 1804, Sergeant Charles Floyd became the only man to die on the journey. He was buried in what is now *Sioux City, Iowa.* The sad group continued on up the Missouri. It was late August, and Lewis and Clark knew that they were getting close to the Sioux Indian territory because they were entering the Great Plains.

The men spotted great herds of buffalo, deer, and elk. The river was teeming with beaver. It must have been great fun to watch these strange creatures building their great dams. Have you ever seen a beaver? They are amazing creatures! God has given them exquisite building abilities, unmatched by the most highly trained human architects. The captains' nature journals were filling up fast; this beautiful, wild country was abundant in wildlife.

It was also abundant in Native Americans, and the expedition met up with their first Sioux tribe, the Yankton. These Indians were peaceful enough, though obviously somewhat disappointed with the gifts offered by Captains Lewis and Clark. The Yankton Indians warned the white explorers about another tribe that lived nearby; the Lakota were not as friendly and would not be so easily appeased by the "cheap" gifts.

The expedition party soon found out just how unfriendly this Lakota tribe really was! They were downright grumpy about this party of intruders crossing their land. Fighting very nearly broke out between the groups, but just at the last minute, the Lakota decided to pull back a bit. Lewis, Clark, and their team took this opportunity to get away up the river. Phew, that was a close one!

NARRATION BREAK

Tell about the journey so far.
What is your favorite part?

Winter was starting to breathe down the backs of our explorers, and the leaves had started to fall. The captains decided to spend the winter in the relatively friendly Mandan Indian territory. They built a fort, which they named Fort Mandan. The city of *Washburn, North Dakota*, now stands close to that location. The expedition crew spent the winter in Fort Mandan, while a group of Mandan Indians camped nearby.

During the time spent at Fort Mandan, Lewis and Clark met a French-Canadian trapper by the name of Toussaint Charbonneau (Too-SONT Shar-bon-OH) and his young Shoshone Indian wife, Sacajawea (Sac-u-ju-WEE-u). Lewis and Clark decided to hire Charbonneau and Sacajawea as guides for the remainder of the journey.

We are not sure exactly how old Sacajawea was at this time, but most historians place her between 14 and 17 years old. Can you imagine? That is very young to be married, and she had a little boy also, but that was the custom among the Indian tribes at that time. However young she was, Sacajawea was brave. She was a very important part of the Lewis and Clark Expedition because she acted as an interpreter for the Indians they encountered. It helped the expedition to appear less threatening to have a young Indian woman and her baby with them.

When spring came to Fort Mandan, Lewis and Clark started preparations to start on their way. It was decided that some of the crew would be sent back to the states with a detailed report on what had been discovered so far. Over 100 botanical and zoological specimens (some still living), more than 60 mineral and rock specimens, and the map, which Clark had painstakingly drawn of the territory they had covered so far, were sent along with the returning party.

Lewis and Clark continued to press on up the Missouri River. They were in what is now *Montana*. Do you remember what is in *Montana*? Yes! The *Rocky Mountains* rise out of the edges of the plains, creating a seemingly impenetrable wall keeping them from their goal, the Pacific Ocean. Still, on they pressed.

On horseback, they passed on through the foothills, following the Missouri River, up, up, up! The Rocky Mountains are often called the "backbone of North America" because it is in the crest of these mountains that the Continental Divide runs. It was a long, hard climb that took more than ten days.

The descent on the other side of the mountains proved to be a bit faster but not any easier! They used canoes to descend the mighty Snake River, which was filled with rapids and turbulent white water. So they came, rushing out of the mountains, down toward the ocean. As they approached Mount Hood, they knew they were nearing the ocean.

"Ocean in view! O! The Joy!" were the words William Clark wrote in his journal. The men didn't have much time to celebrate, though, for winter was closing in on them once more. Lewis and Clark

Lewis and Clark on the Columbia River. Behind the explorers is Sacajawea with her baby and husband.

Sacajawea with Lewis & Clark at Three Forks

decided to build a fort on the South side of the Columbia River. They stayed through the winter there at what is now known as Fort Clatsop, and what a miserable winter it was, too! Wet and wild winds crashed against the flimsy walls of the fort, and the group had a hard time keeping dry. They passed their time by boiling ocean water for salt to preserve meat for their return trip home.

Sacajawea and her now-toddler son were still with the group. Everyone had grown to appreciate her knowledge of the wilderness and her ability to converse with the Indians they met along the way. The journey had been long, and it wasn't over yet!

March 23, 1806, almost two years from when they had first set out on their voyage, they started back down the long trail. The trip home was faster. This time they were floating back down the Missouri River. Lewis and Clark separated for a while to enable them to explore different sections of wilderness. On their return trip, the group did run into some hostile Indians, but no one was killed or badly injured.

The expedition ended September 23, 1806, when they reached St. Louis, Missouri, very near to where they first started out. It was a successful and important journey, for it opened up the country to the many thousands of settlers who wanted to press west.

Some of the most amazing benefits that came from the Lewis and Clark Expedition were the nature journals created on the journey. These journals are truly astounding, with numerous, detailed, and quite beautiful entries. The gathering and preserving of natural data showed future settlers of the west what kinds of flora and fauna were in the land that would become a vast section of our country. Did you know that the men sent a live prairie dog back to President Jefferson?

You, too, can be an explorer and nature journalist. It is through discovery and people just like you journaling that some of the most amazing scientific discoveries are made. Let's get out and explore!

NARRATION BREAK

Tell your favorite part of this adventure story.

CONQUERING THE TERRITORIES – THE EXPEDITION OF LEWIS AND CLARK

Milestones of the Expedition

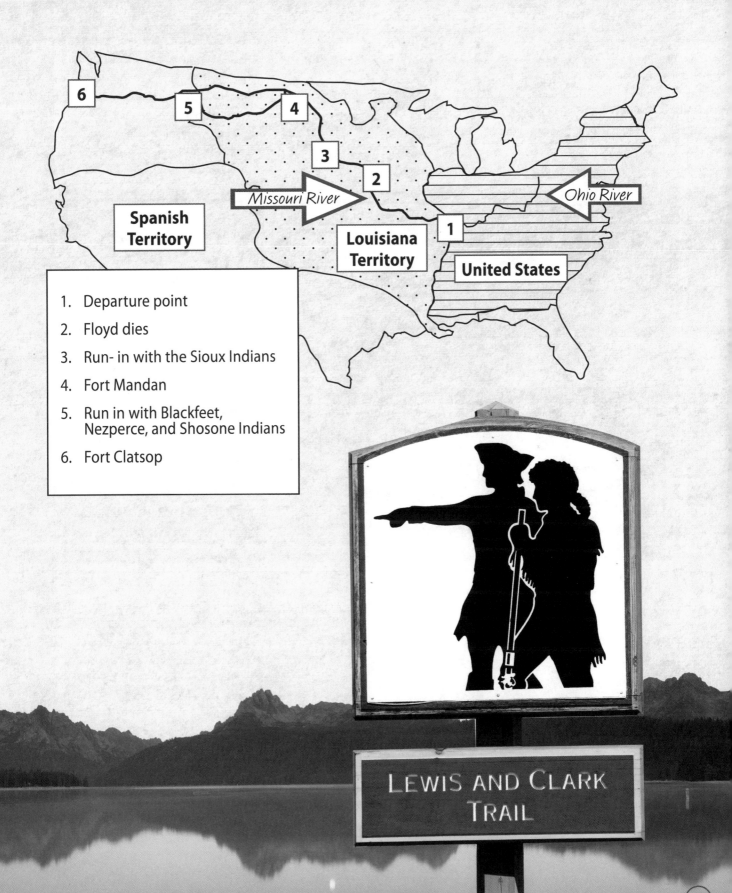

Spanish Territory

Missouri River

Louisiana Territory

Ohio River

United States

1. Departure point
2. Floyd dies
3. Run- in with the Sioux Indians
4. Fort Mandan
5. Run in with Blackfeet, Nezperce, and Shosone Indians
6. Fort Clatsop

LEWIS AND CLARK TRAIL

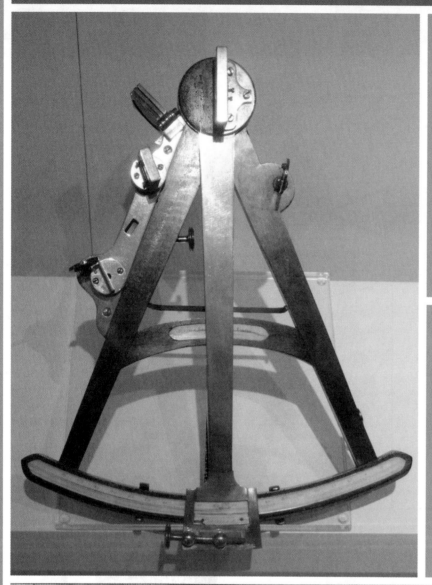

◄ Lewis purchased scientific instruments for their trip, including a quadrant (pictured to the left), compasses, thermometers, a telescope, and a microscope, to aid their navigation and scientific studies.

An important aspect of the trip was mapping the West. Clark was a naturally gifted mapmaker, so he usually drew the maps while Lewis used instruments to determine their position. One of Clark's maps. ▼

◀ Their studies included charting the course of the Missouri River. They also studied its depths and currents.

Beyond making contact with the tribes in the West, Lewis and Clark were also ordered to study their customs and languages. Tribes they encountered included the Blackfeet, Cheyenne, Nez Perce, and Shoshone. ▼

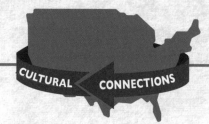
Sacajawea was a knowledgeable guide for the Lewis and Clark expedition. In fact, it is doubtful that they would have survived the journey, let alone actually made it the Pacific Ocean, without her! In our time, people, who are well-informed about the wilderness and want to make a difference in their protection and conservation can become forest rangers. Forest rangers are often the first responders to natural threats, such as forest fires. They also monitor human activities, such as hiking, camping, fishing, and hunting. Forest rangers are considered the peace officers of the forest.

Sacajawea with baby
in a papoose

Forest ranger at Shenandoah National Park in Virginia

THOUGHTS TO REMEMBER

1. Flora and fauna is the plant life (flora) and the animal life (fauna) naturally indigenous to a specific area or region.

2. Lewis and Clark's expedition used keelboats to go up the rivers. While on the expedition, they carved fifteen canoes from logs, and when they came to the Rocky Mountains, they bought horses from the Nez Perce and the Shoshone Indians.

CHAPTER 21

THE STRANGE WAR OF 1812

Spot Light

Starting Point: It's hard to believe just a few decades after defeating the British for their freedom, America would be forced to fight again because of injustices against American sailors and citizens!

Fort McHenry: Fort McHenry is now open for public tours. This star-shaped fort in Baltimore, Maryland, played a critical role in the War of 1812. It was built in 1798 on the site of a former fort called Fort Whetstone. Fort McHenry was named after James McHenry, who was a signer of the United States Constitution.

READY TO EXPLORE?

1. Why were the British and Americans fighting again?
2. Who won the War of 1812?

Around the year 1800, England and France were fighting . . . again. Even though America did not want to become involved, the fighting was causing trouble for the American merchant ships. The British were trying to keep supplies from getting to France, and tried to stop the American merchants trading with Europe. Many Americans depended on the trade with other countries.

Tradesmen who made or grew their goods here in America would sell them to countries overseas. With so many American merchant ships being held up, trade slowed to a grinding halt, and people lost their jobs as ships sat empty in the harbor. The British Navy needed men to fight, so they attacked American merchant ships and forced the crew to work on the British warships. Time after time, American ships were stopped. Time after time, the crews were forced, at gunpoint, onto the English ships.

How could the English get by with this? They said that the men on the American ships were deserters from the British Navy, and therefore traitors. Years went by, and many, many American sailors and ships were captured.

Even though America was a young country and did not have the money it took to fund a war, we were being forced into bankruptcy by these thieving tactics of the British. Finally, America could no longer stay neutral; too many insults and injustices had been endured. But what could we do about it? Didn't the British have the biggest and strongest navy and army in the entire world? We had beaten them once, and we would have to go do it again!

The United States declared war on England in 1812. The first step in America's war strategy was to try to take Canada. That way, they wouldn't have to worry about an army coming from across the sea and down from the north also.

General William Hull was sent to face the English Canadians at Fort Detroit, Michigan. However — General Hull surrendered Detroit without a single shot! This was not a good way to begin a war. Even though the sentence was never carried out, General Hull was sentenced to be shot for treasonous cowardice.

Fortunately, there were some brave men who did some very honorable and heroic acts indeed. The war of 1812 was very different from the American Revolution, for America had grown much larger because of the 1783 "Treaty Land," and the vast Louisiana Territory.

The Canadian English had a naval fleet of six ships on *Lake Erie*. A young American captain, Oliver Perry, was sent to that

Battle of Lake Erie

lake to fight the British there. There was one catch — he was to build his own fleet of ships from the trees growing around the lake!

Captain Oliver Perry and his crew had to be lumberjacks and carpenters before they could be fighting men. They proved to be dandy at both of these occupations, for within several weeks they had built a small fleet of ships and were sailing to meet the British for battle.

Oliver Perry

What do you think the British thought as they saw these rustic, homemade vessels coming at them from seemingly nowhere? I am sure they were surprised! After quite a lengthy fight, the flagship, which Captain Perry was on, was badly damaged with only a handful of men left alive. Captain Perry, who reminds me of Commodore John Paul Jones, leapt into a small boat and, with an American flag waving defiantly in his hand, made his way to another ship in his fleet.

Once aboard the other ship, he sailed straight toward the scattered British fleet, who thought they had won the battle. He fired left and right until they didn't know which way was which! The British surrendered to brave Captain Perry.

This was the beginning of a successful run for the American navy. Time after time, the Americans faced the British and were victorious. As the war raged on, the British had only two victories at sea. In the War of 1812, the British had many more victories on land than they did at sea.

In July of 1814, a large British fleet sailed up *Chesapeake Bay* with close to five thousand men. They marched on *Washington, D.C.*, our young country's capital. The small number of American soldiers stationed there could not hold them off, and the British took over the city. They burned public buildings and even set fire to the White House. Our fourth president, James Madison, and his wife, Dolly, barely escaped in time! I am sure the Americans thought the war was over for sure. Could it be that America would only be free from England for such a short time?

Encouraged by the easy conquest of Washington, the British moved on. *Baltimore, Maryland,* was their next target. They thought now that they had control of the Capital city, they would most certainly not have a problem gaining control of Baltimore!

The White House was set on fire, August 24, 1814.

NARRATION BREAK

Tell what you have learned so far.

The British attack on Fort McHenry, which guarded Baltimore, was relentless. For two days, the British ships hammered away at the fort, but the stubborn Americans would not give in. I am quite sure you have heard the familiar tune of our national anthem. Did you know that this song comes from a poem that was written during this battle?

It was September 14, 1814, and the British warships were shooting continuously at Fort McHenry. On board one of those ships was an American man by the name of Francis Scott Key, a lawyer from Washington. It is unclear why he was on the British ship, but he was unable to leave because of the British bombardment of Fort McHenry.

As Mr. Key spent the long night on board the British ship, he heard the bombs and cannons. He wondered if the British would win, for they had such a mighty fleet leading a strong attack. How long could the Americans hold out against them? All night long, he prayed that his beloved country's flag would still be flying over Fort McHenry in the morning.

Francis Scott Key awakes to see the American flag still waving over Fort McHenry.

BAY: a body of water that is partly surrounded by land (and is usually smaller than a gulf)

What do you think he saw in the wee hours of the morning, when the sun's rays were just bringing the edges of the sky to a pink glow? There it was! The stars and stripes flying bravely against the dark sky showed him the fort had not fallen to the British attack.

Francis Scott Key wept with relief to see the American flag, though tattered and torn, flying victoriously. He put his emotion into a poem. You have heard the words to this poem many times, I am sure, for it was set to music and became our official national anthem in 1931.

Only the first stanza of the poem is used most of the time when we sing our national anthem. Can you hear the bombs, and feel the rocking of the ship as Francis Scott Key wrote the words? Imagine the emotions he felt as he penned these words.

One of the most important lessons to learn from history is the love of our country. How can we appreciate our country unless we learn about the people who built it, and who have fought valiantly to keep it free? My friend, freedom is not free! Don't ever forget this. Wherever there is freedom, someone had to sacrifice immensely to bring that freedom. It is our duty to guard it, and to protect it for coming generations. So many brave men and women have fought and died for our country's freedom.

I would like very much for you to read the whole poem, for it is a beautiful symbol of love for our country. The next time you hear our national anthem being played or sung, remember the story of the brave soldiers who fought and the weeping, young lawyer, who wrote these words for us.

The Star-Spangled Banner

Oh, say can you see by the dawn's early light
What so proudly we hailed at the twilight's last gleaming?
Whose broad stripes and bright stars thru the perilous fight,
O'er the ramparts we watched were so gallantly streaming?
And the rocket's red glare, the bombs bursting in air,
Gave proof through the night that our flag was still there.
Oh, say does that star-spangled banner yet wave
O'er the land of the free and the home of the brave?

On the shore, dimly seen through the mists of the deep,
Where the foe's haughty host in dread silence reposes,
What is that which the breeze, o'er the towering steep,
As it fitfully blows, half conceals, half discloses?
Now it catches the gleam of the morning's first beam,
In full glory reflected now shines in the stream:
'Tis the star-spangled banner! Oh long may it wave
O'er the land of the free and the home of the brave!

Francis Scott Key

And where is that band who so vauntingly swore
That the havoc of war and the battle's confusion,
A home and a country should leave us no more!
Their blood has washed out their foul footsteps' pollution.
No refuge could save the hireling and slave
From the terror of flight, or the gloom of the grave:
And the star-spangled banner in triumph doth wave
O'er the land of the free and the home of the brave!

Oh! thus be it ever, when freemen shall stand
Between their loved home and the war's desolation!
Blest with victory and peace, may the heav'n rescued land
Praise the Power that hath made and preserved us a nation.
Then conquer we must, when our cause it is just,
And this be our motto: "In God is our trust."
And the star-spangled banner in triumph shall wave
O'er the land of the free and the home of the brave!

By late 1814, both sides were tired of fighting. The war had been a strange one; the Americans were victorious at sea, but on land, the English had won many major battles. A peace treaty was written and signed by both sides. It was a strange way to end a strange war, for it simply stated that they were going to stop fighting now. Neither side had claimed victory, and the War of 1812 became known as the war that nobody won.

As we know, in those days there were no telephones or email, so the news of the treaty, which had been signed in Europe, took a long time to get back to America.

The Battle of New Orleans

Neither side knew the war was over, so they kept fighting. In fact, one of the biggest battles of the war was fought after the treaty was signed! In January of 1815, the British attacked *New Orleans, Louisiana.* They marched in with their bright red coats, which made excellent targets for the Americans.

When I was a little girl, my dad taught me a song about this battle. The first lines of lyrics go like this, "In 1814, we took a little trip, along with Colonel Jackson down the mighty Mississip. We took a little bacon, and we took a little beans. . . ."

The Colonel Jackson from the song was none other than Andrew Jackson. He gathered a crew of men from all over the South; some of these men were old hunters from Tennessee. These "soldiers" were sharpshooters, who could knock a squirrel out of a tree from a hundred yards! The Americans were such good shots that the British in their red uniforms didn't stand a chance. By the end of the battle, more than two thousand British soldiers were killed, while the Americans only suffered eight casualties. Finally, the news of the peace treaty reached America, and the fighting was over. Andrew Jackson became known as a national hero for his leadership during the battle of New Orleans.

NARRATION BREAK

Tell what you learned about the writing of "The Star Spangled Banner."

The War Ends...The Battle Continued

The Battle of New Orleans was not a single battle, but came at the end of a series of engagements between British and American forces that began with the Battle of Lake Borgne and the night attack of December 23 and ended with the 10-day siege of Fort St. Philip.

The Battle of New Orleans took place on January 8, and overly eager British troops combined with a lack of communication left their attacks in disarray in the face of concentrated American gunfire. Quick, bloody, with moments of bravery on both sides, the British were defeated in less than half an hour — with 700 killed and 1400 wounded, with hundreds taken prisoner. Sadly, none of the combatants knew of the treaty that had been signed on December 24 ending the war.

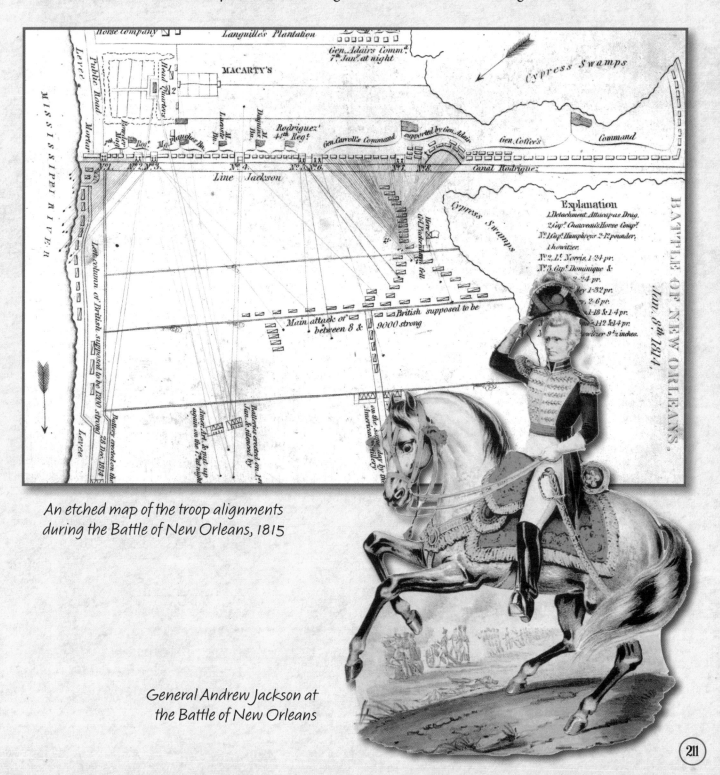

An etched map of the troop alignments during the Battle of New Orleans, 1815

General Andrew Jackson at the Battle of New Orleans

TWO NAVAL BATTLES IN THE WAR OF 1812

The *USS Chesapeake* became a casualty of war in 1813. This depicts the initial shots in the *Chesapeake's* encounter with the *HMS Shannon.* ▶

The ships fire upon each other. ▼

The Defeat of the Chesapeake

▲ The *Shannon* brings her prize, the *Chesapeake,* into Halifax, Nova Scotia.

◀ Moments before the *Chesapeake* is crippled. Soon the Americans surrendered, and the ship was boarded.

Impressment

Seamen had a unique perspective on the War of 1812. Many American seamen had been involuntarily forced into the service of the British Navy in the previous years, and it was especially infuriating to communities along the American coast. It was a deliberate action against the sovereignty of the still young American state and a leading cause of the War of 1812.

If you were an able seamen or even just a man between the ages of 15 and 55, you could become a target of the press gang. Sometimes a community became a target, and hundreds of seamen could be taken.

The 1807 encounter of the *USS Chesapeake* and the *HMS Leopard* created a firestorm of anger among the Americans. The *USS Chesapeake* was fired upon and captured by the *Leopard* while searching for British deserters. The American public were ready to go to war, but President Thomas Jefferson tried to get British officials to end the practice of impressment of American seamen. The British refused. The Americans passed the Embargo Act of 1807 against Britain as their response to the controversy.

The *USS Constitution* as she defeats the *HMS Guerriere*. ▼

The *USS Constitution*, nicknamed Old Ironsides, today. ▼

The Victory of the Constitution

The *Constitution* under fire and being towed with British ships in pursuit. ▶

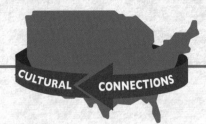
In chapter 21, I mention a song that my dad taught me when I was a little girl. Some of my fondest memories from my childhood are centered around folk songs and ballads about American history. You and your family may thoroughly enjoy this cultural aspect of our American heritage.

Playing lovely ballads across time.

THOUGHTS TO REMEMBER

1. The British and Americans were fighting again because of years of unfair sanctions imposed by the British and the French, while those two countries were fighting among themselves — again. The Americans were tired of and angry about the British's practice of impressment (hijacking ships and kidnapping sailors, forcing them to work onboard the British naval vessels).

2. Neither side won the War of 1812.

CHAPTER 22

THE INDUSTRIAL REVOLUTION CHANGES THE WORLD

Starting Point: An age of great creativity and innovation around the world helped to improve the lives of many as well as expand scientific knowledge! This Industrial Revolution changed the everyday lives of many.

Spot Light

Cotton

Cotton Crop: Cotton harvesting and cleaning was back-breaking work because of how the plants grow. It is difficult to remove the cotton from the 'pod' in which it grows.

READY TO EXPLORE?

1. How did the invention of the cotton gin both help and hurt the slaves of the south?

2. What kind of ship engine did Robert Fulton invent?

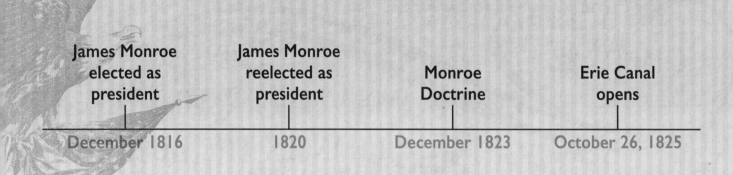

James Monroe
elected as
president

December 1816

James Monroe
reelected as
president

1820

Monroe
Doctrine

December 1823

Erie Canal
opens

October 26, 1825

Have you ever considered the amazing journey of humankind? I am sure that many of you have heard the stories of the Bible. The way people in those times lived is very different from the way we live now!

What are some of these differences? First, let us take a look at our houses. What kind of house do you live in? Do you live in a house with just your family, or do many different families share the roof of your apartment building? Whatever your home looks like, it looks very different than a Bible-time dwelling!

Think back to the beginning of our story, when we learned how people crossed the Bering Land Bridge (now the Bering Strait) and came to the Americas from Asia. Our first chapter in this book was about those people and their ways of life.

As we have traveled down the winding path of our country's history, we have met some very interesting people who did extremely important deeds. We have also noticed America changing, haven't we? There were now many kinds of people in America. The Native Americans, descendants of those who came from Asia, were still here, but there were many other settlers from other countries by the year 1800.

In this chapter, we are going to take a look at a time in our history that is called the Industrial Revolution. Unlike the American Revolution, this Revolution was not a war; instead it was a time of great invention and progress. Many of the inventions of this time are the "great-granddaddies" of helpful items that we use every day.

James Watt and the Steam Engine

INVENT: to create or design something that has not existed before.

We will start with the story of a young lad from *Scotland* who became a famous inventor when he grew up. James Watt was only a boy when he got the idea that steam from hot water might have enough power to move a heavy load or better yet, drive an engine! In the 1770s, before the American Revolution, James invented the first

216

good steam engine, which marked the beginning of true invention progress. His steam engines were used in England for many different purposes.

When American inventors found out about James Watt's steam engine, they, too, wanted to use steam for power. There were several inventors who tried to use steam engines to run boats and ships. One of these inventors, a man by the name of Oliver Evans, actually invented a large enough steam engine to run a boat on the river. However, due to a dry season, the engine was removed from the boat, and instead was used in a sawmill, where it proved to be very productive.

I would like to tell you the story of Robert Fulton. Mr. Fulton was an inventive sort of fellow who liked to work out problems and make life easier through invention. He

Fulton presents his steamship to Bonaparte in 1803.

was determined to make a steam-powered boat that could travel long distances.

Robert lived in *New York*, and he worked on designing his ship to run in American rivers. While he was working on designing and building his ship, he had no other than James Watt designing and building the steam engine to run it. Have you ever heard the story about how everyone laughed at Noah as he built the ark? People did the same thing to Robert Fulton. In fact, they called the ship Fulton's Folly. These were such unkind words, and ones they were soon going to have to eat!

In 1807, Fulton's steamboat was finally finished and ready for trial. There it floated, in the *Hudson River*, ready for its maiden voyage. People gathered around to see what would happen, fully expecting the large boat to remain bobbing in the river current. Some of them laid bets on what

Fulton's First Steamboat

would happen; they said the boat would not go any faster than the current could carry it.

What a strange-looking boat it was, too! Robert Fulton had designed it with large wooden paddles hanging down on both sides. The steam engine would turn the paddles, which would move the vessel through the water. He had invented the design as a boy, when he was tired of moving his child-sized raft up the river by using a long pole to push it. Robert and his friends had built and placed the strange-looking, wooden paddles on the sides of their raft, connecting the paddles to handles which they turned, and therefore powered their craft without nearly as much work as the pole took. What a smart idea! Now grown-up Mr. Fulton did the same thing with the large boat, but using the steam engine instead of hand-turned cranks.

To the amazement of the gathering crowds, the giant wheels on the sides of the ship began to turn, and the vessel started to move! The amazing, steam-powered ship, moving against the current and the wind, traveled up the Hudson River to *Albany, New York*, a journey of 142 miles in just 32 hours! Nothing like this had ever been done before!

1909 Replica of the Clermont

NARRATION BREAK

Retell the story of the invention
of the steam engine.

Another famous inventor I would like very much to tell you about, did not invent something to travel in; instead, Eli Whitney lightened the load of the cotton industry. I have told you that in early America, African slaves were used to work the large farms or plantations. One of the crops raised on these plantations in the south was cotton.

Eli Whitney

Have you ever seen a cotton plant? It is a strange-looking, bush-like plant with the fuzzy, white cotton growing encased in sharp, thorny leaves. It is a very difficult task, indeed, to separate the cotton fluff from the seeds and outer shell that sometimes gets stuck on it. Cotton was very expensive in early America because of the long cleaning process.

In the 1780s, Eli Whitney came up with a helpful invention. He wanted to eliminate the long, hard cotton-cleaning process, so he designed a machine to do it. This was not a large steam-powered engine such as James Watt invented, but it did change America.

You might be wondering how it could do this. Because cotton was so hard to grow, harvest, and then clean, it was very expensive, and therefore the demand was low. With the invention of the cotton gin (short for engine), cotton was much easier to clean, therefore the price came down, driving up the demand for it.

More cotton was planted, and of course, more workers were needed to take care of it, pick it, and clean it (with the new gins). In a way, Eli Whitney's invention helped revive slavery, which had been in a slow decline in the south. I am sure he had no such intentions, but like we learned before, a small pebble dropped into the water can cause a big ripple, and so can the one important invention of one man.

This was a very big growth spurt time in America. One invention led to another, and little by little, manual labor gave way to machine labor. In some ways, America was heading into a darker time, for with the growth of the cruel slavery in the South, came its northern counterpart: child labor in factories. We will see that, as time passed, the demand for the goods being produced kept the demand for cheap labor climbing. It would be this way for a long time, until someone cared enough to step forward to change it.

We will travel away from the talk of slavery and child labor and visit a very interesting story. At the time of the colonies and their fight to become an independent country, our neighbors to our southwest were cheering us on. They too were struggling under the heavy rule of a tyrant. *Spain* had ruled *Mexico* since they conquered the Aztecs in the 1500s, but now Spain was weakened from its wars with *France* and *England*.

There was talk all over the European countries, who felt that they too had a claim in the Americas. Russia wanted Oregon, and wanted others to stay out of that area. France and other European countries offered to help Spain regain control of her colonies in South America.

First Cotton Gin

Our fifth president, James Monroe, was a wise man. He had been a personal friend of George Washington and had even fought alongside the general in the Revolution. President Monroe had great sympathy for the Mexican people who wanted to be free. He was also concerned about the prospect of other European countries gaining control of parts of North America.

James Monroe

To better understand his concerns, let us take a few minutes to study the map you completed in your Teacher Guide for chapter 10. Do you see the United States of America? Canada is to the north, while directly to our west, is the large Oregon territory. Directly south of the Oregon territory, is Mexico. Can you understand President Monroe's concern about the strong European countries gaining control in these areas?

James Monroe had to come up with a plan that would accomplish these things: not lead America into war, but still show the world that America was not afraid to take on anybody, and keep the European countries out of the Americas.

His plan became known as the Monroe Doctrine. He made these three statements in his plan very clear: he warned the European countries not to start any more colonies in the Americas; he told them they could not attack any of the colonies in Central and South America who had won their freedom from Spain; and he promised that the United States of America would not get involved in Europe's business.

President Monroe had an important ally — England had become our friend, and offered to help the United States carry out this plan. The Monroe Doctrine worked, and it played an important part in the history of our country.

Our sixth president, John Quincy Adams, came to office in 1825. He was the son of President John Adams, our second president. President Adams had been helpful to his friend, James Monroe, by helping formulate the Monroe Doctrine.

While he was in office, President John Quincy Adams was known for being outspoken against slavery. He predicted that it would destroy the nation if something wasn't done about it, and he spoke strongly about the corrupt practice of slave holding. He felt that in this country, founded on freedom, there was no room for ownership of humankind. Mr. Adams was not a very popular president and only served one term.

As we continue down our path of history, we will see President Adams' prediction of impending doom growing on the horizon — an ominously threatening storm that would eventually break over our nation.

John Quincy Adams

NARRATION BREAK

Retell the story of the cotton gin and tell about the Monroe Doctrine.

PROTECTING THE AMERICAS

America's fifth president James Monroe was elected in 1816, having served his country holding various public offices since the founding of the country. President until 1825, he is known for his principled stand for the independence of lands in the Americas from European interference and control. His policy became known as the Monroe Doctrine.

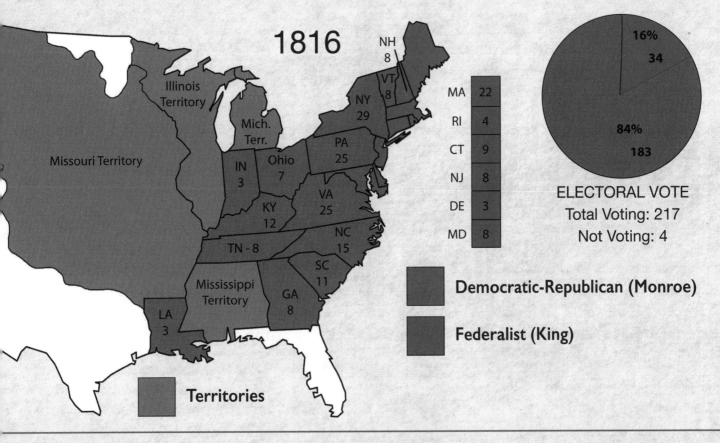

1816

MA	22	
RI	4	
CT	9	
NJ	8	
DE	3	
MD	8	

16%
34

84%
183

ELECTORAL VOTE
Total Voting: 217
Not Voting: 4

Democratic-Republican (Monroe)

Federalist (King)

Territories

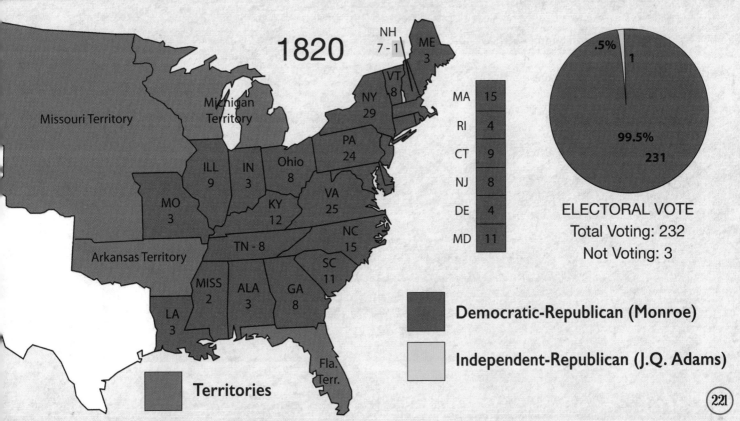

1820

MA	15	
RI	4	
CT	9	
NJ	8	
DE	4	
MD	11	

.5%
1

99.5%
231

ELECTORAL VOTE
Total Voting: 232
Not Voting: 3

Democratic-Republican (Monroe)

Independent-Republican (J.Q. Adams)

Territories

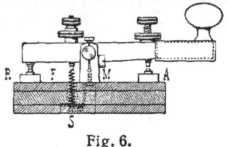

Fig. 6.

▲ While others had produced variations of telegraphs, an early form of transmitting signals to communicate messages, Samuel Morse is credited for creating the first commercially successful model in 1837. His first messages on a telegraph line between Washington D.C. to Baltimore in 1844 was "What hath God wrought." (United States)

▲ In 1799, Alessandro Volta invented the first electric battery, known as the "Voltaic pile." (Italy)

In 1814, Joseph Niépce is the first to take a photograph, but he had other inventions as well. (France) ▶

VELOCIPEDE.

▲ Though not the first inventor to create one, Elias Howe invented a sewing machine. A few years later, Isaac Singer invents one as well. (United States)

▲ Variations on bicycles were a popular form of invention as well, with many varieties being produced. This is a small selection. (Germany)

In 1829, W.A. Burt invented the "Typographer," considered the first typewriter. (United States) ▼

In 1815, Humphry Davy invented the "Davy lamp," a safer lamp for use in coal mines. (Britain) ▶

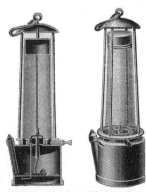

Fig. 192. Davysche Sicherheitslampe

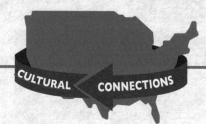
Then and Now: Though other types of simple telephones had been invented, it was Alexander Graham Bell's efforts to broadcast a voice message by way of telegraphs that led to his inventions related to the telephone in 1876. The telephone has seen many improvements since this simple beginning — and today mobile phones are a popular mobile device that works as a camera, a computer, and workspace for many. Bell could have never imagined the successful future of his wonderful invention!

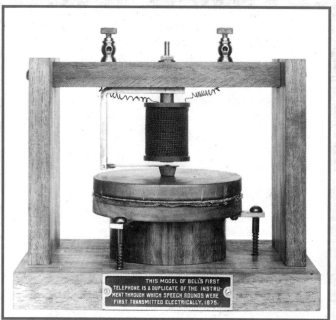

Technology across time.

THOUGHTS TO REMEMBER

1. We learn in Chapter 22, that Eli Whitney unintentionally helped the cause of slavery with the invention of his cotton gin. A shorter cleaning process made cotton production by slaves less time-consuming and less expensive. Cotton growers could now produce more cotton, creating more work for slaves in the fields.

2. Robert Fulton invented a paddle boat, which was powered by a steam engine. This was the first time a ship had been powered by anything except human strength and energy or the wind.

CHAPTER 23

PATHS OF CHANGE

Starting Point: Remember when we talked about slavery dividing many in the colonies? That division would deepen as the country grew. The mistreatment and removal of Native American tribes echoed injustice.

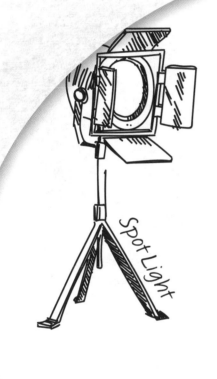

Spot Light

Slave quarters at Boone Hall Plantation in South Carolina

Slave Quarters: Slave housing were rough cabins or shacks that were barely able to provide any comfort at all for their inhabitants. The life of a slave was hard, with very little comfort.

READY TO EXPLORE?

1. What do you think the life of a slave child was like?

2. What was the Underground Railroad, and how did it work?

Part 1: Path to Freedom

(Parents, please read the notes for this chapter in the Teacher Guide. This chapter contains sensitive information related to slavery and the forced relocation of Native American tribes.)

We have learned a little about slavery in America, but today I want to describe the life of a slave in a little more detail. We know that slavery is wrong, but it was widely accepted in America as a necessary way of life, and whole industries were built on slave labor.

In the early 1800s, America was still a very young country; rough around the edges, you might say. There were not many doctors, builders, or any other kind of tradesmen in the west. People moving west had to do things for themselves. They had to learn by doing!

There were big disagreements about allowing slavery in the new parts of the country. As the country grew, there were those in the government who thought it would be fine to let slavery grow right along with it! There were those, however, who did not want slavery spreading all over the country. They worked hard to keep it contained to the South. As new states were added to the union, they made laws about making these new states "slavery free."

Harriet Beecher Stowe

There were many people, in the North and the South, who made fighting slavery their life's work. Do you remember what we call these people? That is right, they are called abolitionists. These people did not like slavery. In fact, they made quite a ruckus about the evils of it! I would like very much for you to meet one lady in particular. Her name was Harriet Beecher Stowe. Raised by

Little Eva reading to Uncle Tom

an outspoken religious leader, Harriet grew up to receive an education that only a man would normally have received at that time in history. Then Harriet married Calvin Stowe, a very outspoken abolitionist. In 1850, the Fugitive Slave Act was passed to reinforce existing laws that made it illegal to help escaped slaves and required they be returned to their owners.

"The fugitives are safe in a free land." From *Uncle Tom's Cabin*

What do you suppose she did? She wrote a book! This book would be destined to change the course of American history. Remember the ripples of a pebble? This one little lady, a 40-year-old mommy of seven, made some HUGE ripples with this book about a slave's life. *Uncle Tom's Cabin* became the bestselling book of the 1800s, second only to the Bible. I think it is important to learn a little about a slave's life. Mrs. Stowe's book portrayed what she thought it was like to be a slave; some of what she wrote was accurate, but some of it wasn't.

America did not invent slavery, for it has been around since ancient times and still exists today in some places in the world. We need to remember, however, that when Jesus died on the Cross for the sins of the world, He died for everyone, including slaves. He wanted everyone to be free. America was founded on the basic principle that all men are created equal. Do you remember the words that Thomas Jefferson penned at the beginning of the Declaration of Independence?

> *We hold these truths to be self-evident, that all men are created equal, that they are endowed by their Creator with certain unalienable Rights, that among these are Life, Liberty and the pursuit of Happiness.*

Some people did not think that the phrase "all men are created equal" included the black slaves. Why would they think that? It could be because slaves were considered to be "belongings" of their "owner," no different than a horse or a dog.

Some slave owners were kind to their slaves and treated them well, but others were cruel and did not care whether the slave was sick or weak. Many, many slave families were split up when the owner would sell them to different plantations.

NARRATION BREAK

Please talk with your children about what you have read so far.

I know that this is a hard topic, and I don't enjoy writing about it, but it is important to understand the hardships that the slaves endured for hundreds of years. There were many slave children, too, not any older than some of my friends reading this story. I am going to ask you to do something very difficult. I want you to imagine that you are there, in the South, on a plantation where the fields of cotton, tobacco, and peanuts stretch endlessly in all directions. None of us can possibly imagine what it would be like, but I am here with you, and we will do our best to do so. Hold onto my hand, as we step back through the years and into the slave cabin where a young slave lives with his family.

As we step together into the one-room slave cabin, the first thing we notice is the floor. It is made of dirt — dust really, and it is very dry. The windowless walls make the interior very dark, and it smells of dirt and sweat mixed with the smell of something cooking over the open fireplace on the far wall.

Our eyes travel around the room, which is crowded, for it is the kitchen, sleeping area, and family area for the four-member slave family who lives here. We press our backs against the rough wall behind us; we do not want to be noticed or in the way.

A small, dark brown child is sitting cross-legged in the middle of the floor expectantly holding out his bowl to be served. Our attention is sharply drawn away from this darling child by a sound coming from a dark corner.

It is the sound of agony followed by a deep voice: "Hold still now, Henry, I's gotta wash this out!"

As we peer into the darkness, we see the form of what seems to be a teenage boy lying face down across a mattress of sorts. A larger man kneels beside him, carefully sponging the boy's back. We both gasp when we realize that the young man's back has open wounds running the entire width of it; wounds caused by a slave master's whip!

"I done tol' you to stop talkin' about freedom! I done tol' you, Henry!"

"I know Pa, I know! But I can't hep it! I just can't! I's so tired of workin' for ol' man Harlin! I's not a dog, Pa, I's amos' a man!"

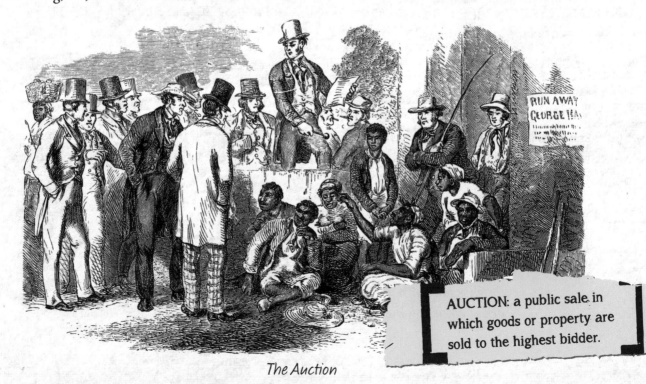

RUN AWAY
GEORGE HA

AUCTION: a public sale in which goods or property are sold to the highest bidder.

The Auction

The woman at the fireplace turns, and we can see the tracks her tears have made in the dust on her cheeks. In one motion, she scoops up the small child on the floor and, grabbing a folded quilt off of the end of one of the sleeping pallets, hurries outside into the cool night air. We are afraid to move, wanting to see what happens with the boy on the pallet.

The low, soft voice of the woman outside drifts back to us through the door left ajar. It's a comforting sort of voice, the kind mommies use when their children wake from a nightmare.

Swing low, sweet chariot, comin' for to carry me home!

Swing low, sweet chariot, comin' for to carry me home. Well, I looked o're Jordan an' what did I see, comin' for to carry me home? A band o' angels comin' afta me, comin' for to carry me home.

We listen, spellbound, as this brave woman holds her child closely; reassuring him, rocking him. The man in the corner stands to his feet, and we get our first, good look at him. He's a big man, having to duck his head to not brush the low ceiling. His eyes are full of sorrow; his hands hang limply at his sides. He stands looking down at his son lying on the bed.

The injured boy is asleep now, his bare back turned to the wall, hiding the rough bandages covering his wounds. Even in his sleep, his face shows the pain. His father stands motionless, gazing down at him. What must he feel? There are no words to describe the pain in a parent's heart when his other child is hurt. What would become of these people? Would they ever be free?

We slip into the night; neither of us is in the mood to talk about what we have seen and felt in that dark, one-room cabin. Slavery is a horrible thing, and by putting a human face and human emotion on it, we both feel the pain of it. There are thousands of slave families back here in the year 1816. How many other slave families are dealing with this kind of sorrow tonight? Who can own the soul of another human? No one can.

Our story has been sad, and to brighten it up a bit, I am going to tell you the story of some very brave heroes. Sometimes a hero doesn't wear a cape and fly to save someone in distress; sometimes, it means secretly helping with a cause that brings freedom to the oppressed. This is true heroism!

There were many, many people in America who did not like slavery. They believed with all of their hearts that God truly did create all men equal, just like the Declaration of Independence says. More and more people were becoming outspoken abolitionists.

There were those who made helping slaves to freedom their life work. These people helped the slaves by giving them a safe place to stay and by helping them get north to Canada. These houses were called "safe houses." This line of safe houses stretched all over the nation! This escape route was known as the "Underground Railroad."

The escaping slaves were moved from one safe house to the next one farther north in the dark of the night. They used the brightest star in the "Big Dipper" constellation to lead the way. "Follow the drinking gourd to freedom," is what they said.

It is said that the slaves had many ways of communicating about plans for escape. Some say that there were quilts sewn in certain patterns, which were actually maps of the Underground Railroad. There were songs, which parents taught their children, the lyrics being coded directions, telling them how to reach safety.

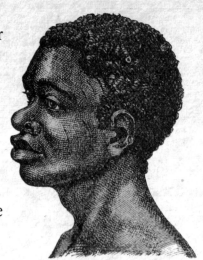

We will revisit the Underground Railroad in our next chapter and meet some of the most renowned heroes of that time. Isn't it comforting to know that there were hundreds of people who risked their own safety to help slaves escape to freedom? Do you think if we lived in those years, we would open our homes as safe houses? I think we would!

NARRATION BREAK

Please take the time to talk to your children about this part of the story.

Indian Reservation

Part 2: The Trail of Tears

Have you ever wondered what it was like for the Native Americans to see the "white man" moving farther and farther into their land? Ever since the Europeans started crossing the ocean to explore and settle the Americas, the Indians were forced to move over and give up lands that had been "theirs" for centuries.

There had been Indian uprisings throughout the years, and the Indians had joined the French in fighting the English in the French and Indian War. They had been angry when the English won that war and had retaliated by attacking settlers, but not all of the Native Americans were violent toward the white settlers. Many of them were satisfied to leave the settlers alone as long as they were allowed to live their lives separately on their own land.

As the United States grew and spread out across the great continent of North America, the Indians were moved into smaller and smaller areas. In the 1830s, the United States government started removing whole tribes of Indians from their homes to other, less desirable lands. As the states' populations grew, there was more of a demand for good farming land.

Our seventh president, Andrew Jackson, was in office at this time. President Jackson had won favor in the American people's eyes in the war of 1812, when he lead the American army to victory at the Battle of New Orleans. Now he was working to end a dispute in the southern states, for many of the states in the South felt that they should have land that belonged to the Cherokee Indian nation.

Have you ever wanted something that wasn't yours? One of the Ten Commandments warns that this is not a good thing to do. You have probably heard, "Do not covet your neighbor's belongings." Covet means wanting something that does not rightfully belong to you. That is what the plantation owners from some of the southern states were doing.

President Jackson thought that by removing the Cherokee Indian nation from the state of Georgia he would solve the problem. He didn't want the plantation owners starting a war with the Indians over the land. It seemed like a simple solution to the problem to just give the Indians other land somewhere else.

Davy Crockett

Louisiana Indians Walking along a Bayou

There were many people who were against the Indian Removal Act. They did not think that it was fair that the plantation owners got land that wasn't theirs. There was one man who was very much against this unfair law. Davy Crockett was a congressman from Tennessee, and he was very outspoken about his disapproval. For a while, it looked like the Cherokee, and several other southern Indian tribes, would be able to stay on their land.

In 1830, to the surprise of many, President Jackson signed the Indian Removal Act, which told the Indians they had to move to certain land in what is now *Oklahoma*. The Cherokee, Creek, Chickasaw, and Choctaw tribes, living in *Georgia* and *Mississippi*, were forced from their lands. Their long, sad journey to Oklahoma became known as the Trail of Tears. Thousands of Indian families traveled together to their new home. By the late 1830s, more than 45,000 Indians had been forced from their homes.

The removal of the Cherokee nation was perhaps one of the cruelest acts in American history. Thousands of Cherokees were rounded up by militiamen from several of the southern states, and forced into camps in Tennessee. It was from these camps that the Cherokee people began their "walk" of over a thousand miles. Thirteen thousand men, women, and children endured this nightmare. Cold, hungry, and without clothing that was warm enough, four thousand people died on this journey to Oklahoma Territory.

President Andrew Jackson

In this chapter we have learned about two "trails" in American history. One of them led slaves to freedom, while the other led Native Americans to live in a place that wasn't their home. Some things that happen in history are hard to understand — they make us sad, or even angry. Today's stories have been like that, haven't they? The puzzle pieces of history are sometimes oddly shaped and very dark. Be comforted that God holds the whole world in His strong, capable hands, and not a sparrow falls, that He doesn't know about.

NARRATION BREAK

Talk about what you read today.

Forced to Move

As Americans began settling farther south and west from the lands of the original 13 colonies, Native Americans who lived on those lands protested, leading to numerous disputes that would finally end in the forced removal of Native Americans in an "exchange" of their lands to other land in the Midwest under the Indian Removal Act of 1830. Remember that Native Americans were not considered citizens, and through a series of treaties that never seemed to be honored by those seeking more land, they were either left without options and at the mercy of the American government or they chose to fight which was futile. Between 1830 and 1850, members of the Cherokee, Chickasaw, Choctaw, Muscogee, and Seminole nations were moved. Many of those forced to move died on the difficult journey to their new lands.

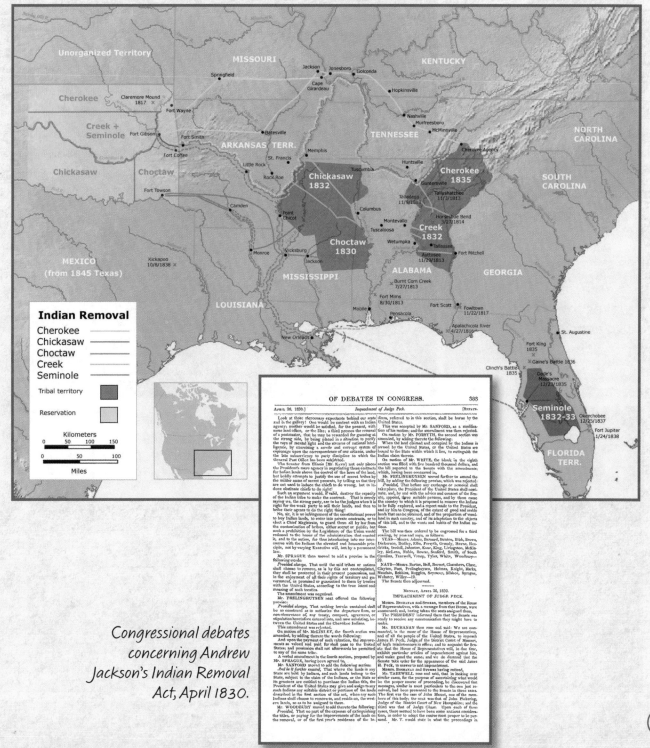

Congressional debates concerning Andrew Jackson's Indian Removal Act, April 1830.

Some slave children were rescued through a process called redeeming — where the child was purchased by someone who brought them to a free state and cared for them. Some were even adopted by their rescuers.

▲ Isaac and Rosa, slaves from New Orleans

▲ Slave cemetery in Georgetown area of Washington, D.C.

◀ Slave balcony of a church. (Charleston County, SC)

◀ *Formerly the slave quarters at a plantation in Hale County, Alabama, photographed in 1935*

After her son was illegally sold, Sojourner Truth won a court case to get him back. ▼

Many assume that slaves were only in the South, but as we have learned at different times in America's early history, slaves could be found throughout the colonies and states. (Montgomery County, MD) ▼

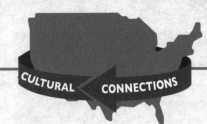

In our chapter we "visited" the home of a slave family. In our story, the momma sang a song to comfort her small child. This song is a well-known and loved "Negro spiritual." This genre of music has a powerful history and a unique place in our heritage and culture as a nation. There are many African American churches that still integrate these beloved songs into their modern worship practices. You may enjoy listening to some of these songs. Ask your parent or teacher if you may listen to a recording of "Swing Low, Sweet Chariot."

Fisk Jubilee Singers in 1882. They were the first to record "Swing Low, Sweet Chariot."

Fisk Jubilee Singers, 2012

THOUGHTS TO REMEMBER

1. None of us will truly know what the life of a slave child may have been. We can imagine the fear and uncertainty from having a mom, dad, or sibling sold, never to be seen again. Or the despair of never having freedom. Slavery was a cruel and heartbreaking condition.

2. We learn in Chapter 23 that the Underground Railroad was a network of safe houses where escaping slaves could find safety and help.

CHAPTER 24

HEROES OF THE ABOLITION MOVEMENT

Starting Point: Many people were willing to risk their lives and property to oppose slavery. These brave men and women defied the law and social customs of the time to stand firm on the need for all people to be equal and free.

Spot Light

Douglass around 29 years of age.

Frederick Douglass: Frederick Douglass had an unconquerable spirit. He spent his entire life working to educate himself as much as he could. His eloquent words went a long way toward destroying what white people believed about the black slaves.

READY TO EXPLORE?

1. Why was it illegal to teach a slave how to read?
2. Why was Harriet Tubman called "Moses"?

Nat Turner's
Rebellion

The life of
Frederick
Douglass

The life of
Harriet
Tubman

August 1831

1818–1895

1821/1822–1913

Words are powerful. Like the pebble that causes ripples spreading out in all directions, words cause change. Sometimes those words come from unexpected places. They do not always come from big, powerful people; sometimes they come from children, or, as we will learn in today's story, a slave.

I would like very much to tell the story of a young man who started out in life as a slave. We learned yesterday that it was a very unpleasant to be a slave. It meant that someone owned you and treated you any way they wished.

Frederick Douglass was born in 1818 in *Maryland* and was given the name Frederick Augustus Washington Bailey. That's a big "handle" for a baby, isn't it? His mother died when Frederick was only a small boy, so he lived with his grandmother for a short while before he was sent to live on another plantation.

At this time in history, it was against the law to teach a slave to read. Why do you think this was? If you know how to read, you can learn about all kinds of things, and when you learn new things, it makes you want to know more new things. This is exactly why the slave owners did not want their slaves to learn to read. They would not have been able to control them as well.

When Frederick was a boy of ten or so, his owner's wife started teaching him to read. What a kind lady! She had already taught Frederick his letters and how to read simple words when her husband found out what she was doing. He was very angry and made her stop immediately, but he was too late; Frederick already knew how to read well enough to know that he wanted to know more!

By playing with other boys who knew how to read, Frederick learned how to read better. Soon he was reading fluently, and read everything he could get his hands on. Frederick was exceptionally intelligent and soaked up knowledge like a thirsty little sponge! The more he read, the more he learned slavery was wrong. The more he learned, the more he spoke out against it. The more he spoke out against slavery, the angrier the "white folks" became.

When Frederick was 16, he was sent to work for a farmer who was known to beat his slaves into submission. He was extremely cruel, but his evil and violent tactics did not break Frederick. You see, a strong mind and convictions based

The last time he saw his mother

238

Anna Murray-Douglass

on the truth can stand up to evil. Frederick knew that God had created him with a strong mind and body for His glory, not to be used or owned by man.

In 1838, when he was 20 years old, Frederick escaped to New York City. Can you imagine what it felt like to finally be free? What gladness filled his heart! The year before, Frederick had met a young, free, black lady and now that he was free, he decided he wanted to marry Miss Anna Murray.

Frederick quickly became involved with the abolitionist movement. His eloquent way of speaking stunned many of the highly educated white people with whom he became acquainted. His story made people sit up and take notice, for he completely contradicted everything many people thought slaves to be.

Many people of that time tried to justify slavery by saying that the black people were inferior to white people. Do you know what inferior means? It means less than or below something or someone else. In other words, many white people thought they were smarter, better, and worth more than the slaves. Such thinking makes Jesus very sad, indeed! He died for the whole world, and that means He loves everyone.

It seems that America, land of the free and home of the brave, is truly trying to become just that, doesn't it? It had taken many years, but the voices demanding freedom for all Americans were getting

louder. Slaves were not the only ones who were considered non-equal with white men; women did not have equal rights either. They were not allowed to vote or own land, and many times girls were not allowed to go to school for very long.

I think back to when I was a little girl, and I know that I would have been very upset if someone told me that I could not have an education because I was a girl. I love to learn and did very well, learning to read at four years old. Do you like to learn new things? Our friend Mr. Frederick Douglass believed that women and girls deserved a good education, too, so he became an advocate for the Women's Rights Movement.

Mr. Douglass soon became quite a well-known author. You will probably read some of his writings when you get to your high school years, for they are usually required reading at that level. Many white people, who did not own slaves and had never been

Slave Irons

to the South, had never heard about it from a person who had lived it. Frederick's books touched people's hearts in a powerful way.

Frederick finally was able to buy his freedom when he was 27 years old. He became known all over the world and met some very important people. Frederick Douglass, an extremely important puzzle piece of American history, lived to be 78 years old. His life caused a ripple effect in our nation. He was one man who changed many, many lives with the power of words.

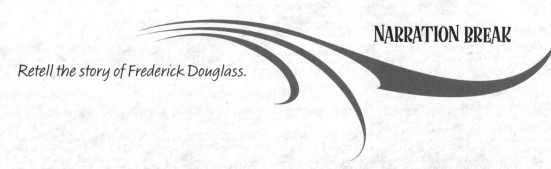

NARRATION BREAK

Retell the story of Frederick Douglass.

The next part of our chapter is a wonderful story about another amazing American hero. This hero was nicknamed "Moses." That is an odd nickname, isn't it? Well, you will see why this is the perfect name for her. Did I just say "her"?

We are going to learn the story of Harriet Tubman, born Araminta Ross in 1821 or 1822. Araminta was a third-generation slave, which means her grandparents had been brought over from Africa, her parents had been born into slavery, and she and her siblings were also born into slavery. That is a long legacy of slavery, isn't it?

Just because the family had been in slavery for a long time doesn't mean they had the hearts of slaves! Araminta (her family called her Minty for short) inherited her mother's spunky attitude, and dreamed of freedom from the time she was a small child.

Harriet Tubman

Minty had a hard time growing up as a slave. She lived in constant fear that she would be taken from her parents, or that her family would be divided. When she was still a young person, her three older sisters were sold to another plantation owner. Poor Minty was terrified, and more determined than ever to become free.

The life of a slave was hard, and Minty suffered from beatings and mistreatment. Once she was hit in the head, and she suffered from seizures, epilepsy, and a terrible sleeping disorder for the rest of her life.

MISSION: an important assignment carried out that typically involves travel.

240

Minty was a devout Christian and believed God had saved her from death for a reason. She was determined to find out what that purpose was and fulfill it.

In about 1844, she married a free black man named John Tubman, and soon after changed her name to Harriet. Things were complicated for them, for he was free and she was not. In 1849, Harriet escaped from Maryland to Philadelphia. Do you recall the name of the widespread network of "safe houses," where slaves could hide when they were escaping? It was called the "Underground Railroad," and Harriet used it to get to freedom.

Once she was in Philadelphia, she got a job because she wanted to save as much money as she could. Harriet had a mission! She felt that God wanted her to go back to get her other family members. This would be no small feat. Nobody had ever escaped, and then turned back to help others do the same.

Harriet started making return trips to rescue her family. First she rescued her niece, who was going to be sold along with her children. Harriet worked with her niece's husband, a free black man, to keep this from happening.

Other abolitionists started taking notice of Harriet, and offered to help her with her mission to rescue her friends and family. She became good friends with Frederick Douglass, who wrote about her in some of his newspaper articles. Who would have thought that a petite lady, who had occasional seizures due to an old head wound, would be brave enough to return again and again to lead her people to freedom? Isn't it amazing that she was able to do this without being caught?

Harriet worked hard and saved the money to fund her missions. Somehow, she would get word back to Maryland, requesting the names of the slaves who wanted to come with her. Spunky Harriet carried a revolver to protect herself on her journeys, and she was known to use it to coax a faint-hearted slave, who was threatening the mission by wanting to turn back. Her missions were very dangerous for all involved, and once she was on her way back toward freedom, there was no turning back! The law said that if you saw an escaped slave, you had to take them to the local authority, and there were many people who tried to earn reward money by hunting for escaped slaves. Many of them had hunting dogs that were trained to be vicious!

Tubman with her family in 1887

It took 13 trips and 11 years, but Harriet rescued her entire family and many of her friends. In fact, she personally rescued over 70 slaves and helped hundreds of others to find freedom. It is no wonder that her nickname was "Moses!" On one of her last rescue missions, Harriet brought her parents out of Maryland and took them all the way up to Canada.

Harriet's bravery didn't stop when her missions stopped. She would go on to become a nurse and a spy in a war that nearly destroyed our nation. We will learn about that war in our next history storybook, *America's Story, Volume 2*. She also became good friends with the president of the United States during that war. You may have heard of him before — his picture is on our penny!

I hope you have enjoyed our story about these unlikely heroes! We have learned that it does not take a big, super-strong person to be a hero, for bravery is most often born from the need to help those we love. You, too, can be a hero by doing what you know is right and standing up for those younger and sometimes weaker than yourself. Sometimes bravery isn't big and noticeable. Sometimes it is small and quiet. Take time to think about how you can be brave and courageous today.

Harriet Tubman

NARRATION BREAK

Retell the story of Harriet Tubman, "Moses."
Why was she called this?

242

SEEKING FREEDOM

For slaves seeking freedom, even the Underground Railroad was a dangerous path. Some people who opposed slavery decided not to wait for the American government to outlaw the practice, choosing to help the runaways in any way they could. Soon a network of "stations," private homes or other locations, were used to house runaway slaves for a brief time before moving them onto the next stop. This became known as the Underground Railroad. It was illegal to help the runaways — and very dangerous. Those who did not make it to freedom could be returned to their owner to face harsh punishment or even death. Even making it to a free state was not always enough if the slave catchers could track a runaway there and abduct them. Anyone helping them could be punished or, in some cases, even killed.

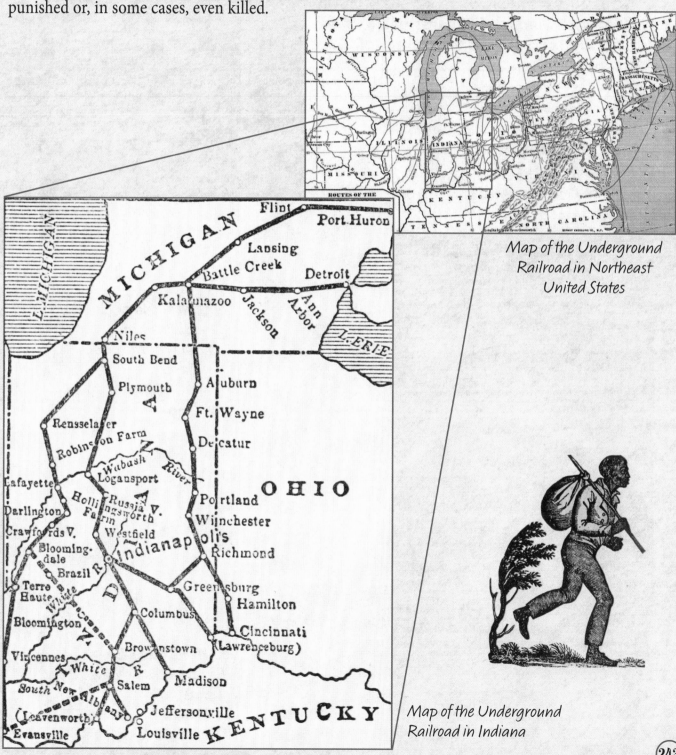

Map of the Underground Railroad in Northeast United States

Map of the Underground Railroad in Indiana

An effort was made by the American government in the 1930s to get firsthand accounts and images related to slavery for historical preservation. The Civil War in the 1860s ended the practice of slavery in America. Here is a collection of images of ex-slaves living in America from the Library of Congress archives.

▲ Mrs. Mary Crane — 82 yrs. old ex-slave, Mitchell, Indiana

◀ Minerva & Edgar Bendy, Woodville, Texas

◄ *Will Adams,
ex-slave*

Adeline Cunningham ►

*John Barker, ex-slave,
Abilene, Texas* ▼

◄ *Old Aunt Julia Ann
Jackson, age 102, and
the corn crib where
she lives*

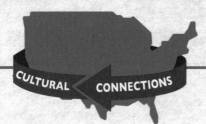

CULTURAL CONNECTIONS

One of the cornerstones of our American culture is the right to a good education. Along with the basic necessities of survival — food, clothing, shelter — is the inborn need for us to better ourselves and to learn and grow mentally, physically, and spiritually. We are blessed to live in a country that has made homeschooling and Christian schooling legal. This right to education is something for which we should be extremely thankful.

The Chance to Learn: Past and Present

THOUGHTS TO REMEMBER

1. We learn in Chapter 24 that it was illegal for slaves to learn to read. Learning to read opened their minds to a much bigger world, therefore bringing even more discontent to their impoverished and controlled existence. The owners wanted to keep them "poor and ignorant" and therefore easier to control.

2. We also learn that Harriet Tubman was called "Moses" because she returned time and again to lead groups of her people to freedom.

CHAPTER 25

THE STORY OF THE ALAMO

Spot Light

Starting Point: Mexico allowed American settlers into Texas, but disagreements followed. A group of Americans seeking freedom from Mexico's rule faced an overwhelming army in a small mission and became legends!

Memorial at the Alamo in San Antonio, Texas

Remember the Alamo!: Sometimes in history special events happen that provide inspiration for people to work even harder to reach their goals. The loss of the legendary Texas soldiers in the Alamo was a rallying cry for others to join the fierce fight for Texas independence from Mexico. In 1836 that dream would finally be realized.

READY TO EXPLORE?

1. What was the battle of the Alamo all about?

2. What famous men were killed at the battle of the Alamo?

Around this time in our story, Spain was losing her grip on her colonies in *Central and South America*. Little by little, colony after colony was shaking off the hand of tyranny. In 1821, Mexico, too, finally became free from Spain. When we see *Mexico* on the map now, it is a lot smaller than it was then. Then, it included what are now the states of *Texas, New Mexico, Nevada, Utah,* and *California*. All of this had belonged to Spain since the 1500s.

This area, which would become California and the southwestern states, was large, but not very many people lived there. Mostly there were several Indian tribes, old Spanish missions, and forts.

America was growing, and there were many settlers who wanted to move westward. Among these people was a man named Stephen Austin, who had a contract with the Mexican government. This contract said that if he brought a certain number of settlers there, he would receive a large parcel of land in return. Since Texas belonged to Mexico, the settlers would have to obey the Mexican government.

At first, the Mexican government welcomed the new settlers, but as more and more of them came bringing their slaves, disagreements sprang up. Pretty soon the settlers outnumbered the Mexican people in Texas, and the settlers did not want to obey the Mexican laws, especially laws banning slavery.

In 1836, Texas told Mexico that they wanted to become independent. Of course, this was met with great disdain by the Mexican president, General Santa Anna, who was quite the tyrant! Of course there was going to be a fight about this; there are always wars about land.

Texas Ranger

The Texan settlers and some American reinforcements turned an old mission called the Alamo into a fort. It was not a very good fort because it was really an extremely old mission, and its walls were not strong. Among the men in the Alamo were Colonel James Bowie, the creator of the famous Bowie knife, and a brave young man named Colonel Travis. Davy Crockett, the congressman from Tennessee and famous woodsman and fighter, was also there.

Altogether, there were only 175 men in the Alamo. There they stayed, determined that they would die before they would give in. They gathered as much gunpowder and as many weapons as they possibly could. I am quite sure they all knew that it would take a miracle for them to actually win this battle! Still, they did not run away; they stayed to face their enemy head on. General Santa Anna's army came marching on, three thousand strong. When the Mexican army attacked the Alamo, the brave men inside drove them back. Santa Anna was very angry! How dare these impudent men stand up to him and his highly skilled army? He demanded that the Texan army inside surrender immediately, or be killed.

The men inside refused, so the fighting continued. It took the Mexican army 11 days to capture the Alamo. Every single man inside was killed. The battle of the Alamo has gone down in history as an example of bravery in the face of unbeatable odds. Even today, when people are faced with seemingly insurmountable odds, the cry "Remember the Alamo!" comes to mind.

It is important to remember that even though there were many Americans who had moved there, and more had come to help fight, Texas was not a part of the United States and it was acting very much like a separate country.

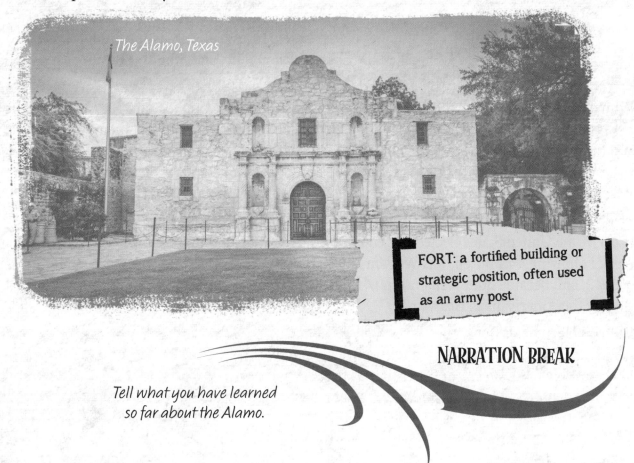

The Alamo, Texas

FORT: a fortified building or strategic position, often used as an army post.

NARRATION BREAK

Tell what you have learned so far about the Alamo.

The Mexican army marched on, and again won a crucial victory, causing high casualties for the Texans. However, Santa Anna was not ready for the tough stubbornness of the Texans or the fighting spirit of their army's leader. Sam Houston, an American from Tennessee, was friends with the fiery-tempered Andrew Jackson. These two men had fought in the War of 1812 together and were a lot alike, too. Both of them were stubborn, tough, and fighters to the bone.

Sam Houston

Sam Houston rallied his men by yelling, "Remember the Alamo!" As General Santa Anna smugly marched his men toward the location of his next battle, Houston hid his men "Indian style" in the brush alongside the road, where the

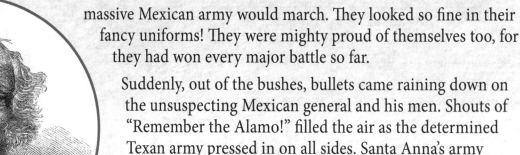
Martin Van Buren

massive Mexican army would march. They looked so fine in their fancy uniforms! They were mighty proud of themselves too, for they had won every major battle so far.

Suddenly, out of the bushes, bullets came raining down on the unsuspecting Mexican general and his men. Shouts of "Remember the Alamo!" filled the air as the determined Texan army pressed in on all sides. Santa Anna's army was completely destroyed, and the general himself was captured!

Sam Houston forced the indignant Santa Anna to sign a paper of surrender. Texas had won its freedom; it was now called the Lone Star Republic, and proudly flew its own flag with a single star on it.

Who do you think became the first president of the Lone Star Republic? Sam Houston, of course! However, Texans didn't want to remain an independent country, for most of them were Americans, and they wanted the Lone Star Republic to be part of the United States of America. Not everyone was so sure they wanted "far away" Texas to be part of the United States. People in the northern states didn't like the slavery in Texas, and others were afraid of Mexico starting a war trying to get the land back. After nine years of debate, Texas finally became a state in the Union.

In 1837, the United States elected our eighth president, Martin Van Buren, who served only one term. Following Van Buren, was William H. Harrison in 1841. Harrison was a general in the War of 1812, and became quite well known when he led his men to victory in one of the biggest battles won by the Americans in that war.

William Harrison is not known for being a great and wonderful president though, no matter what a great job he did as a general. President Harrison was the very first president to die in office, and this is what he is remembered for. I am sure he would have been a good president, for he had many helpful ideas for our country, but he never got to carry them out. He died only 32 days after taking office.

William Harrison

The early 1800s was an interesting time in the history of our country. There was widespread growth, invention, and abolition in America. In our next chapter, we are going to ride along with some families as they travel the trails west to the unsettled American frontier.

NARRATION BREAK

Retell the story of the Alamo. What is William Harrison remembered for?

A Battle Lost, but Glory Found

The historic fortress of the Alamo was an unlikely scene for the historic battle that would bring it fame and to those defeated within, glory. As you see below in this plan of the Alamo interior, its walls were thick and tall, but numbers were not on the side of the valiant Texans in this courageous final stand for freedom.

Having beat back the first two assaults, the third and final one overwhelmed the smaller force of Texans. Their legendary courage still remains a rallying cry in the face of impossible odds.

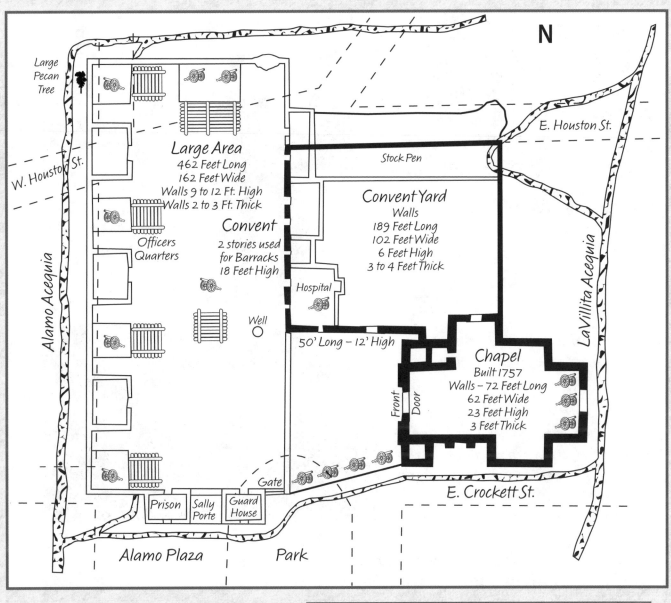

N

Large Pecan Tree

W. Houston St.

E. Houston St.

Stock Pen

Large Area
462 Feet Long
162 Feet Wide
Walls 9 to 12 Ft. High
Walls 2 to 3 Ft. Thick

Convent Yard
Walls
189 Feet Long
102 Feet Wide
6 Feet High
3 to 4 Feet Thick

Convent
2 stories used
for Barracks
18 Feet High

Officers Quarters

Hospital

Well

50' Long – 12' High

Alamo Acequia

La Villita Acequia

Chapel
Built 1757
Walls – 72 Feet Long
62 Feet Wide
23 Feet High
3 Feet Thick

Front Door

Gate

Prison

Sally Porte

Guard House

E. Crockett St.

Alamo Plaza

Park

AUSTIN

Road

Tenoxtitlan R.

Washingt

Bastrop

La Grang

Llano

Medina R.

Old Presidio

San Marcos R.

Colorado R.

Salado

Cibolo R.

San Felipe de

San Antonio de Bexar

Ft. Alamo

Columbus

Gonzales

The Alamo on an old Texas map

▲ *A romantic view of the battle of the Alamo*

After being captured, Santa Anna surrenders to the wounded Sam Houston of the Texan army. ▶

Susanna Dickinson, wife of Captain Almaron Dickinson, and her child Angelina were among the few survivors of the Battle of the Alamo. She hid with other women and children in the chapel. According to her account, she saw her husband briefly after the Mexican Army breached the wall. He warned her and asked her to save his child as well, then returned to the battle. Susanna identified many of the dead following the battle. ▶

REMEMBER THE ALAMO!

It's a story that embodied the American spirit for freedom. A small group of determined and principled Texans, fighting to form the Republic of Texas, facing an immense Mexican army at the Alamo in what most knew was a valiant, but lost cause. Fighting to give others in the Texan army time to make plans, the group, including the famous Jim Bowie and Davy Crockett, were all killed following a 13-day siege and fierce final battle.

Some families had taken shelter in the Alamo's chapel as the Mexican army approached, and a few Texas soldiers had been sent from the mission carrying messages and other information to the Texan army. These people survived the battle. At least one young boy, mistaken for a soldier, was killed by the Mexican army in the chapel.

The survivors traveled to Gonzales and found Sam Houston who commanded the Texas army leading a group of 400 men. General Santa Anna had hoped that the survivors telling of the utter defeat at the Alamo would stop the building rebellion, but it merely served as a rallying cry for the Texans.

For the next few months, Texans — both military and civilian — raced to get out of Santa Anna's path in what was known as the Runaway Scrape. The Battle of San Jacinto was the site of a decisive defeat of the Mexican Army. Texas had fought hard and won its freedom.

A 1906 reunion of the Army of the Republic of Texas veterans. The soldiers of the Texan Army were volunteers. L-R are William P. Zuber, John W. Darlington, Aca C. Hill, Stephen F. Sparks, L. T. Lawlor, and Alfonso Steele. All participated in the Battle of San Jacinto, as well as other skirmishes. ▶

Map of the Battle of San Jacinto ▼

Battle of San Jacinto ▼

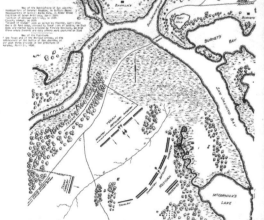

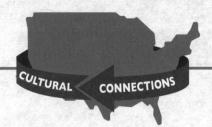
The Mexican American segment of the American population has a deep-rooted part in our heritage and modern culture. The southwestern and western states of California, New Mexico, Arizona, and Texas have the highest percentage of people with a Mexican heritage and ancestral line. Their influence is visible in the architecture, art, and music of those states. If you live in one of those states, you have probably seen the Mexican flavor in many aspects of life. Thankfully, even if you live in the upper midwest, like I do, you still have the ability to visit Mexican restaurants that serve deliciously authentic ethnic dishes!

Mexican heritage flavors many aspects of life.

THOUGHTS TO REMEMBER

1. We learn in Chapter 25 that the battle of the Alamo was a showdown between just a handful of Texans who were fighting for their independence from Mexico and Mexico's tyrannical president, Santa Anna.

2. Among other fighters killed at the Alamo were Colonel James Bowie (the creator of the Bowie knife), and Davy Crockett (the famous congressman from Tennessee, woodsman, and fighter).

CHAPTER 26

THE GREAT JOURNEY WEST – PART 1

Starting Point: The story of America is one of defying limitations and boldly seeking a new beginning. Families would pack up and take a perilous journey to have the chance for land and a bright future!

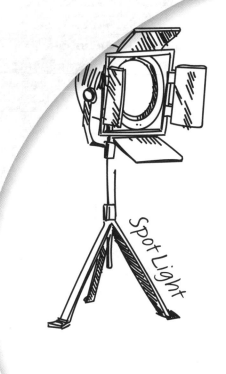

Spot Light

Passing through the Erie Canal, 1890

Erie Canal: The walls of the original locks of the Erie Canal were made with stone in the 1800s. About one hundred years later, in the early 1900s, the locks were replaced with concrete structures.

READY TO EXPLORE?

1. What is the Erie Canal, and who built it?

2. How did people move West without cars, trucks, or airplanes?

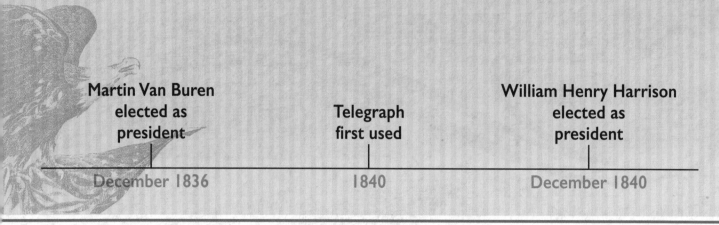

Martin Van Buren elected as president

December 1836

Telegraph first used

1840

William Henry Harrison elected as president

December 1840

America had been settled by people wanting more room, and people from all over the *Eastern Hemisphere* had moved here for many different reasons. It didn't matter that their reasons were different though, for the settlers of America all had something in common — a spirit of adventure! That adventurous spirit is what kept the settlers pushing west. It is what enticed Daniel Boone to try to find a passageway through the Appalachian Mountains, and it was the constant companion of Lewis and Clark on their trek to the Pacific.

Along with an adventurous spirit, Americans shared individuality and independence. America truly is a unique country, for there is a little of many different cultures here; some even call it "the melting pot of the world."

As we have learned, the first generation of European settlers settled along the east coast, and only a few generations later, explorers were pressing through the mountains to *Kentucky* and *Tennessee*. After the war for independence, adventuresome folks were pushing into *Mississippi*, western New York, and even the Ohio River valley. By the time of the War of 1812, little boys and girls were growing up hearing stories of the lands that lay out west. These children would grow up to be the generation that pressed west to *California, Oregon*, and *Texas*. They, and their children, would be the ones who saw our great country stretch and grow all the way from coast to coast. What an exciting time in history!

How did these Americans get out west? There were no cars, vans, or airplanes; in fact, there were no roads — only rivers, prairies, and dusty trails that stretched on for miles. There were thousands of miles between the settled lands of the East Coast and the wild expanse in the West, and the journey from one to the other took a long time.

Before we learn about exactly how all these people moved west, let's talk about why they moved. Just like the people who came hundreds of years earlier, many people chose to move for religious purposes. One very large group of people pushing further west were the Mormons. There are still large groups of Mormons living in *Utah*. Other people moved west to claim land in a homestead, while still others were looking for gold, adventure, or a new life.

Whatever the reason was for moving west, the decision to do so had to be made seriously. It was a very long journey, and many people died attempting it. Still, by the 1840s and 1850s, there were thousands of people making the journey.

Mormons on their journey westward

Have you ever seen a covered wagon? There are two different types — the prairie schooner is short and lightweight, while the Conestoga wagon is almost twice as long and is built to carry a heavy load. Both of these types of wagon were used to cross the continent in the settling of the West. Great trains of them crossed thousands of miles every year. I think the best way to learn how these pioneering settlers travelled is to go along for a ride. It seems the wagon train heading to Oregon has enough room for one more wagon. Which kind of covered wagon should we take? I think a prairie schooner would be good for us; they are quite a bit smaller than the Conestoga wagons, and hopefully, a bit easier to drive!

We need to know where we are going to be traveling, so let's go look at the map at the end of this chapter. Let's look carefully. We will be leaving from *Rochester, New York,* because it is the closest town to where we are. There we will take the *Erie Canal* to *Lake Erie* in *Ohio*. Once we are there, we will catch a steamboat, which will take us across the lake to Cleveland, Ohio. In Cleveland, we will catch a train to Cincinnati, a town on the Ohio River. In *Cincinnati*, we will board another steamboat that is going to take us down the *Ohio River* to the Missouri River. On the Missouri, we will travel all the way to *Independence*.

In Independence, we will meet up with the wagon train that is going to take us to *Oregon*. There are three major trails heading west; the Santa Fe Trail, which leads to Texas and the southwest, and the Oregon Trail, which travels through the *Rocky Mountains* and branches into two trails. One of those trail leads northwest to Oregon, and the other branch leads southwest, to California. We are going to go on the Oregon Trail all the way to Oregon. I hope you are rested up for our trip! We start bright and early tomorrow morning. It is early spring now, but by the time we get to Oregon, we will scarcely have time to build a cabin before winter sets in.

NARRATION BREAK

Discuss the route for our up-coming journey!

We are up bright and early this morning! As we make our way to the Erie Canal, we discuss how this amazing, man-made waterway works. The Erie Canal is 363 miles long, and every inch of it was dug by hand. It has only been open for use for 24 years at the time of our great wagon train adventure in 1849. When work started on the canal on July 4, 1817, there was no easy way for people

CANAL: a man-made waterway for transportation or irrigation

1829 drawing of the Erie Canal

to cross the Appalachian Mountains. People who wanted to move west had to figure out how to get over the mountains before they could do anything else.

As the country expanded its borders, it seemed the Appalachians would forever divide the eastern and western United States. A man by the name of DeWitt Clinton decided to make it his life accomplishment, and against common opinion that it was an impossible feat, he raised money to start the project. You might think that digging a 363-mile ditch by hand is a big enough job; but what if I told you the canal had "steps" in it? These "steps" are called locks, and there are 83 of them in the Erie Canal.

The canal stretches from the Hudson River in New York, to Lake Erie. Lake Erie is more than five hundred feet higher in elevation than the Hudson River. It truly is like climbing a massive set of stairs. It is simply amazing to think that boats can "climb" this three-hundred-plus-mile "staircase"! The Erie Canal made it possible for people in the east to more easily cross the Appalachian Mountains, therefore connecting the east and the west. Very clever!

As we load our belongings onto the canal "packet boat," we run through our list to make sure we have everything with us. Besides our own personal belongings, we had to pack a lot of food and clothing for the trip. You can find this list in the Teacher Guide in the section of pages for this chapter. Let's take a few minutes to look at it right now. That's quite a list, isn't it? We have had to pack our provisions very carefully for this trip; there are going to be many transfers, and it would never do to be disorganized.

As we settle in for our ride down the Erie Canal, the other families on the boat are talking about the journey in front of us. There are folks who have been on the canal all the way from Albany, New York, which is where the canal begins. We sit on our crates on the top of the boat and watch the shore line slowly pass by. The canal does not have a strong current to push us along, and the packet boat does not have a steam engine or a sail. A tow-path runs along the canal of both banks, where teams of mules walk along, hauling us and all our belongings down the canal. No wonder it's slow going! Have you ever heard the Erie Canal song? This song was sung by the mule team drivers, who walked the banks of the canal.

I got an old mule and her name is Sal.
Fifteen miles on the Erie Canal.
She's a good old worker and a good old pal.
Fifteen miles on the Erie Canal.

We've hauled some barges in our day,
Filled with lumber, coal, and hay.
And every inch of the way we know,
From Albany to Buffalo.

Our long, slow canal trip is over, and after we unload our crates and barrels from the canal boat, we head over to the wharf, where we will catch the steamboat to cross Lake Erie. This is a fascinating vessel! We know that we can thank Mr. Robert Fulton for making the steamship a popular mode of transportation. The journey across the lake is much faster than the mule-dragged canal barge we have been on for the last few days. Soon we are pulling into the docks in Cleveland, Ohio.

Excitement is in the air! The swarms of people unloading their belongings from the steamship make it difficult to keep track of our own crates and barrels. After carefully checking to make sure we have everything, we load our belongings into an ox-drawn cart, which is standing nearby for these purposes, and pay the driver to take us to a hotel. We are going to be boarding the train to Cincinnati in the morning.

The train trip is bumpy, and we find ourselves wishing for the comfortable seats in our van at home! We are thankful we will be on the train for only three days before switching to another steamship in Cincinnati. By this time, we are getting to be experts at keeping our many crates, barrels, and bags organized! As the train puffs into the Cincinnati train station, we start gathering our belongings again. The transfer to the steamship will be easier if we know where everything is. A kind man whom we met on the train is going to be traveling with us on the steamship to Independence. I think he may even be joining the same wagon train as we are. He is going to California to prospect for gold!

As we board the steamboat, we are shown to our cabin where we will be spending the nights. They are surprisingly comfortable and cozy. We will be on this boat for five days as we travel down the Ohio River to the Mississippi and then the Missouri. We decide to gather our belongings and then take a nap. All of this pioneering is exhausting, and we are not even halfway through our journey to Oregon! Rest now — in a few days we will be joining up with our wagon train. We will need to purchase the remainder of our supplies, find a wagon and team, and repack our belongings for the last half of our adventure.

NARRATION BREAK

Retell the story of the Erie Canal. What do you think of our journey so far?

PIONEERS ON THE PRAIRIES

As states filled up with people in the East, others seeking land and possibly a fortune began to migrate to the western lands of the United States. Unlike today when you have a huge highway system that is maintained, back then people followed popular routes known as "trails" to get them to their destination. Some went to make a new home. Others went to the gold fields of California. There were many hardships on the journey — from Native American attacks to sickness and death.

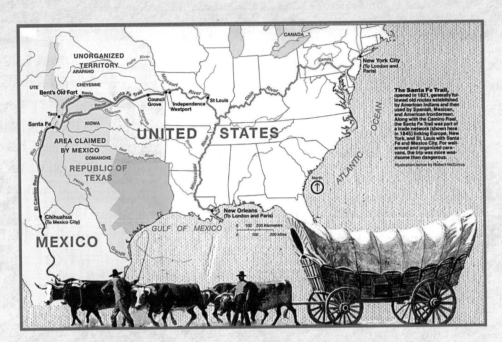

The Santa Fe Trail, opened in 1821, generally followed old routes established by American Indians and then used by Spanish, Mexican, and American frontiersmen. Along with the Camino Real, the Santa Fe Trail was part of a trade network (shown here in 1845) linking Europe, New York, and St. Louis with Santa Fe and Mexico City. For well-armed and organized caravans, the trip was more wearisome than dangerous.
Illustration below by Robert McGinnis

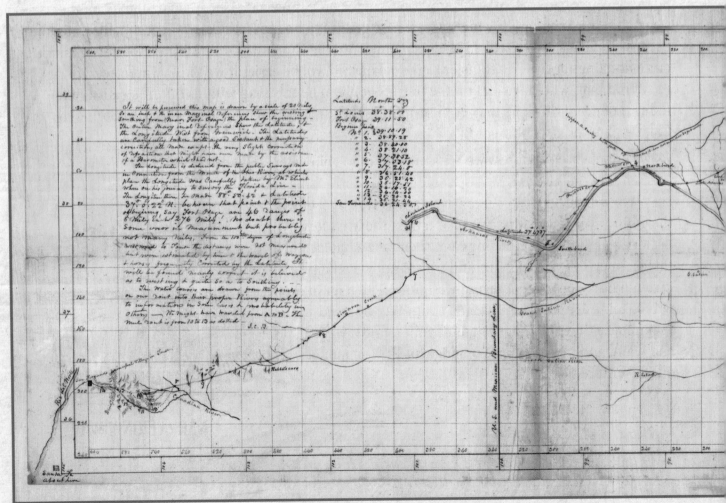

Santa Fe route

Some of the "trail" that led people to the western coast of the United States

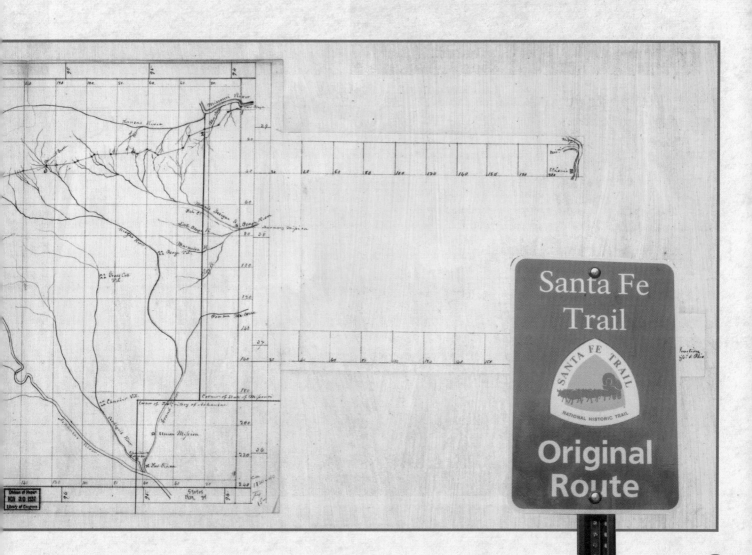

THE OREGON TRAIL

We know much of what life was like along the Oregon Trail from the experiences of those who lived it and recorded it in letters to families back home or diaries in the case of several women.

Their accounts tell of a dangerous journey, where many died of illness and they would see the remains of other travelers and their wagons along the way. At least one artist made the trip, leaving visual images of the journey. His name was Alfred Jacob Miller.

▲ Self-portrait of Alfred Jacob Miller

Fort Laramie pre-1840, on the Oregon Trail by Alfred Jacob Miller ▶

▲ *Our Camp*, Alfred Jacob Miller

Heading west in the painting *Breaking up Camp at Sunrise* by Alfred Jacob Miller ▼

▲ Oregon Trail Re-enactment at Scotts Bluff National Monument in Nebraska.

▲ Oregon Trail Re-enactment

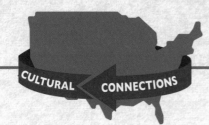
In our chapter, we discovered some of the many ways the American pioneers made their way to the West. Their modes of transportation were slow, crowded, uncomfortable, and dangerous! Have you ever taken a long road trip with your family or perhaps flown on a plane to a destination too far away to drive? Compare and contrast the methods of travel with our modern travel options. How are they similar? How are they different? How does the ability to move around inside of our nation affect our culture?

THOUGHTS TO REMEMBER

1. We learn in Chapter 26 that the Erie Canal is a 300+ mile, hand-dug canal that connects the Hudson River to Lake Erie. It was designed by De Witt Clinton.

2. We also learn that many people moved west by wagon train. It was a long, difficult journey, but thousands did it every year! Between these wagon trains, boats on the rivers, and even trains, the American west was being settled.

CHAPTER 27

THE GREAT JOURNEY WEST – PART 2

Starting Point: While many wanted to find new land they could build their futures upon, some headed west for shinier reasons. Gold and other precious metals created mining towns and opportunities to become wealthy!

Spot Light

Native gold in quartz, found at Eagles Nest Mine, Placer County, California

Golden Opportunity: Because there were no easy routes across the land from the east to the west, many fortune seekers traveled the entire length down the east coast of South America, around the southern tip of that great continent, and then back up the western coast. Now that's taking the long way to California!

READY TO EXPLORE?

1. Why were people so anxious to get to California in the late 1840s?

2. What is a covered wagon, and how were they used?

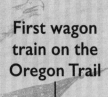

First wagon train on the Oregon Trail	Harrison dies, John Tyler becomes president	James Polk elected as president
1841	April 4, 1841	December 1844

We have a long journey and a lot of work in front of us; I hope you have slept well in our comfortable steamboat beds! Over the last five days, we have had a wonderful time meeting other folks also heading to Independence, Missouri. There are so many stories! There are all kinds of adventure seekers, mostly young men who want to strike it rich out in California. It seems like we are going to have a passel of them on our wagon train. We got to know our friend, Joe, from the train better when we spent a whole day talking to him about the Gold Rush going on in California.

It seems like the whole world has an itchy foot and gold fever. (Don't worry, it's not the kind of fever that will make you sick!) Gold fever is an expression that means a person wants desperately to strike it rich by finding gold. Joe explained to us how the United States had won California from Mexico in 1846, and in January of 1848, gold had been found in Sutter's Mill.

The Gold Rush, Sutter's Mill, California

News of the gold had spread like wildfire, and soon people from all over the world were stampeding to California. Everyone thought they would be the lucky one to strike it rich. The thought of finding gold turned a lot of people into crazed fortune seekers. If you were in California during this time, it would not have been uncommon to see a "junk" (a type of boat) all the way from Asia in a California harbor!

Many Americans living on the eastern side of the Appalachian Mountains didn't want to take the time to cross the great continent of North America, which lay between them and the longed-for gold. Instead of traveling across the continent, they went on "clipper ships" all the way around the southern tip of South America! The fastest time recorded for one of these trips was 89 days. To understand how outstanding this was, take a look at a world map, and follow the route starting in New York City. Now go south, all the way down to Cape Horn at the very southern tip of South America. Next, go straight north up the west coast of South America, past Mexico, and then up to California.

Joe tells us that his brother has already made the trip to California to stake a claim. To stake a claim, a person has to show up and ask to be assigned a plot to prospect on. His brother had sent a message to Joe, asking him to come and join him in California. Joe says that he is excited but very nervous. He used to be a schoolteacher in Maine, so this is a very different life for him! Joe explains that the life of a gold miner is pretty rough.

Mining was hard, dirty work, and dangerous too. Fighting broke out often when miners "claim jumped," trying to mine someone else's claim. Mining towns sprang up all over the place. Where there was once only a small general store, shacks and tents turned into a "town." The law enforcement in these mining towns was not very good, and arguments often times ended in violence.

The Gold Rush

NARRATION BREAK

Talk about the journey so far. Why do you think gold made people act so crazy?

The Courthouse in Independence, Missouri, 1855

As we pull into Independence, the hustle and bustle of people is overwhelming; it reminds me of Christmas shopping at the mall! Joe helps us to locate our belongings among all the hubbub. We are happy to have the assistance. We make our way to the general store to purchase the rest of the needed provisions. I cannot even imagine where we are going to put all of these belongings!

After finding a sturdy wagon, a strong pair of oxen, and a riding horse, we are exhausted . . . and broke! Joe shows us how to yoke the oxen and hitch them to the wagon. Our work is still not done; the wagon needs to be loaded because we are leaving at first light tomorrow morning. All of our barrels and crates are piled on the ground along with the provisions we purchased this afternoon.

We sit on our pile to take a rest and watch the action around us. It seems that everything is in mass confusion! Men yell at oxen and other livestock, cows moo, and women call for their children who are running here and there. We are amazed at all the different kinds of people we see here. There are men in big beaver hats, Mexicans in huge sombreros, Indians in blankets, men in buckskins, and of course, people like us, in sturdy homespun clothing.

After we finally get our wagon loaded, we head to the hotel where we will get our last hot bath and good night's sleep before heading out on the trail. Joe said he will keep an eye on our wagon and belongings, since he is sleeping in his wagon right next to ours. We eat supper in the hotel dining room, which is crowded and noisy with excited people. Both of us are practically sleepwalking as we climb the stairs to our room. Tomorrow will come bright and early, and we need to sleep.

The next day, as we bump along, we recognize some of the land from the exploration we took of the Louisiana Territory. For the most part, the land we are traveling through is flat and rather dusty, with the miles stretching on endlessly. We take turns driving the oxen, allowing each other a chance to get down and walk to stretch our legs. It sure is hot! The sun is mercilessly beating down on us day after day, and our skin is starting to resemble shoe leather. We have learned to draw our wagon into the circle at night. Doing this creates a corral of sorts for the livestock.

Nighttime is a welcome break from the bumping and jarring of the hard wooden wagon seat and the sweltering sun. After we draw our wagon into the circle, we make a fire and cook up a simple meal. Usually, we have biscuits, bacon (which is salted), and beans. We both would really like a nice, fresh, leafy, green salad right about now, but there are no fresh fruits or vegetables out here.

Sometimes after supper has been taken care of, someone in the wagon train brings out an instrument. Either a banjo or a guitar, and sometimes a fiddle start to play softly. At first it amazed us that these people, who had walked or ridden all day long, had the energy to sing and dance, but as we got used to the travel, we too started joining in.

Wagon train life is very much like a traveling town. There are 60 wagons in our train and 215 people. There is a chaplain, a lawman, a midwife (she has delivered three babies so far!), about a dozen scouts, hunters, and of course a trail master. The trail master is the boss on the trip. If anyone has a problem they can't work out, he is the one they go to for help. He is a fair and honest man, and he has made this trip at least a dozen times.

Through the day, each person is responsible to gather fuel for that night's and the next morning's fire. Out on these plains, there are very few trees, and at first we were bewildered about how we were going to make a fire. We soon had our question answered in a very surprising way! Joe showed us what seemed to be strange, round, dried-out pieces of mud. He was collecting and piling them in a barrel in the back of his wagon. He called them "buffalo chips," which is another name for dried out, crusty buffalo droppings!

Neither of us liked to pick these "chips" up, and both of us were just a little concerned about the smell when we burned them, but after realizing there wasn't much of a choice, we decided to do what we had to do. Now we are picking the chips up without another thought. We really are becoming quite the pioneers!

Not all aspects of wagon training are bad. Every night we spread the butter we made that day on our biscuits or cornbread. Our "neighbor" wagon has a milk cow that has a calf. Our kind neighbor gives us a small jar of cream every day. She also showed us how to make butter by tying a tightly lidded crock full of cream to the back of our bumping, bouncing wagon. By the end of the day, we always have a crock full of creamy sweet butter. What a yummy treat!

As we travel across the plains toward the mountains, we are always on the lookout for Indians. The wagon master tells us that he has never had an Indian raid on any of his trips out to Oregon. This is comforting, but we have heard enough stories from other people in the wagon train to know that there is always a threat. The Indians are not happy that they are being crowded off of their hunting grounds.

We discuss the difference between the way white folks, like us, and Indians view the land. The Indians see the land as a natural element, like the air or the sea. They do not believe man can own land any more than he could own these other elements. The white man views land as something to possess, and if need be, change. If there is no waterway between two points of land, no big deal, we

Wagon Train

will dig one, even if it is more than three hundred miles! If we can't plant because there are trees, we cut the trees down; nothing stands in our way.

The Native American Indians had lived here for hundreds and hundreds of years without changing the land. The "white men" had brought many changes in a relatively short time. These opposing views of the land brought a lot of trouble. We just hope we are not in the middle of that trouble! The families in this wagon train are looking forward to farming and living peacefully in their new homes on their new land, and the gold miners are anxiously awaiting their chance to get rich. Both groups are full of hopes and dreams, and it's easy to catch their fire. The fire of the American dream burns brightly in the hearts of these people.

As we sit around the campfires tonight, we watch the tired faces around us. Yes, this is America, growing right in front of our eyes. These men and women, working together to build our country, have no idea that they are going to be thought of as American pioneers, settlers of the West! Tomorrow, we are forging a river that lies about ten miles west of us. The wagon master says that this is the best time of year to cross this river, for the rains of spring have subsided and the dryness of the summer has lowered the water levels. After the river crossing, we will be heading into the foothills of the Rocky Mountains. There are passes through the peaks, but the going is still tedious and hard.

These people simply amaze us with their "go getter" spirits! As we wrap up in our bedrolls under the wagon, our minds drift back over the journey we have taken. The puzzle pieces we have put together sketch out over the first half of our country's history; from those first wandering Asians who discovered a now-non-existent land bridge shortly after the Tower of Babel, to George Washington, brave woodsman and first in the hearts of his countryman, from Benjamin Franklin's inventive spirit to the 363-mile, hand-dug Erie Canal that helped open up the American west.

Yes, my friend, it's been quite a ride. We have learned a lot, and there is so much more to learn, for we have only barely touched on some of the most interesting puzzle pieces of our history. I hope you read and learn more for yourself. Coming up in our last chapter, we will discuss our place in history.

NARRATION BREAK

Talk about life on the trail in a wagon train. What is your favorite part?

San Francisco Harbor, 1850

BY WAY OF CAPE HORN

While many took on the rugged and perilous landscapes of America in their trip west to find their fortunes in the gold fields of California, some would choose a different route — by way of Cape Horn off the coast of South America. But that was a journey that held perils of its own. Strong winds along with larger and steeper waves proved hazardous at time, as well as ice at certain periods of the year. The route is considered by many to be among the most dangerous routes for ships in the world — having cost many ships and the lives of sailors.

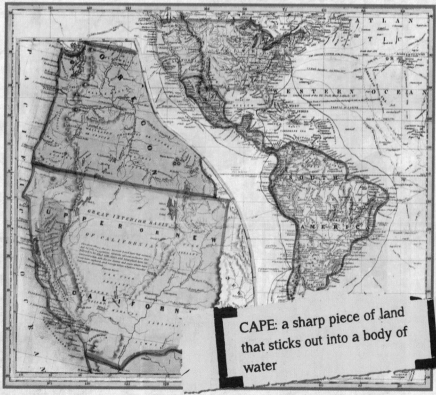

CAPE: a sharp piece of land that sticks out into a body of water

The gold fields of California are denoted in yellow in these maps. Above, you also see the Americas — highlighting the distance taken by those who chose to sail around South America to the western coast of America.

◀ This, Cape Horn, is the site that would cheer travelers on the sea route to the fields of California. There were a series of gold rushes as well as silver rushes in various parts of the western United States as discoveries were made.

While individuals began the gold rushes, it wouldn't take long for mining companies to set up shop. ▼

▲ Packers ascending the summit of Chilkoot Pass, Yukon, Alaska, during the gold rush of 1898

◀ Angel Camp, gold rush boom town today

◀ A prospector

Sailing card for
the clipper ship
California, depicts
the Gold Rush ▶

◀ Gold miners,
El Dorado,
California

CULTURAL CONNECTIONS

In our previous Cultural Focus sections, we have discussed the heritage of our country's ballads and songs, and our poetry and art. In this chapter, we are surprised that the pioneers have the energy to dance and celebrate at the end of a long day of traveling in a wagon train. What kind of dancing did they do? During the pioneer time period, most people knew how to dance and enjoyed doing so! From a very young age, children were taught the steps of dances such as the waltz, the jig, the reel, the minuet, and other similar dances. These dances required the participants to thoroughly know the steps — one misstep would be extremely embarrassing . . . and dangerous!

Irene and Vernon Castle, c. 1912

Modern-day Tango

THOUGHTS TO REMEMBER

1. We learn in Chapter 27 that many people from all over the world were going to California because gold had been found there!

2. We also learn that a covered wagon was a simple box on high wheels. The wagon box was covered by a large canvas stretched over wooden or metal bows. These wagons were usually pulled by oxen.

CHAPTER 28

OUR PLACE IN HISTORY

Starting Point: There are so many reasons America always has been and remains unique among the world of nations. The freedoms and opportunities here are sought by many still today!

Spot Light

The United States of America Flag: Freedom is not free. The future of our country depends on us.

READY TO EXPLORE?

1. Do you have any relatives or family friends who have served in our country's armed forces?

2. How has what you've learned this year in history taught you your responsibility as an American?

United States declares war against Mexico

May 13, 1846

Zachary Taylor elected as president

November 1848

California Gold Rush begins

1849

Have you ever asked yourself, "Why should I study history? I mean, it's interesting and all, but is there really a need to know history? Will I ever use it in real, nowadays life?"

When I was a young girl, my dad took me on his knee and told me a real-life story about some important men in our history. I had never heard these stories before, and I thought he was making them up! When I got a little older, I read some books written about these men. The stories were true. How exciting!

History is exciting, but that is not the only reason to learn it. As Americans, we have a rich, godly heritage. We have learned that many of the original settlers of this country came here for religious reasons. They came because they could not worship the way they felt was best in their own countries.

As generations passed, some of the descendants of these original settlers forgot why their great-great-grandparents had braved the hard journey across the Atlantic Ocean to come to this new land. God reminded them by sending a Great Revival to remind them of who He is. God raised up men and women to lead the way, when the 13 colonies grew and wanted to become independent.

FIFE: a small, high-pitched flute, that is similar to the piccolo, but louder and shriller.

Although there has always been controversy about the founding fathers' personal faith, no one can deny they were men of integrity. Our Declaration of Independence and our Constitution are based on sound principles that are grounded in truth. America has had its faults, for we are a nation made up of imperfect people, but no other nation on earth has ever been founded on principles such as these.

As we have learned through the stories of the American Revolution and the War of

Three patriots, two playing drums and one playing a fife leading troops into battle

1812, freedom never comes at a low price. This is something that I want all of my friends to know. Learn this, and learn it well — America is free because people stood up for what is right. That is our responsibility as American citizens.

Maybe you have a family member who serves in our Armed Forces, or perhaps a grandparent or great-grandparent who served in World War 2. If you do, I want you to write them a thank you letter, and I want you to pray for them, and pray for all of the young men and women in our armed forces, who work hard to protect our country.

You might be asking, "What can I do, I'm just a kid?" My friend, you are America's future. Learn to do what is right; follow Jesus with all of your hearts. Learn from the great men and women in our history. Learn from their achievements, but also learn from their failures. As you grow, learn about what is going on in the world and in our country. Be educated and pray for those in leadership.

You may not think that you have an important part in history, but you never know! In America, any child can grow up and become president. Even if you never do anything that goes down in history books, you are an important part of our country and the human race in general. God uses those who are willing to do whatever He wants them to do. Sometimes that "whatever He wants them to do" is small, but as we have learned, small changes lead to big changes. We are like the small pebbles dropped in the pond; the ripples of our lives reach out and touch the ripples of others' lives.

Did you know that God knew you before you were even born? It says in the Bible He knew you before there was even time! Isn't that amazing? He chose you to be born at this time in history for a reason. He could have made you a pioneer boy or girl, but that wouldn't have fit His plan. You see, we are put here for a reason — to touch the world for Him.

Generation by generation, history goes marching by. In our next American history adventure, we will learn how the battle over slavery nearly ripped our great country apart. In a later volume, we will watch as two brothers attempt to fly the first airplane, and we will watch as evil men are stopped as they try to take over the world.

This has been exciting journey through the beginning of American history, and I promise you, it keeps getting more exciting! You have been a marvelous travel companion, and I hope we meet again in *America's Story Volume 2.* I hope you have learned a lot, and more importantly, I hope I have helped fan the fire of your love of learning. God bless you, my friends; you are precious to Him.

NARRATION BREAK

Talk to your parents about what you can do to honor the men and women who have given their lives for our freedom!

FROM MANY, ONE AND IN GOD WE TRUST

Below is a map of the United States today (minus the territories it still oversees), with the year that each was granted statehood in the union and their capitols.

This map truly reflects the unofficial motto of the nation, *E Pluribus Unum* or "From Many, One," first adopted by Congress in 1782 on the Seal of the United States. It was not until 1956 that the official motto of "*In God We Trust*" was adopted by the United States.

As part of the union, the states are governed and protected by the Constitution of the United States. Article Four of the Constitution lays out the relationship of states to one another, including their rights and privileges, the process of gaining statehood, and the obligations of the federal government to the union of states.

Close-up of E Pluribus Unum on the back of a 1967 United States Quarter

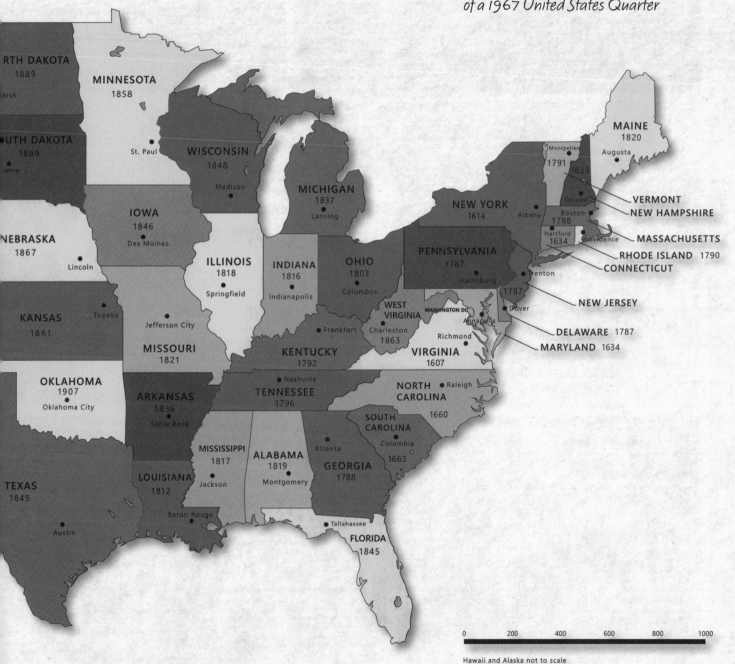

Hawaii and Alaska not to scale

◀ The First Battle of Bull Run — Civil War

Women serve in the armed forces and support roles like industry and health care. ▼

Korean War, 1950 ▲

World War I – A group of men gather for military service in Los Angeles in 1918. ▼

LOCAL BOARD #17
815 ME
NOV. 11, 1918.

African American Air Cadet, c. 1940s — World War II ▶

▲ American forces in Vietnam, 1968

◀ Afghanistan, 2005

ST QUOTA

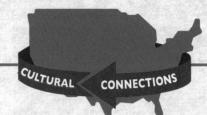

Are there any aspects of our modern culture that you would like to change? What are they? Why and how would you change them?

Orchestra music has not changed much in the last 100 years, but the presentations have.

YOU ARE AMERICA'S FUTURE

1. It is an honor to have family that have served in the armed forces. These men and women have played a vital and important part in helping to secure our country and resolve conflicts with other nations. Some have even lost their lives in service to America.

2. Answers will vary but should include: being proud of our country, realizing freedom is never free, defending our country, praying for our country, etc.

GLOSSARY

Auction: a public sale in which goods or property are sold to the highest bidder.

Boycott: to stop buying or using goods or services as a protest.

Escort: accompanying another for protection or security, or as a mark of rank.

Expedition: a journey taken by a group of people with a particular purpose.

Feast: a large meal, usually in celebration of something.

Fleet: largest group of naval vessels under one commander, organized for specific purposes.

Fort: a fortified building or strategic position, often used as an army post.

Globe: spherical representation of the earth, usually on a pedestal or stand.

Heroic: having the characteristics of a hero or heroine; very brave.

Inauguration: a ceremony celebrating the beginning of a leader's term of office.

Invent: to create or design something that has not existed before.

Mission: an important assignment carried out that typically involves travel.

Patriot: someone who feels a strong support for their country.

Pilgrim: a person who journeys to a sacred place for religious reasons.

Quakers: members of a historically Christian group of religious movements.

Slavery: a law allowing humans to be classified as property.

Sphere: an object having a round, solid, 3-dimensional shape like a ball or globe.

GEOGRAPHICAL TERMS

Archipelago: a group or chain of islands clustered together in the ocean or sea

Bay: a body of water that is partly surrounded by land (and is usually smaller than a gulf)

Butte: a rock or hill with a flat top and steep sides

Canal: a man-made waterway for transportation or irrigation

Canyon: a deep valley with very steep sides

Cape: a sharp piece of land that sticks out into a body of water

Channel: a narrow body of water that connects two larger bodies of water

Colony: a country or area under the full or partial political control of another country.

Continent: a large body of land. The earth is divided into seven continents.

Cove: a small horseshoe-shaped bay that is surrounded mostly by rock

Delta: a triangular-shaped area of land in which a river divides into smaller streams before emptying into a lake, sea, or ocean

Dune: a hill made in sand by the wind

Equator: the imaginary "belt" which runs around the middle of the earth, halfway between the North and South Poles

Fife: a small, high-pitched flute, that is similar to the piccolo, but louder and shriller.

Fjord: a long, somewhat narrow inlet from the sea. It is usually bordered with high rock cliffs.

Island: a small piece of land completely surrounded by water

Isthmus: a narrow strip of land connecting to large pieces of land

Nation: a large group of people with common characteristics and customs.

Peninsula: a piece of land surrounded with water on three sides

Surveyor: a profession in which boundary lines of property are decided.

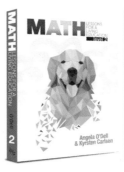

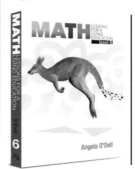
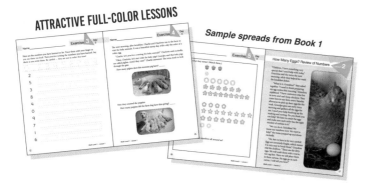

CHARLOTTE MASON INSPIRED
ELEMENTARY CURRICULUM THAT CONNECTS CHILDREN TO
AMERICA'S PAST... AND THEIR FUTURE!

Through this unique educational style, children develop comprehension through oral and written narration, and create memories through notebooking and hands-on crafts. This is not just facts and figures; this is living history.

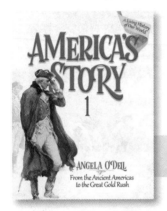

FROM THE ANCIENT AMERICAS TO THE GREAT GOLD RUSH - 3RD GRADE

Part 1: Begins at the infancy of our country and travels through the founding of our great nation, catching glimpses of the men who would become known as the Founding Fathers.

America's Story Vol 1   *Teacher Guide*
978-0-89051-979-0   978-0-89051-980-6

FROM THE CIVIL WAR TO THE INDUSTRIAL REVOLUTION - 4TH GRADE

Part 2: Teaches students about the Civil War, the wild West, and the Industrial Revolution.

America's Story Vol 2   *Teacher Guide*
978-0-89051-981-3   978-0-89051-982-0

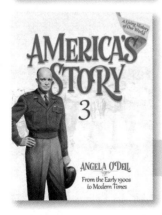

FROM THE EARLY 1900S TO OUR MODERN TIMES - 5TH GRADE

Part 3: Carries the student from the turn of the 20th century through the early 2000s, seeing war through the eyes of the soldiers in journals and letters.

America's Story Vol 3   *Teacher Guide*
978-0-89051-983-7   978-0-89051-984-4